The Sign in Music and Literature

The Dan Danciger Publication Series

The Sign in Music and Literature

Edited by Wendy Steiner

 University of Texas Press, Austin

Requests for permission to reproduce material
from this work should be sent to:
     Permissions
     University of Texas Press
     Box 7819
     Austin, Texas 78712

Library of Congress Cataloging in Publication Data

Main entry under title:
The Sign in music and literature.
   (The Dan Danciger publication series)
   Bibliography: p.
   1. Semiotics and the arts.   I. Steiner, Wendy, 1949–
NX180.S46S53   700'.1   80-27915
ISBN 0-292-77563-6

Contents

The Sign in Music and Literature

CHAPTER 1

Introduction
BY WENDY STEINER

The promise of semiotics is the promise of every universal language: a system that will encompass all meanings for all people. With a subject matter as broad as the sign, any cultural entity, in fact any object of perception whatsoever, falls under its rule. It is this breadth that made the sign crucial to the Unified Science movement of the mid-century, and that now makes it the focus of a revolutionary field of inquiry, the semiotics of art.

The disappearance of aesthetics as a discipline has left students of the arts particularly open to sign theory. It is tempting to embrace semiotics as a new gospel whose mere application will turn art theory from a chaos of speculation into a systematic field of study. But the replacement of chaos by order can backfire, and the application of semiotics to the arts threatens to reveal a murkiness in the neat categories of the theory quite in keeping with the militantly "unclear thinking" of art. The semiotics of art thus comes to serve as the testing ground of sign theory as a whole; work in this subject is as vital to theoretical semioticians as to students of the arts.

The essays in this volume demonstrate the struggle involved in formulating a semiotics of art. The arts treated—particularly literature and music —have a good deal in common, but what separates them—the absence of semantic reference in music—would seem at first glance to stop semiotics in its tracks. The old metaphors, "the language of music" and "the music of language," quickly lose their appeal if we are asked to take them literally, and the "linguistic imperialism" of current French and Russian semiotics appears to be doing just that. If language is considered the "primary modeling system" upon which not only literature but all the arts are based, the comparison of the arts would be merely a description of the means by which each art implements this common material. While several of the papers on music here demonstrate the merits of understanding music in terms of language, a number of them voice considerable discomfort with this approach.

But semiotics need not be taken as generalized linguistics, and the studies in this collection raise many more fundamental issues regarding the semiotics of art. In order to isolate these issues it will be necessary for me to outline what I take to be the "argument" of this diversely authored book.

We begin with Benjamin Hrushovski's broadly conceived introduction to the subject in which he proposes a three-dimensional model which would accommodate all possible aspects of any semiotic object. He derives the model primarily from literary texts, but argues that it is equally valid for any other kind of text. The three dimensions—of Speech and Position, of Meaning and Reference, and of the Organized Text—are versions of Charles Morris's three dimensions of semiosis: the pragmatic, semantic, and syntactic, each of which Hrushovski skilfully adapts to the particular needs of literature. It is in the second of these dimensions, that of meaning and reference, that the validity of the model for music would seem to be most questionable, but, as we shall see, this level presents some of the most difficult problems for literary theorists as well.

The semantic dimension of art in fact dominates the next three articles. The first two, by Seymour Chatman and Charles Altman, begin with similar questions. Chatman asks what happens when we do not understand a text, though we may understand all the sentences from a strictly linguistic point of view. Altman describes "the disconcerting feeling of walking into a movie late. . . . The actors are familiar, the surroundings recognizable, the sound track perfectly clear, and yet we remain convinced that we are not hearing everything, not seeing everything, not understanding everything." In other words, in what way does textuality differ from language?

The answers that Chatman and Altman offer exemplify the diametrically opposed approaches that seek a common home in semiotics. Chatman claims that our failure to understand is the failure to select an adequate extra-artistic code with which to interpret the text. It is in the implementation of such codes, which he associates with the topoi of Greek rhetoric, that a text engages reality, and its consistency within the conventions of that code creates its verisimilitude. Altman, on the other hand, argues that the difference between speech and textuality lies in the self-enclosure of the text. He goes so far as to claim that a text is not merely an element of *parole*, but constitutes its own *langue*: "While I do not wish to suggest that texts lack intertextual, or precoded, meaning [such as Chatman describes], I do suggest that the text's most radical and disconcerting method of making meaning is that which derives from its status as secondary modeling system. The experience of reading draws its special nature from the necessity of learning a new language in the course of reading."

The argument between Altman and Chatman is itself one of the topoi of twentieth-century art criticism. If the text is meaningful, then it is one of the innumerable cultural products that contain this meaning. How then can we account for the uniqueness and specificity of meaning that everyone claims in art? On the other hand, if the artwork has a unique meaning, how do we learn this meaning, and how do we share it?[1]

Nancy Armstrong explicitly raises this issue in the next essay as she explores the nature of the literary character:

> Conventional readers have always seen characters in fiction as examples of social and psychological laws and thus have tended to confuse the meaning of a character with an ostensible referent in the world of human phenomena. Critics in the formalist tradition have sidestepped this problem by restricting their treatment of character to the level of the signifier, that is, to purely formal relationships within the text. But . . . after all, we tend to talk about characters the same way we talk about real human beings because authors have employed the same cultural codes in composing fiction as those used in ordinary descriptions of social experience. It is not surprising, consequently, that literary characters should appear to be both autonomous and referential.

What Armstrong argues is that the meaning of the text must be discovered as an interplay between coded and internal values. Using a Greimasian approach to explicate *Pride and Prejudice*, she shows how the ironic and sentimental possibilities in the opening statement of the book are transformed in the course of the novel. Thus the narrative process restores meaning to the beginning of the novel by proving that "initially disjunctive systems of meaning are in fact isomorphic." Armstrong shows, however, that this harmonious solution applies more to the conventional novels of the "great tradition" than to modernist texts, so that the accommodation of centripetal to centrifugal meaning is not as easy to generalize as one might wish. And stating in theoretical terms how aesthetic meaning can be both sharable and unique remains a challenge.

The answer most frequently offered in semiotics is that the peculiar organization of art is responsible for the problematic mode of reference that characterizes it. This is Hrushovski's dimension of the Organized Text, and it is the area explored in the other three articles here on literature. The first of these, by Elemér Hankiss, isolates contradiction as the central fact about literature: "Every stylistic and poetic device—rhymes and metaphors, parallelisms and inversions, epic and dramatic structures, syntactic and semantic patterns—serves to create and perpetuate an intense oscillation . . . that is probably an aesthetic universal and one of the main sources of aesthetic experience." Hankiss illustrates in some detail what Altman terms the level of "intratextual rewriting," that is, the constructive factors in a text whose organization "teaches" us the unique "language" that the text allegedly is. Moreover, Hankiss reveals oscillation in such unlikely areas as Jakobson's metalinguistic and phatic dimensions of the text. Art is thus ambiguous in its relation to the linguistic code and even in its very gesture toward the reader.

Hankiss's theory prepares the way for some of the remarkable observations in Miroslav Červenka's depiction of the literary artifact. Following in the tradition of the most venerable structuralist school, the Prague Linguistic Circle, Červenka shows the aesthetic sign not as a simple unity of signifier and signified, but a hierarchical structure in which each level is alternately the signifier of the next higher level and the signified of the level below it. In this way, the sphere of the signifier encompasses virtually the whole artwork. But at the same time, since the components of this signifier are, except for the material level, created by meanings and their complexes, virtually the whole work constitutes the signified. A constant oscillation thus goes on in the semiotic nature of almost every component of the art sign. Červenka concludes that "to be a signifier" and "to be sensorily perceptible" do not have the same extension in the literary artwork, nor do "to be sensorily perceptible" and "to be given."

In the purest tradition of the Prague School, Červenka argues that the essential materiality of the text is oral rather than visual, making temporal successivity the fundamental fact of poetic experience. He constructs a continuum of concreteness for the literary work, from the abstraction of successivity as such (pure auditoriness) to the concreteness of fully realized speech sounds in the related art of recitation. This continuum of materiality has many important implications for the art of music. It is here that the problem of where the artifact of the work lies—in the score, a performance, all performances, or the description of any or all of these—is so crucial. No other art seems at once so purely material and so ideal.

The essentially oral nature of literature is supported by the findings of Nicolas Ruwet's study as well. Ruwet tries to discover the exact relation between the typographic and linguistic structure of a poem, to isolate the content of the notion *stanza*. After an exhaustive search for possible connections between the form and functions of stanzas, Ruwet concludes that the relation is often arbitrary. In this way, the arrangement on the page of blank spaces and type resembles both orthography and musical notation in reflecting only some of the structural features of the system it represents while omitting or distorting others. The perfect closure of the work of art and the mutual implicature of all its parts do not hold as far as the graphic representation of the poetic work is concerned, and so with Ruwet's and Červenka's position we come up against the very definitional basis of art. There is no doubt that the same problem applies to music, with some contemporary compositions functioning very much as paintings. If there is an imperfect isomorphism between this aspect of the literary or musical work and the rest of its structure, the wholeness of the aesthetic artifact is much more questionable than most structuralists would like to believe, and the disjoining of form from function is a disturbing possibility. Concrete poetry under such circumstances becomes a decidedly peripheral enterprise.

Ruwet, a major figure not only in poetics but in musicology, is a fitting bridge between the literature and music essays in this book. The music section opens with a contrast at least as violent as that between Chatman and Altman. Here Henry Orlov discards the notion of music as a secondary modeling system based on language. Instead, he argues that musical semiotics should proceed from only the primary reality of the text—music as sound. By this statement he means performed sound, for each single tone, unlike each word in speech, "is contemplated and experienced by the listener as an inimitable multidimensional object, a piece of reality itself alive and rich with all sorts of meaning." This very richness is what makes music a promising subject of semiotic study according to Orlov, because it is the purest system of abstract relationships presented in concrete form.

Allan Keiler, on the other hand, centers his study on the relation between language and music, particularly in reference to deep structures, the antithesis of Orlov's emphasis on music as sound. He quotes Jean Jacques Nattiez's division of musical semiotics into three levels (Nattiez 1974): the poietic (production, encoding), the esthesic (process of perception), and the neutral or material level (the object of study seen in its material reality). (The contrast between this classification and Hrushovski's is instructive, for there is no referential level here; moreover, the pragmatic level has been differentiated into that of the encoder and that of the decoder, reflecting the special status of performance in music.) It is on the material level that Keiler claims musical semiotics must concentrate, but like Červenka and Ruwet he stresses the need to see this level not as a mere given but as something that must be approached through theory and hypothesis. He believes that the study of music will significantly contribute to semiological research only when there are viable theories about the complex musical systems of the world; and that only this understanding of musical competence will make it possible to deal with "the even more intractable cognitive issues of musical behavior."

But the other studies on music are unwilling to stop at the level of competence. Alan Perlman and Daniel Greenblatt are specifically concerned with performance, since they find a homology between the improvisation of jazz and the speaking of sentences. A jazz solo, though impromptu, is constructed according to specific harmonic and melodic constraints. Thus, command of these principles is equivalent to linguistic competence, and executing ideas according to these principles corresponds to linguistic performance.

The ethnomusicologist John Blacking, also faced with "music for which there is no written score, and in which the structure emerges only in performance," argues against the splitting of the musical work into material and pragmatic aspects. He claims that this distinction is inappropriate even for music with a written score. Since different artists can perform Beethoven's *Hammerklavier* differently, he asks whether there really is a distinct phenomenon, "*the Hammerklavier*" which can be subjected to semiotic analysis. Blacking goes on to argue that the scientific rigor of many musical analyses is illusory since signs have no meaning until that meaning is shared. Thus, "the *processes of sharing* become as crucial to the semiotics of music as the sonic product which provides the focus for analysis." However, where Perlman and Greenblatt find that that process of sharing can best be described through the analogy to language, Blacking dismisses the notion of language as a primary modeling system. He regards music instead as more appropriate than verbal language for revealing the purely structural requirements of a symbolic system.

David Lidov bases his paper on this claim, arguing that music, like consciousness, is temporal, continuous, and without spatial boundaries. Thus, music "engages an unlimited semantic field" which is not translatable into language, but which the semiotician can describe. Lidov demonstrates the process of description through Schoenberg's twelve-tone method, which he finds homologous with certain structures of belief: "The advantage of Schoenberg's harmonic theory is that, unlike Schencker's, it does not portray all possible departures from the key as ultimately strengthening the dominion of the single tonality. His theory of monotonality is compatible with a concept of a weak and fading center." Expressionism, Lidov argues, accepted weakness as a condition of knowledge, but in its rigorous exclusion of variants that do not conform to the row, the twelve-tone method becomes an "imitation of moral will."

This homology between musical structure and other cultural structures is what Judith and Alton Becker term *iconicity*, following Peirce and the mainstream of theoretical semiotics. Not only is this feature of art a definitional trait; in many cases "the major source of power of a kind of music or literature is associated with the iconicity or 'naturalness' of the coherence system which informs that music or literature." The Beckers illustrate this idea with an analysis of Javanese gamelan music, showing striking similarities between its structure and that of the local description of the days of the week, the date, the year, and so on. They conclude that "musical systems or languages are always more than organized sounds, vocabularies, and syntaxes; they are instances of the way a specific people understand and relate to the phenomenal world."

The final essay in this book is one of the very rare studies of the semiotics of dance. Here Marianne Shapiro outlines the historical controversy between those who consider dance an abstract, "pure" art and those who find it a representation of the extra-artistic realm. This is the essential semiotic issue for any art, and Shapiro addresses it through the story-ballet *Giselle*. She asks what dance can signify—sexual roles, societal relations, narrative progression, and so forth—and the semiotic modes—icon, index, symbol—by which it can do so. Shapiro even goes so far as to analyze the audience's relation to the ballet, discovering a homology between the elaborate clothing of dancers and audience which decreases with the distance of the viewer from the stage. This discussion provides the basis for her provocative hypothesis that "classical ballet comments reflexively on modalities of thought and on social institutions, both maintaining and undermining them through its critique of institutions and personages."

Such is the range of opinion in this volume. Music and ballet are direct icons of thought or of culture; they are languages with purely systemic meaning. The essence of music is in its structure; the essence of music is in its performance. Literature is meaningful because it engages semantic codes exterior to it; literature is meaningful in that each text is its own code; literary meaning arises from the intersection of external and internal codes. The essence of literary aesthesis is pan-structural oscillations; the essence of literary aesthesis is the oscillation between each level's functioning as a signifier and as a signified. Literature is like language and music in the imperfect "fit" of its notational system; literature is oral in essence because typography renders it imperfectly.

If this collection of essays reveals anything, it is not the solutions that semiotics offers the arts but the system of questions that it poses. The questions themselves are not new—neither is semiotics for that matter. But the semiotic frame of reference organizes these questions in a more coherent way than before and provides a common terminology and an institutional forum for issues that were previously dispersed throughout the humanities. The mechanisms of this coherence unfortunately make semiotics appear to the uninitiated as an esoteric Procrustean bed, a closed, restrictive system, whereas to the initiated the Tower of Babel seems the more apt analogy. Where the truth lies is something that I leave to the reader to decide. It is to be hoped that collections like this one will aid in that decision.

Notes

This book contains the papers on literature, music, and ballet delivered at the International Conference on the Semiotics of Art held in May, 1978, at the University of Michigan in Ann Arbor. The organizing committee was headed by Richard W. Bailey, Ladislav Matejka, and myself, and included Marthalee S. Barton, Alton L. Becker, Judith Becker, Arthur W. Burks, Vern Carroll, Michael Clark, Herbert J. Eagle, Emery E. George, Diane Kirkpatrick, Gwynn S. McPeek, John Mersereau, Jr., Walter D. Mignolo, Michel J. Pierssens, and George G. Rosewald. Funding for the conference was generously provided by the National Endowment for the Humanities, the International Research and Exchange Board, and the University of Michigan. My personal thanks go as well to Professors Bailey and Matejka for their invaluable assistance in the preparation of this volume.

1. I have discussed this issue in regard to the clash between the New Critics and Charles Morris and between the structuralists and post-structuralists. The articles here belong to the latter disagreement. See Wendy Steiner 1979.

CHAPTER 2
The Structure of Semiotic Objects: A Three-Dimensional Model
BY BENJAMIN HRUSHOVSKI

Introductory Remarks

The purpose of this essay is to present the argument that literary texts can be apprehended fully only through a three-dimensional model. For purposes of understanding or analysis we may have to observe one dimension (or certain aspects of it) at a time; we cannot, however, disregard its relations with aspects of the other dimensions. Theories based on properties of one dimension only will remain weak and limited in solving the problems of literary texts in their aesthetic or communicative functions, because bridging between the abstract model and concrete descriptive analysis requires relegating too much to "context," whereas this "context" is merely part of a different kind of organization.

Furthermore, though literary texts—in their wealth of structuration and meaning-relations—most readily display typical properties of sign-complexes, such properties are by no means confined to literature. The three-dimensional model applies actually to all kinds of texts—indeed, to all objects which may be considered "semiotic."

This model is a very general, abstract one, which, I hope, will become clear through a number of concrete examples (however sketchily illustrated). At the same time, it is a simple model, reflecting the simplicity of our basic cognitive operations. Three different kinds of operations—it is argued—combine to grasp any specific complex configuration in language texts or in other objects which convey meanings to us—and this is precisely because meanings are conveyed through objects which possess these three dimensions.

This model is not meant to remain abstract: it is intended to serve as a framework to accommodate all possible aspects of various semiotic objects within one system of description (though this can obviously not be shown here). It is hoped that readers who are interested in concrete texts or concrete aspects of literature, or of buildings in a city, will not shy away at this point, since the theoretical argument which follows should be pertinent to the understanding of concrete stories and individual texts.

Semiotic Objects

Semiotics is said to be the science of systems of signs or of sign-processing. If so, it must recognize that signs rarely appear in isolation. We usually confront sign complexes, to be understood in a variety of ways. Moreover, signs are not floating ideas; they appear in objects in the world, which have their own structure and influence the nature of the sign. They may be either objects made of language, i.e., "texts," or of any other material, such as buildings, nature, colors in painting, etc. Without considering the nature and organization of such objects, we cannot properly understand their signifying functions.

Semiotic objects may be intended for sign-functions or not. In the second case, they become "semiotic" if they are interpreted as signs by "understanders." For example, while walking in a city we read the forms, sizes, or density of buildings to signify "office buildings," "middle-class homes," "slums," etc., even if such messages were never intended by the producers of those objects. While reading such objects as signs, we select and abstract some parts and aspects of the observed objects, which convey the reconstructed message, disregarding other aspects which serve other, nonsignifying functions. For example, a multilobed arch signifies Islamic architecture in Spain, while a pointed arch represents Gothic architecture. In both cases, there are of course further qualities symptomatic of their respective "styles," but there are clearly nonstylistic properties as well, such as the existence of walls, the sturdiness of the construction, etc., which make the "coherence" of the object, enable its existence in the world, and make possible the performance of its primary, nonsemiotic functions. Clearly, structural considerations (in the sense of the material structure of buildings) influence the expression of any architectural style. The same, however, holds for semiotic objects strongly intended for aesthetic, nonutilitarian purposes. Thus, the conventional length of films limits and frames the possibilities of cinematic expression (as was pointed out long ago by Eikhenbaum). And the necessity of a linear presentation, segmented into parts, dictates a great deal in the nature of the presented "world" in works of fiction (as has been demonstrated in detail in Hrushovski 1976 and elsewhere).

In recent years, attempts have been made to base literary theories on speech act theory or linguistic functions (in Jakobson's sense); previous theories have discussed literature in terms of a fictional "world" or literary "meaning," or, on the contrary, reduced everything to "structure." The point of my argument is that it is impossible to account for all aspects and elements in works of literature through any one of those models. On the other hand it seems to me that one can analyze texts exhaustively while organizing their elements into three separate, though highly interdependent, dimensions: the dimension of Speech and Position; the dimension of Meaning and Reference; and the dimension of the Organized Text (or structured object). In each particular text, patterns of the three dimensions may be intersecting, partly overlapping, embedded in each other, motivated by each other, or even constituted by means of each other. Nevertheless, the dimensions always remain autonomous and are not reducible to any one of them, requiring, therefore, separate and complementary methodologies for their study.

One Example: Words in Architecture

Speech and embedded speech surround us wherever we go. Before analyzing the complex phenomena in this dimension, I would like to present one, rather simple, illustration. A building in Berkeley has a number of inscriptions on its walls. Four of them were recorded by my informant (Figure 2-1). Insofar as the whole building may be considered a semiotic object, it clearly has embedded linguistic texts, which relate variously to the building itself or to related phenomena. Inscription 3a, "Boalt Hall of Law, 1911," refers to the building itself and to the date of its construction. On the other hand, Inscription 4, "School of Law," refers to a social institution which is located in that building (and may or may not occupy all of it, or not be located entirely here). Again, Inscription 3b, "McEnery Library 1951," clearly refers to only part of the building and presumably does not include the walls of the library, since the date indicates that it was established much later than the building itself. The interpretation made so far is not based on any sign or any syntactic means presented to the viewer. It is a construct which any understander has to make, applying words to specific "frames of reference" (see below), while using logical argumentation based on knowledge of such social institutions. There may always be knowledge unavailable to the understander which would make his or her understanding incomplete or approximate. For example, someone who is not in the field of law may not know whether Boalt or McEnery are famous lawyers or donors (both conventions exist in name-giving in American universities).

A more difficult case is Inscription 1. Its second-person form of address implies a speech situation, in which a person named Cardozo appeals

1. YOU WILL STUDY THE WISDOM OF THE PAST. FOR IN A WILDERNESS OF CONFLICTING COUNSELS, A TRAIL HAS THERE BEEN BLAZED. YOU WILL STUDY THE LIFE OF MANKIND, FOR THIS IS THE LIFE YOU MUST ORDER, AND TO ORDER WITH WISDOM, MUST KNOW. YOU WILL STUDY THE PRECEPTS OF JUSTICE, FOR THESE ARE THE TRUTHS THAT THROUGH YOU SHALL COME TO THEIR HOUR OF TRIUMPH. HERE IS THE HIGH EMPRISE, THE FINE ENDEAVOR, THE SPLENDID POSSIBILITY OF ACHIEVEMENT, TO WHICH I SUMMON YOU AND BID YOU WELCOME.

Cardozo

2. [The trees—in full bloom—covered up the wisdom in spring. The letters are all capital—in iron on granite.]

3a. BOALT HALL OF LAW 1911
   b. McENERHY LIBRARY 1951

4. SCHOOL OF LAW

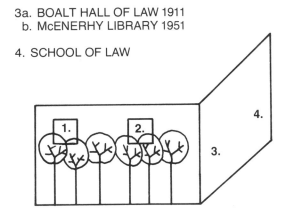

Figure 2–1. Texts in Architecture. University of California, Berkeley, Law School Building.

apparently to students of a law school. It is, however, a speech act within a speech act: the style and the direct solemn message of Cardozo's language cannot possibly be taken without a smile by present-day students. It is as if the heads of the present-day institution were saying to their students: "We would like to tell you something like this if it could be translated into a present-day message." This inscription relates neither to the building nor to the institution within it but to people who attend that institution. Furthermore, it refers to qualities in the minds and behavior of such people. For me, walking by that building has even further embedding because, since I am not a law student, I am not the addressee of that message. I don't even know who Cardozo was and therefore I don't know whether he addressed students in this law school or elsewhere. Therefore I must further process this message to convey something about the moral purposes which the founders of this school had in mind, possibly as opposed to what lawyers are considered to be in society.[1]

Inscription 2 was not legible to my informant, because the trees, which seem to be part of the organized architectural space, had grown since the school was built and covered the inscription. What remained was the aesthetic function alone ("iron on granite"), or the "poetic function" in Jakobson's terms.

As this case shows, speech embedded in architecture may be used in a variety of modes. An understander has to construct the intended speech events, relate words to frames of reference and perceive their place in the larger object. In our case, the words are not related directly to their physical "context" and have to be processed in a variety of ways, referring to the building itself, one part of it, the social institution located in it, people attending that institution, and attitudes of such people. Though physically all these inscriptions are embedded within the building, some are meant to be above it, to embed it, naming it or describing it, and some are merely part of it. Only when the building is processed through such verbal material can we abstract further sign aspects from the nonverbal parts of the building. (Even an observation that there are no overt "law-school features" in the architecture may be processed as a sign of modesty, seriousness, etc.) Of course, our analysis is not complete, since within that building, and within the institutions located in it (school of law, library) there is an enormous amount of verbal material pertaining to it, some of which describes the nature of the institution as a whole (programs, schedules, student announcements, textbooks, etc.).

This is an example of how nonverbal and basically nonsemiotic objects may use verbal material to guide their understanders' processing of its signification. Verbal intermediaries may be used even where no words are presented overtly, e.g., in medieval paintings. On the other hand, verbal texts constantly use our knowledge of nonverbal objects, without which semiotic processing or "understanding" is impossible. Any theory which separates the verbal from nonverbal modes of communication, or overlooks their interaction, is limited in explaining the separate modes as well. Meaning is not simply "given" in objective signs, but depends largely on interactional constructs. Separately studied signs are merely potential units, assignable sign-forms, which become meaningful only in larger constructs.

The Dimension of Speech and Position[2]

All information conveyed in language is produced, and presented, directly or indirectly, by "speakers" and from particular positions. In fact, all knowledge we acquired about the world via language was originally presented to us from specific positions. Our mothers, friends, teachers, mass media, etc., were never entirely neutral sources of information. The same holds for President Carter's opinions about inflation, given to us through a selection of words he chose to use at the particular moment, mediated by a White House spokesman, again excerpted by a specific journalist, printed by the *New York Times*, the position of which we may or may not accept even if we are interested in the factual information. When such a complex series of embedded speech and positions is presented to us it may be important to know precisely whose position is reflected in specific sentences, and it may be quite hard to know it.

Literary texts can be seen as chains of embedded speech. The most general form of speech embedding is:

$$A \, (S \, (\underline{C_1 - C_2}) \, D) \, R$$

A = author, S = speaker, C = character, D = addressee, R = reader. The underlined symbols represent language in the text; A and R are constructs.

In various texts specific elements of this formula may be missing, or may be multiplied and complicated. Since a literary text is usually divorced from a single speech situation, the author (or the so-called "implied author") is a construct to be made by the reader, and may be constructed variably, may be coherent or not, may be identified with the writer (W) or not, etc. On the other hand, there may be a variety of reader constructs; a contemporary reader, a "proper" reader, a present-day reader, an actual reader, etc. In this formula, I used the term "speaker" rather than "narrator" in order to cover poetic as well as narrative texts. In fiction too a main speaker is not necessarily a "narrator" in the strict sense: one may present words about a "world" without intending to tell a "story."

It is important to note that such embedding cannot be understood merely through the formal linguistic presentation. Thus, the first person in lyric poetry may represent not the poet but an object or character distinguished from the poet; and, on the other hand, the second-person form is often used to express the first person of the lyrical "I"; or the third person may be identified by the reader as the "poet." The same holds for fiction. Any impersonal narration including language about a character may be reconstructed by the reader to represent that character's speech, thought, feelings, or general position. Quite often special linguistic devices are used to indicate this phenomenon (such as "free indirect style"), but in many texts or parts of texts this is not the case. In general, any "higher" speaker, while talking about a person embedded in his or her speech, may represent some of that person's language, thoughts, feelings, and positions. When studied from the speaker's (or narrator's, or author's) side, this phenomenon is seen as one-directional—simply as "embedding." When seen from the reader's side, however, this is "combined discourse,"[3] in which two voices may intermingle. It is not at all true that texts are monolithic in this respect, and are written either from the narrator's point of view or from a character's center of consciousness. Even when one of the two possible voices is dominant, the other voice may occasionally interfere or take over. Where linguistic indicators are lacking, the understander has to separate the two (or more) voices by making general hypothetical constructs about the possible positions of the intersecting voices. For example, in Joyce's story "Eveline," the reader realizes that most of the text is presented from Eveline's point of view (though she is described in the third person, in an impersonal narration), but a number of generalized sentences betray the narrator's intrusions. The sentence "Everything changes" is suspect due to its generalizing nature. It is only when we finish the story and realize that nothing really changes that we understand that it cannot represent the narrator's position. The sentence is clearly limited to Eveline's position at this particular moment and confined to the particular circumstances. I use the term *position* precisely in order to avoid an assumption that such a sentence must be Eveline's own speech "represented" by the narrator, or even her thought at the moment.

The same technique of combined discourse is used widely outside of literature; e.g., in a recent historical account of Adolf Hitler's life we find many passages like the following:

> By May 3 Munich was secured but at the cost of sixty-eight Free Corps lives. These, of course, had to be avenged. Thirty Catholic workers of the St. Joseph Society were seized at a tavern while making plans to put on a play (Toland 1977: 112).

The second sentence clearly does not represent the author's position, but the point of view of the Nazis. Nevertheless, the third sentence shifts back easily to an objective historical account.

In combined speech, there is no symmetry of represented positions when we move from left to right or from right to left. As has been observed, any "higher" speaker, in whose language a person or a position is embedded, may represent parts of the speech and position of the "lower" voice. The reverse is only marginally true, e.g., in the newspaper headline

"Brezhnev Says: Russians Won't Budge." Clearly the language of the higher speaker has intruded into Brezhnev's voice, since Brezhnev presumably would not have said it so bluntly and would never refer to the Soviet government and people as "Russians." More important, however, is the understanding that we have when encountering a "lower" (or quoted) speaker that his or her speech may have been selected, misrepresented, or even distorted by a higher authority. Often it is not clear how far to the left we must go: if a character is presented in an ironic light, it may be either that the narrator is the source of the irony or that the narrator is a naïve observer and is viewed ironically in turn by the author of the text. It is a quotation within a quotation: an author presents a narrator who quotes a character (who may quote another character in turn), and a distortion may occur at any stage. For example, in Gogol's "The Overcoat," the opening paragraph makes an elaborate excuse for not mentioning the name of the department in which the story occurred because if it did all Russia would be offended. This is clearly done tongue-in-cheek because anonymous presentation is even more typical and the device has been laid bare, the reader's attention being called to the problem of an intentional criticism of the whole social system. Nevertheless, it is not clear whether the narrator is being ironic or is presented as a simple-minded person who believes anything he hears and is presented ironically by the author. The reader's decision on this matter is a very difficult one (if possible at all) and clearly involves an interpretation of the whole story.

I shall not discuss here all possible complex presentations of positions within positions and the reader's reconstructions. In many cases there is no single narrator, and even when there is one, the presentation of the fictional world is often divided among a number of characters. The formula I have presented above and a more detailed apparatus derived from it enables us to discuss in one conceptual framework a variety of phenomena which have been dealt with under such headings as "point of view," "irony," "implied author," "narratee," "implied reader," "clashing norms," etc. Within this framework, and only here, can one apply speech act theory or Jakobson's functions of the speech event. The interpretation of such factors, however, can be made only from the second dimension, the dimension of Meaning and Reference. For example, when Dmitri Karamazov threatens to kill his father, we may assume that the "force" of the speech event is a "threat," but toward the end of the novel we realize that there was no such intention and understand his words to represent merely an emotional outburst.

Many semiotic objects are perceived as such without any intentional speech act. The reconstruction that we make from features of period styles when we say that they are "expressive of" merely uses a model of speech events: a period or a culture seems to "talk" to us through some of its creations.

In any case, all voices in a text refer to the same frames of reference and are placed in such frames of reference. In order to understand what a speaker refers to or in order to be able to reconstruct the speaker's position, we must construct the Field of Reference to which the words refer and in which the speakers operate.

The Dimension of Meaning and Reference

Meanings presented in texts cannot simply be considered on a single level. Nor are concepts like "context" and "coherence" sufficient to explain how meanings integrate in texts. Let us define meaning as everything an understander can understand from a text. Meaning so perceived is a result of a three-story construct:

RP = regulating principles, s = the level of "sense," fr = frame of reference.

The sense of a word, combined into "utterance meanings," is related to specific "frames of reference"; it obtains its truth value or figurative status and is specifically qualified by the frame of reference. Regulating principles, such as point of view, irony, and generic mode, derive from the speaker or the maker of the text. They explain in what sense to take the senses of the words (and can be dealt with within the first dimension).

It seems to be less clear how senses of the words depend on the frames of reference they relate to. Let us take an example. The sentence "This is a dirty hotel" when used in a dirty hotel preserves its literal meaning. If, however, the floor is not dirty, the word "dirty" becomes metaphorical (acquires a moral sense). An observation of the referent (within a specific frame of reference), independently of the words and their senses, influences the decision on the meaning to be assigned to this sign. The same sentence, if spoken by a man to the woman he lives with, changes its entire meaning. The word *hotel* when referring to an apartment cannot be accepted literally. The sentence then has to be re-understood to imply "I consider this apartment a temporary place," or "I am not going to stay here any longer." Such processes of re-understanding the words occur constantly in everyday life. It is not only that senses of words add information to known referents, but vice versa: the information we have about referents qualifies the meanings of words.

Let us define a frame of reference (fr) as any semantic continuum, to which signs may refer. There may be frs which are real or are ideal, e.g., a theory of grammar or an ideology. A frame of reference in space and time will be called a "scene." frs may be fixed in time or extended in time (e.g., the biography of a person). While using language we may refer to present frs or to absent frs, known to the listener or unknown. If an fr is present, simple pointing or labeling of a referent will enable us to obtain further information from the real referent. The same holds for frs known to an understander. Newspaper articles do not provide all the information needed for their understanding, since they rely on previous information the readers had about the same frs.

A Field of Reference (FR) is a hypothetical continuum of frames of reference, e.g., the world of a novel is a highly complex multi-directional Field of Reference. A character may be presented when he was two years old, and then at the age of forty; the presented frs are not directly continuous with each other but are perceived to belong to one wider FR. There may be in a novel frs which cannot be integrated as directly continuous with the major FR, e.g., the legend of the Grand Inquisitor in *The Brothers Karamazov*.

The necessity of the level of frs can be seen in the following example:

He opened the door. A few pieces of clothing were strewn about. He caught the fish in his net.

The first two sentences are not connected by any syntactic means. If we want to make a coherent text, we must provide a hypothetical fr, e.g., a room. In spite of the fact that many aspects of the room remain indeterminate, the two sentences can easily be accommodated within a normal concept of a room. But the third sentence cannot be accepted. It is normally turned into a metaphor. This sentence has no metaphor when seen separately and becomes metaphoric only when related to such a hypothetical fr. It is, however, possible, though less likely, to construct a hypothetical fr which would accommodate all three sentences in their literal meanings, e.g., by assuming that it is a backyard with a pool belonging to an eccentric in California. Such an assumption, however, will make the fr highly specific and limit any additional information provided by further parts of the text. The interdependence of meanings and frs becomes clear.

A further possible understanding construct of the same text can be seen from a slightly different version:

He opened the door. A few pieces of clothing were strewn about. The beach was beautiful in the light of the early morning. To his satisfaction, he saw he had caught the fish in his net. She was not to be seen anywhere. But he attended to his business of pulling the net out of the water.

Now we realize that in the first example we understood the word *opened* to mean "opened and entered," but it could just as well mean "opened and went out,"[4] especially if the building is near a beach. In our second example, metaphorical relationships are still possible, especially in certain genres of fiction (e.g., the metonymic transfer from the sea-scene to the human relationships) but all literal meanings can be accommodated in one fr as well.

A work of literature is different from other texts in one respect: it creates at least one Internal Field of Reference (IFR). There are some referents, such as characters, places, times, for which we have no evidence outside of this text ("intentional" objects in the phenomenological sense). We construct the IFR and its specific frs using models from the world or from literary and other conventions, and we have access to knowledge about them only from what is given and what may be constructed in the text. At the same time, however, many sentences in a literary text may refer to an External Field of Reference (ExFR). For example, geographical or historical names of persons, places, or events refer both outside and inside the text. Many generalizations about human nature refer to both inside and outside. The reader judges such statements both from the values of the IFR and from the values of the ExFR (the real world).[5]

It must be stressed that the employment of this integrational procedure does not necessarily imply that a work of literature must have one unified "meaning" or "message," or even make sense. In any case the interplay of elements which have any semantic aspect works through such patterning.

Double (or multiple) referring is a widespread feature in texts. An argument about politics by characters in a novel or in real life presents us with information on both the political situation discussed and the positions of the discussants. Nature scenes are conventionally transferred to the moods of characters in poetry. We may distinguish between direct reference to a specific fr and "referability" to other frs. We may then analyze the modes, forms and validity of such transfers (metaphoric, symbolic or other). In painting, though usually no direct statements are made, the continuity of an fr plays an important role in the organization of representational elements or constructs.

The Interdependence of the First Two Dimensions

The information obtained from texts, which refers or is related by an understander to frs, is presented by speakers or from specific positions. Such positions may be either personal or collective ones, e.g., social and moral norms or accepted opinions. Therefore an understander constructs intentional "worlds" of fiction or an understanding of reality by using the positions of speakers as regulating principles. There can be no analysis of meaning or of the information about specific referents and frs without considering the dimension of Speech and Position. (This dimension includes, of course, the generic properties of texts and other semiotic objects.)

The same is true in reverse. In a text, speakers are embedded in frames of reference and in a specific Field of Reference. We do not usually encounter in literature simple quotation within quotation. A speaker presents a piece of the "world" (an fr) and within that world he presents another speaker. In order to grasp the position of a speaking character, we must understand his place in the IFR or fictional "World." This relationship may be represented in general in the following diagram:

$$
\begin{array}{l}
\text{Dimension A} \qquad\quad S_1 \quad S_2 \quad S_3 \quad S_4 \\
\text{Dimension B} \quad (fr) \quad |fr \quad |fr \quad |fr \quad |fr
\end{array}
$$

S = any speaker.

A text may start either presenting "objectively" a world within which speakers are placed or it may start in a speaker's voice ("personal narration"). In both cases, we have to reconstruct each dimension separately. Even in drama, where it seems that we encounter only speech acts, we understand only by integrating words by different speakers relating to the same frs outside of their speech. The assumption that behind each text there is a creator (or implied author) creates merely an illusion that a text as a whole is an independent speech act. Clearly the author too is placed in a world, a tradition of literature, language, and culture.

The Dimension of the Organized Text

The understanding of meanings relating to a Field of Reference involves reorganizing the information in a whole network of heterogeneous patterns, hierarchically related to each other. While reading a novel, we reconstruct from discontinuous elements the characters, plot, the order of time, space, society with its norms, world-views, as well as other relationships. This hierarchical complex, however, must be presented in the medium of each semiotic object, e.g., in linear language in a novel. The organization of the *text continuum* is separated from the reconstructed meanings.

Texts are organized primarily by means of *segmentation*. Segments may be overlapping and variously divided. Segments are not at all parts of "macro-structures" (of meaning, or plot), or "surface" manifestations of "deep" global patterns. They may be constituted by rather "trivial" means. But they are the necessary *floor* from which all constructs are built. To some extent they are constituted by formal devices, such as strophic structure, chapters, paragraphs. To a large extent, however, texts use for their organization the other two dimensions. For example, scenes in a drama are divided by changing the grouping of speakers. A major means for segmenting a text is the use of thematic material, or shifting from one fr to another fr.

The motivations for introducing segments or discontinuing them, too, are derived from material of the other two dimensions. For example, in *The Brothers Karamazov* Alyosha's curiosity (a character trait) and his mission in the world (a role) are responsible for his going from one place to another to hear what various characters have to say, dividing and linking thereby the chapters of the novel. This cardinal role which thematic material plays in the organization of the structure of a text is responsible for the enormous variety and the individuality of structure of literary texts.

On the other hand, patterns in the dimension of the Organized Text may be related to the other dimensions. Thus, structural properties are said to participate in the "meaning" of a novel, sound patterns are related to the meanings of words in poetry, etc.[6]

Space does not allow me to discuss here similar phenomena in non-literary or nonlinguistic texts. Clearly, newspaper articles must have their own structure in order to be printed on a page and in order to be read, or to be read throughout. Here, too, thematic material is used for segmentation. For example, in a specific news article, the headline summarizes (part, sometimes a sensational part, of) the topic; the first paragraph presents a more detailed summary; the second paragraph may summarize background information on the fr discussed; the third paragraph may describe in detail one item; the fourth paragraph may quote from one person's views on the issue at hand, etc.

In representative painting, the composition of a picture uses elements of the fr for its organization. In cubist painting, on the other hand, relations of forms and colors may intrude into the organization of the fr. In any case, if signs are used, they must be presented in objects, which must have their own conditions for existence and coherence. Even nonmaterial presentations of signs, e.g., in conversation, must have their own coherence. For example, conversations are linear, cannot be held endlessly, must use shifters to move from one part to another, "attentional" devices to focus the listener's interest, etc. This is true even more for objects which are read as signs but are not intended primarily as such. Buildings, cities, cars, clothing have their own structure and functions which can only then accommodate the semiotic aspect.

Some Concluding Remarks

The three dimensions discussed here are interdependent, in part overlapping; each may use patterns of the others for its own constitution, but must be considered separately in an analysis. Each requires a very different methodology, because they have their separate modes of integration and cannot be reduced to each other.

Where are artistic norms and values located? Aesthetic or other functions of semiotic objects are based on selections of elements and patterns in all three dimensions. Sometimes an aesthetic function may be located primarily in one dimension, e.g., in the dimension of meaning and reference by Marxists or in the dimension of the organized text by structuralists. Separating the patterning in each dimension in an analysis of any semiotic object must be supplemented by an observation of the relations between them. It seems to me that the separate concerns of recent theories (such as fictionality, metaphor, speech act theory, parallelism) must be seen within one overall framework.

Notes

A previous version of this article appeared in *Poetics Today*, vol. 1, no. 1–2 (Autumn 1979). The theory outlined here will be presented in full in Hrushovski (forthcoming) and was published in summary form in Hrushovski 1976. My thanks to Merlinde Beckelmans and Debbie Ellis for their assistance.

1. Further embedding may be imagined if I think of the students and authorities of this school today, who perceive (ironically?) what the message was to the builders of the school, who, in their turn, quoted Cardozo and his immediate audience.

2. The ideas in this section have been elaborated in detail in Tamir-Ghez and Hrushovski (forthcoming).

3. This term was coined in the Israeli school of poetics, probably by Menakhem Perry and myself, in interaction with a pioneering paper by Harai Golomb (1968). The theory was developed in great complexity and

shown in numerous works of literature by Menakhem Perry and others after him.

4. A further possible hypothesis—that the door was without a building (as in a Bergman movie or surrealist painting)—would, again, impose global restrictions on the whole Field of Reference (or genre of the text).

5. See the discussion in my analysis of *War and Peace* (Hrushovski 1976), especially Chapter 2.

6. I have suggested a general theory for sound-meaning relations in poetry in Hrushovski 1968.

CHAPTER 3

How Do We Establish New Codes of Verisimilitude?
BY SEYMOUR CHATMAN

I have been preoccupied of late with three constellations of ideas: (1) the
ancient concept of the *topoi*, that is, the notion of stores of special and
commonplace knowledge supposed to exist and therefore presupposed by
authors to be in their audience's competence; (2) the Renaissance notion
of *verisimilitude*, that is, the seeming-real, a name for the aesthetic effect
of the proper application of the *topoi*, as recently recovered by the French
structuralists; and (3) the method of textual analysis performed by Roland
Barthes in *S/Z* (1970). Fortified, even solaced by these, I feel emboldened
to ask a simple, a dangerously simple question: what happens when we do
not understand a narrative text though we may understand all the sentences from the strictly linguistic point of view? I shall argue that this
incomprehension (about what the text means, as opposed to what it says)
can be usefully seen as an uncertainty about which *topoi*—or to use the
modern name—which *codes* apply.

" . . . I who am dead." Thus the narrator of Julio Cortázar's short
story "Las babas del diablo," translated as "Blow-Up," the basis of Antonioni's movie. But he adds immediately, "And I'm alive, I'm not trying to
fool anybody." How to make sense of this and similar demands of modern
fiction is, I would argue, a question of verisimilitude. Verisimilitude entails not only the linguistic surface of the message, but also those other
aspects of the communication between encoding author and decoding
reader which reflect unmentioned and presupposed but powerful cultural
conventions. The latter are obviously of special interest to the semiotics of
art, where presupposed meanings abound, indeed knit together the critical
bones of the textual skeleton.

Verisimilitude—based on the *topoi*—is shared by poetics with rhetoric.
The topoi bridge the two disciplines, cement their interdependence. Poetics we confidently define as literary theory, the theory of literariness, as
the Russian formalists put it. Rhetoric's relation to modern thought, however, especially to semiotics, is murky and worth consideration. Rhetoric

is traditionally the art of persuasion in the real world. Or better *suasion*—making the best of a case—since even a superlative argument may not actually convince an audience. In this narrow sense, rhetoric concerns itself with texts which (1) refer to a situation in the real world, and (2) urge the audience actually to behave in a certain way in respect to that situation, or at least to adopt a stance or disposition to so behave. Yet some texts which meet only one of these conditions are also said to have a rhetorical aspect. On the one hand, a newspaper article may recount an incident in the real world without explicitly or implicitly urging anything upon the audience. On the other, a lyric poem, though cast in imperative form, need not and indeed cannot refer to the real world since it is a fiction. The poet cries, "For God's sake hold your tongue, and let me love." But of course it is not I, the real Seymour Chatman, who can fulfill that request. The poem only works insofar as "Donne's" persona, a fictional person, the lyric counterpart to the narrator, addresses another fictional person, not me as real reader. The poem communicates with me only as I muster the appropriate fictional surrogate, that is, an adequate implied reader.

Fictional narratives, which I am particularly interested in, meet neither condition, that is, neither refer to a situation in the real world nor urge the audience to behave in certain ways. So how *can* I—how can Wayne Booth—speak of the rhetoric of fiction? I can do so, in a relatively uninteresting way, by redefining *rhetoric* to mean the nonprescriptive study of any text whatsoever, nonsuasory as well as suasory. Rhetorical analysis would then be separate from and the next step beyond linguistics: it would simply be discourse analysis or "text-linguistics." A more intriguing solution, because it preserves some of the original sense of "rhetoric," is to extend the notion of *suasion* to fictional texts as well. But what does that mean? If the world invoked by a fiction is not real, has no truth value, what are we real readers playing the role of implied readers suaded to do? Obviously we can do nothing *in* that world, but we can do something *with* it, namely, accept it. The suasion urged by a fictional text, then, is that the reader imaginatively accommodate its premises, its assertions, its representations—in short, its autonomy, the autonomy of its world. In this view, the rhetoric of *Madame Bovary* is an invitation extended by its implied author to accept as plausible that a given bourgeoise in nineteenth-century provincial France would in fact feel the feelings and do the doings ascribed to Emma. To the extent that we real readers are suaded of that plausibility, the novel is a rhetorical success.

"Plausibility" is Aristotle's *TO EIKÓS* (*Poetics*, Chapter 9): poetry treats not of "events that have actually happened, but rather, events such as *might* occur and have the capability of occurring in accordance with the laws of *probability*," probability as regulated by the topoi, the storehouses of special and common "places" of knowledge. History differs from fiction as actuality differs from "like-seeming." "Like-seeming" consists of the necessary and the probable. If a man kills his father and marries his mother, it is probable in ancient Greek culture that certain other—and dire—events will occur, for example, that he will be punished by fate. On the other hand, necessity, the *Rhetoric* tells us, controls nonhuman affairs. When air gets colder than thirty-two degrees, rain will necessarily turn to ice or snow. But it is only probable that a wifebeater will also prove ungentlemanly in other ways.

Probability operates in the sphere of character, too. Character, in Aristotle's view, consists of traits superadded to the agents of plot actions. These are treated at length in Book II of the *Rhetoric*: for example, a young man tends to be—will probably be—eager, easily incensed, brash, lusty. In fiction, the likelihood that a young man will manifest such traits crystallizes a general or universal truth distinguishing fiction from the more particular, more "erratic" truth of history. It is that which makes poetry more "philosophical." Special cases are acceptable to history but scorned by fiction.

Since the Italian Renaissance, verisimilitude has been viewed as the convention which accommodates a work "to the prejudices, limitations, and knowledge of the audience," that is, to common opinion rather than scientific demonstration. Now opinion is a psychological matter, that is, it entails audience reaction. So poetic probability must be a rhetorical question. It is impossible to conceive of any text (indeed any semiotic act) apart from the implicit psychology of an implicit audience, though one can agree that what actual audiences do with messages is not significant to poetics, whatever it means to history. Our most perceptive literary theorists argue that each text inscribes a model of the audience, or more precisely of appropriate audience behavior. Meanings cannot mean independently of those who potentially interpret them. They mean for *somebody*. Every text must provide the clues to its own interpretation if it hopes to be interpreted. Literature, as Stanley Fish puts it, is *in* the reader. Or at least partly so. Therefore we must consider the reader's psychology: not its broadly behavioral aspect, but specifically its mechanisms of comprehension.

Now "plausibility" must not be confused with realism. It is not simple lifelikeness, or mimesis of what there *is* in the real world. What constitutes plausibility is radically cultural, hence varies, not only from society to society, but from era to era and from genre to genre. We are quite content to accept the plausibility of a supernatural text if its peculiar demands on our credulity are consistent. Flying carpets, robots, unicorns, and other magical objects, beings, and actions are decorous in texts that are recognizably "fantastic" throughout. What would injure the plausibility of such a text is not the continued proliferation of supernatural elements but precisely the opposite, their sudden and unexplained disappearance. The reader could well feel that a decorum had been breached and that the text was no longer to be trusted, no longer "believable." Unless, of course, some other convention was taking over, playing with the distinction between fantasy and reality.

So we can divide the suasion of texts into two sorts, according to the direction of its reference: whether to the world or to itself, whether extratextual or intratextual. A text urging an audience to take action in the real world (an advertisement, a legal brief, a speech in Congress, a public encomium) is extratextually suasive, though, if well done, it may have intratextual values. It reaches out of itself to get people to take a stand, to change (or to reaffirm) their views about real issues, and to act or at least to feel differently about them. Of course, it must utilize a textual form to do so, but the textual form is secondary, transparent, invisible even, not itself the focus. Indeed, in some cases it must *not* call attention to itself. A jury so awestruck at the beauty of a lawyer's logic might well forget or even suspect the object of his plea. He wants to sound logical only to the extent that that will help his case. He may do so, for example, if by a kind of metonymic contagion he can make his client's behavior sound logical. If evidence is slender and his witness pitiable, rhetoric demands that he switch to a purely emotional appeal.

A fictional text, on the other hand, must be intratextually or *form*-suasive. In Jakobson's metaphor, we attend the formal beauties of the stained-glass window, not what lies beyond. "Form" is used here in a broad sense—not only surface properties like diction, meter, and rhyme, but deeper structural elements: narrative voice, point of view, even the implied author's selection and arrangement of details. What seems essential for a text to succeed in its formal aspect is a certain integrity or cohesiveness, a recognizable consistency of intention throughout. This proves its claim to autonomy, that is, to acceptability as a single, homogeneous (however complex) thing in itself. For all its bizarreness, Emma Bovary's gruesome death is appropriate and plausible. Suicide by other means would somewhat weaken the novel's autonomy; accidental death would considerably weaken it; allowing her to "live happily ever after" would destroy it. It would seem that every theory of interpretation must respect this cohesiveness, seek it through confirmations and redundancies.

A modern view of the function of rhetoric in fictional texts is well characterized by David Lodge on the back cover of the paperback version of Wayne Booth's *The Rhetoric of Fiction* (1961):

"Rhetoric" is Professor Booth's term for the means by which the
writer makes known his vision to the reader and persuades him of
its validity.

Yes, providing we see in "vision" not "that which might be" (in the
"visionary" sense) but "that which holds for the particular world invoked
by this text," and in "validity" not "scientific or other truth-value" but
simply "aesthetic coherence or self-consistency."

So rhetoric is both in the text (put there by the author) and in the
reader. Any real reader has a potential ability, a competence, to become a
successful implied reader, that is, to recognize what is needed for a satisfying interpretation of a text, including the conditions for making it plausible and autonomous. That competence derives from knowledge acquired
and stored over years of reading and living, stored in the topoi, the codes.
Where the text is highly innovative, or otherwise troublesome, the reader
also has the capacity to experiment and to invent codes to accommodate
it. How to characterize this ability—the reader's creativity in working out
textual coherence, that is, the text's verisimilitude—is a subject of some
interest.

The topoi or "places," so the metaphor goes, occupy the mind's
space, a space in which information, common and technical, is stored.
(The metaphor continues in the circuitry of artificial intelligence, with
its "memory banks," "storage," and so on.) We can look at these stock-
piles the way linguists used to look at their counterparts in language (for
semiotics has not yet advanced to its Chomskian phase). Narrative structure presents reservoirs or paradigms, visualizable in the form of vertical
slots intersecting the horizontal dimension of the actually constructed narrative syntagma. From the paradigms of possible forms, the implied author
selects one or a few to actualize a narrative-syntactic element. Syntax combines these elements into well-formed narrative complexes. Narrative artists design narrative constructs—novels, ballets, comic strips, films—according to codes which they assume the audience can identify. They rely on
the audience's knowledge of codes to permit a successful interpretation of
their narratives. The readers presume as a working procedure that the artifact is well-formed and search their memories for the codes—and, more
narrowly, the terms in those codes—to meet each textual demand.

But what happens if readers find no code in their minds to accommodate a given textual demand, or feel that the codes that come to mind are
not really up to the task? As when, in Cortázar's story, we read one moment that the narrator is dead and the next that he is alive. A standard
recourse, I think, is to try out several codes, alone or in tandem. For instance, I have acquired, through my experience with narratives, the code

of "narrator." I know, for instance, that narrators may be relatively vague presences or fully established (if fictional) human beings, and if the latter, that they may be characters or simply authorial surrogates. In "Blow-Up" I know that the narrator is "I," first person, with all that entails, for instance, that the speaker of the discourse is the same person as the protagonist of the story. However, other complications arise later when the protagonist starts being called "he." Another code, that of commonsense physiology, tells me that human beings are either dead or alive but not both. Now the code of figurative language suggests that "dead" may be metaphoric. Or the code of the fantastic allows a literal interpretation: the "living dead" may be possible if the rules of nature are otherwise suspended. And so on. In short, I have potential means for negotiating the text by picking and choosing among the codes that I decide might be relevant. We could define the "correct" set of codes as that chosen because of its optimal explanatory power. In any case, we have laid to rest the notion that reading is a passive activity. The view of the reader actively ransacking various codes to make sense of a text is now widely accepted.

But why call them *codes*? For one thing, to insist that they are learned, not "natural" conventions. We get better at interpretation as we acquire new codes and broaden and subtilize the old. For another, to emphasize their covert character. The text need not and generally does not explain a code like that of the voice of the narrator. It simply presupposes it. A reader who is unacquainted must by hook or crook, like a good handyman or *bricoleur*, gather, imagine, project "facts" and invent or rig out codes to meet the case. (As we all did when we read our first second-person narrative, e.g., Butor's *La Modification*.) Whether consciously or not, one must ask oneself such questions as "Under what set of circumstances could I accept the characterization of a narrator as both alive and dead?"

The third and most important reason to call them codes is that they are structured, that is, they follow nonrandom distributions. By raising to a conscious level the process of code negotiation, we demystify some important elements of the interpretive process. Roland Barthes has already given us brilliant analyses of codes in highly conventional or "readerly" (*lisible*) narratives by Balzac and Poe.

But what about the problems raised by problematic texts like "Blow-Up"? In such cases we recognize the travail of interpretation, the work of deciding which are the maximally informative and cohering codes and subcodes. My own early efforts to come to terms with this story, insofar as I was even conscious of them, are now too buried by the struggle itself to be of use as illustrations of the process. So I shall discuss another interpretation by a critic named Henry Fernández (1968–1969). His interpretation fails, as my earlier interpretation did, in quite understandable ways. The verisimilitude he utilized is inadequate because he chose the wrong codes and, in one crucial place, refused to choose a code at all. Errors of omission in interpretation are perhaps more serious than errors of commission. Here is his plot summary:

> "Las babas del diablo" . . . takes place in Paris. . . . The title . . . is a Spanish commonplace about being right in the devil's drool and escaping before Satan closes his fangs, i.e., a close shave. . . . the protagonist is a photographer [only by avocation; professionally he is a translator] . . . . he is idly walking around when he sees a couple whose picture he snaps and later blows-up in his studio. . . . The couple . . . is a very young man and an older woman. The photographer conjectures that she is a prostitute making a pick-up and is glad to see his picture-taking creates enough confusion to allow the embarrassed boy to flee. . . . However, there was a man sitting in a parked car, who enters the scene during the argument between the woman and the photographer. The [photographer] cannot understand this man's role until after the shots are blown-up and the realization that this was a homosexual pick-up becomes clear. Since the photographer is also the narrator the reader discovers the truth along with him. In a nightmarish scene, the photographer discovers that he, who by arresting time in his photograph saved the boy, must now live out the entire experience as the blown-up shot in his studio comes to life. The boy is saved again and the moving photographic image of the homosexual turns toward the photographer with open mouth. . . . After being tormented by the images in his blow-up, the narrator sees only a sky with moving clouds. . . . (Fernández 1968–1969: 27–28)

Plot summaries, of course, are not innocent: they stem from and embody an interpretation. Here is what Fernández expressly makes of these events; in other words, this is his view of the story's "theme."[1]

At the end of his plot summary—where he left the hero and narrator Michel facing the open mouth of the homosexual—Fernández ventures this observation: Michel "too must experience the feeling of being right in the devil's drool before order can be restored." He goes on to argue that order is in fact restored: at the end of the story Michel is "*content* to merely sit and watch the clouds go by" because, in Fernández's word, he has mastered the hubris, the overweening pride, of trying to capture the encounter with an inappropriate medium, his still camera and darkroom—that is, through a temporal medium. Thus, Fernández implies, Michel is an artist who has learned a valuable aesthetic lesson (the code invoked is the code of philosophy), the lesson that one medium cannot copy another. Though it was scary, the experience was not deeply traumatic or profoundly impactful on the character of Michel. Hubris with media is a mistake that anyone or at least any artist could make and, indeed, it is the same mistake, Fernández argues, that Thomas—Michel's counterpart in Antonioni's film —makes. Fernández predicts that Michel, having corrected the mistake, will "now move in a world beyond the grasp of his camera," that he has been cured of his hubris by the experience.

Let us consider Fernández's basic view, that Michel is an artist who gets into a conflict because he violates aesthetic decorum by trying to do with a still camera what can only be done with a typewriter or some other time-respecting medium. There is no evidence that Michel's obsession with the blown-up photograph is aesthetic: on the contrary, he says himself that there was only one shot on the roll, that of the Conservatoire, that was "worth so much work"—"worth" presumably meaning "aesthetically worth." So quite another code than the aesthetic must be operating. At first glance, perhaps the code of simple curiosity, of detection, the code of the *roman noir*: Michel thinks of looking at the photo from an oblique angle because it "might . . . divulge different aspects" and so on. But what is he looking for? The detective code would say that it is to find out what was going on between the boy and the woman. But why is the inspection so compulsive? Why so many fantasies and speculations? Why is he so emotionally invested in the boy? As one critic notes, why should this presumably street-wise Parisian view a heterosexual pick-up with relative complacency but a homosexual one with such abhorrence? Above all, why should his preoccupation lead to the astounding penultimate paragraph, in which the characters in the photograph begin to move, the photograph takes on a third dimension, and Michel finds himself, apparently against his will, being sucked back through time and space into the very scene of the encounter, into the awful mouth of the vile seducer? It is here that Fernández's aesthetic interpretation really falters; and it is precisely because he refuses to take responsibility for his codes, to make them add up. All he says of the blown-up photograph is that "it acquires movement; it becomes a narrative by coming to life." Period. But in what *sense* does it move, come to life? Literally? Is the code of the supernatural invoked? Metaphorically? Is the code of figures invoked? Hallucinatorily? Is the code of psychopathology invoked? One cannot duck this question: to do so leaves the story uninterpreted. If pressed, Fernández might say that the appropriate code is the figurative. The story is realistic and Michel quite sane: he is simply a sensitive artist who comes to realize that he cannot mix his media, that straining too hard to unearth the true history of that photograph causes him ever so momentarily to "see things," slightly hallucinatorily perhaps but mostly artistically, and that thereby he learns his lesson and will in the future avoid trying to tell stories except through appropriately temporal media.

My purpose is not to denigrate Fernández's interpretation to the glory of my own, but rather to ask how interpretations come to us and what makes us satisfied or dissatisfied with them. The interpretation of a difficult narrative or of any text rests on the procedure popularly called "reading between the lines." How might semiotics characterize such a procedure? Is it not our postulating—after parsing the purely linguistic sense of a text—a theory of its implication or net of implications? And what constitutes the most satisfying interpretation if not a net of implications whose explanatory power is great enough to account for all or as many as possible of the questions that a reading gives rise to? And what would prove that explanatory power if not the occurrence of redundancies, as incidents, traits of character, and so on check each other out? Redundancy and explanatory power strike me as the critical operational principles for weighing the merits of interpretations.

My own early interpretation of the story satisfied me no more than Fernández's. Many questions were unresolved. I shall not give an account of my struggles here (a record of sorts will appear in a forthcoming article in *Poetics Today*). Implicit in it, implicit in all such struggles, was the search for codes as well as for meanings, for finding meanings *through* codes. The master code I finally hit upon was the code of psychopathology. The idea came to me as I puzzled over that bizarre penultimate paragraph. In that paragraph, Michel, who has been busy at his translation, looks up from time to time at the blown-up photograph tacked to the wall. Suddenly, he says, there was nothing left of him. Without warning, movements start taking place in the photo, including the entry of the man in the grey hat from off-frame. Even more bizarrely, Michel says that he himself began to move, passively, toward and *into* the picture. In his words: ". . . in the foreground, a place where the railing was tarnished emerged from the frame. The woman's face turned toward me as though surprised, was enlarging, and then I turned a bit, I mean that the camera turned a little, and without losing sight of the woman I began to close in on the man." Finally the woman is cut out of the frame as if by a movie camera "dollying" forward. The man in the grey hat stays center but ultimately goes out of focus as the camera approaches (this is what would happen with a real lens if it got too close to its subject). What struck me first was that the movement is described precisely as the movement of a *movie* camera. Before, Michel identified himself with his Contax, his still camera; now he has become *malgré lui* a movie camera. But also a movie projector. There is no strong evidence that a code of metaphor is invoked. He seems to be hallucinating, not aesthetically but really. Further, the hallucination occurs during his post hoc survey of the events, not during the events themselves. For in the report of the events as he claims to have actually experienced them, the man had not even come down into the square yet. I recalled that "projection" is a term in psychoanalytic theory, and it occurred to me that what Michel describes might be an instance. I consulted two popularizations, Charles Brenner's *An Elementary Text-book of Psychoanalysis* (1957), and Eric Berne's *Layman's Guide to Psychiatry and Psychoanalysis* (1968). I now see the rhetorical suitability of dipping into such texts: they are themselves storehouses of modern-day psychological topoi, compendia of accepted opinion about mental illness. *Projection* I found defined as "a defense mechanism which results in the individual attributing a (conscious or unconscious) wish or impulse of his own to some other person or for that matter to some nonpersonal object of the outside world. A grossly pathological example of this would be a mentally ill patient who projected his impulses and as a result incorrectly believed himself in danger of physical harm from the F.B.I., the Communists, or the man next door" (Brenner 1957: 101). And the psychosis marked most prominently by projection is paranoic schizophrenia. Now what impulse, I asked myself, could Michel be projecting? And upon whom? Three possible and coexistent projections occurred to me: first, the fear of being homosexually seduced, which he projects onto the boy; second, the more deeply repressed fear of recognizing his own homosexual impulses to seduce an "angelic" boy, which he projects onto the man in the grey hat; and third, the conscious longing to be at peace with the universe, to turn his obsessions off, which he projects onto the passing clouds and birds. The latter projection I could see as a withdrawal, possibly even a catatonia—Michel seems trapped in his top-floor room, doomed to watch the clouds pass, for all intents and purposes dead (his own word) to the world. As I read further about schizophrenia in my latter-day paperback *Topics*, I discovered other symptoms to explain aspects of Michel's behavior hitherto unclear to me. Grandiosity, for example, which explains puzzling statements like: "One of us all has to write, if this is going to get told. Better that it be me who am dead, for I'm less compromised than the rest." Another symptom is that for which the disease is named, the splitting of the personality, which would explain Michel's enormous difficulty with identity: for instance, ". . . nobody really knows who it is telling it, if I am I or what actually occurred or what I'm seeing." The split is even more sensationally manifested in the grammatical flounderings and solecisms of the first paragraph, and in the shifts from self-reference as "I" to self-reference as *he* or *Roberto Michel* throughout the story. Paranoia is also amply present even before we get to the expression of fear that he feels for the man and the woman. Relatively early in the story we

read a mysterious unfinished sentence with clear paranoic import that begins "If they replace me, if, so soon, I don't know what to say ... "
Michel thinks of himself as some mechanical instrument, like his camera and typewriter, an instrument to be replaced by some "them" if it does not function as it is supposed to.

To present all the inferences that flooded in once the code of psychopathology was invoked would take a hundred pages; I limit myself to one that arose fairly late in the game. Assuming that Michel is projecting his own homosexual impulses onto the scene, it occurred to me that the events and characters, the putative villains, may have been quite other than as he depicts them. Going back over the only paragraph in which the man in the grey hat is actually reported to play a role, I find no independent evidence—that is, evidence outside of Michel's own surmise—that the man is in fact a homosexual working in league with the blond. Indeed, at the one moment when something might have been said by him and directly quoted by the narrator to that effect, I found only: "The clown and the woman consulted one another in silence." Is it not conceivable that the man was a total stranger and was simply coming over to find out what was going on, perhaps to help the woman deal with this agitated fellow? All we really know about what happened out on the Ile St. Louis on November 7 is strained through Michel's consciousness, and, given the weird hallucination of the penultimate paragraph, he does not seem to be the world's most reliable narrator.

If we accept Barthes's distinction, "Las babas del diablo" is either *lisible*, 'readerly', or *scriptible*, 'writerly'. If the latter, "il n'y a peut-être rien à dire" (Barthes 1970: 11).[2] The rest is silence. Since every reading of every such text is an independent act of productivity, it is not only impossible but undesirable to ask the questions I have asked, let alone to try to answer them. "Son modèle étant productif (et non plus représentatif), il abolit toute critique, qui, produite, se confondrait avec lui: le ré-écrire ne pourrait consister qu'à le disseminer, à le disperser dans le champ de la difference infinie" (ibid.)[3] If that means what I think it means (who can be sure when it comes to Infinite Difference?), there's not much point in struggling with codes, since there can be no principle of selection for all these readers-become-"writers" to agree upon.

> Le texte scriptible, c'est nous *en train d'écrire*, avant que le jeu infini du monde (le monde comme jeu) ne soit traversé, coupé, arrêté, plastifié par quelque système singulier (Idéologie, Genre, Critique) qui en rabatte sur la pluralité des entrées, l'ouverture des réseaux, l'infini des langages. (ibid.)[4]

Texts like that (if only he had named some!) must make semioticians desperately nervous. Dedicated as we are to the analysis of meaning and of how things come to mean, and assuming as we must that any theory of meaning must reject solipsism, we can hardly agree to a theory of reading some of whose objects are literally unreadable and exist only as disparate nonce constructions by nonce perusers. There must be *some* degree of closure for communication to take place at all. There must be *some* agreement between two or more readers about what a text seems to be saying. In short, *texts*—literary works conceived as webs, as tissues, as sets of interlocking parts—are *only lisible*, or readerly. That is their defining criterion. If there is another art form which relies on the audience's ability to manipulate printed words, let us distinguish it by another term. Perhaps it is something like music, that is, score notations for a performance. But a musical score is not a literary text.

As soon as we insist that our texts are circumscribed and are not simply the infinite play of signifiers, we are back to the same old questions: how do readers and critics decide what texts mean? Or in a more suitably pluralist vein, how do they determine the range of meanings? An old question, but one that will continue to be asked long after the dust storms of *différence* and *différance* have blown themselves out. "Las Babas del diablo," I think, means something, not just any old thing. Even if it means several things, it doesn't mean everything (and so nothing). I don't think it is an infinite play of words. I think it says something of genuine significance, of genuine import to my life. If I didn't think that, I wouldn't struggle to understand the story, and I certainly wouldn't cite it as an instance of the rhetoric of difficult fiction. Nor would I be interested in what someone else thinks it means.

Notes

Some of the material in this essay has appeared in "The Rhetoric of Difficult Fiction: Cortazar's 'Blow-Up'," *Poetics Today*, Vol. 1:4 (Summer 1980).

1. *Theme* is a troubled word in poetics; let me offer my definition. The theme of a fiction I take to be a nexus of story-wide or global assertions of general—that is, extratextual—purport that can be made about it. Thus themes concern the world at large, the world beyond the confines of this text, with its particular characters in their specific situation.

2. "There may be nothing to say." (This translation and those in the following two notes are from Barthes 1974, a translation of *S/Z* by Richard Miller.)

3. "Its model being a productive (and no longer a representative) one, it demolishes any criticism which, once produced, would mix with it: to rewrite the writerly text would consist only in disseminating it, in dispersing it within the field of infinite difference."

4. "The writerly text is *ourselves writing*, before the infinite play of the world (the world as function) is traversed, intersected, stopped, plasticized by some singular system (Ideology, Genus, Criticism) which reduces the plurality of entrances, the opening of networks, the infinity of languages."

CHAPTER 4

Intratextual Rewriting:
Textuality as Language Formation
BY CHARLES F. ALTMAN

We have all had the disconcerting feeling of walking into a movie late. One character is making gestures which do not square with his words; another is reacting to this seemingly banal speech as if it contained a verdict of life or death; a third keeps glancing out the window even though it is dark as pitch outside. The actors are familiar, the surroundings recognizable, the sound track perfectly clear, and yet we remain convinced that we are not hearing everything, not seeing everything, not understanding everything. For during the earlier part of the movie, meaning has somehow come to these images and sounds; a supplementary signification system has been grafted onto the primary photographic and linguistic systems. It is this supplementary system that interests me in this paper. How is it that a film —or any other text for that matter—comes to signify in a way that the late-comer can never understand completely? In sum, how does textuality differ from language? Is the text just another *parole*? Or does it enjoy a special status differing from *parole* as well as from *langue*? This is not a new problem; I shall thus be constantly borrowing from, as well as eventually criticizing, previous responses formulated by Roland Barthes, Christian Metz, and Jurij Lotman.

A child, in first reacting to human sounds, confuses cries of emotion, nonsense syllables, and other nonlinguistic phenomena with the sounds of language itself. Only slowly does the child learn to distinguish language from other sounds, that is, to isolate language's spoken chain. This is not to say that other sounds do not carry meaning: the slam of a door may mean that Daddy is home, the rush of water that he is in the shower, a sudden yelp that he has cut himself shaving. Language is not the only road to meaning in the child's world, nor is it at first the most effective; nevertheless, it is clearly of a different order from alarm clocks, noonday whistles, and cries of pain. The child soon learns to distinguish those sounds that enter into a system from all other sounds. The child progresses from hearing sounds to identifying meaningful sounds to isolating the spoken linguistic chain to learning the language.

A precisely analogous progression, I will claim, governs the reader's construing of a text. Many people have claimed that texts are like languages, but they have generally meant known languages. The analogy which I will set up likens the text to an unknown language, the text constituting both *langue* and *parole*, such that the system of the one must be learned before it is possible to understand the message of the other. As a secondary modeling system, to borrow Lotman's term,[1] every text, whether literary, cinematic, or nonfictional, displays all the attributes of an unfamiliar language, except that of being a shared human institution. In order to support this claim, I will first put aside certain possible objections, for which purpose I will continue to exploit the convenient analogy between the child learning language and the reader reading the text.

Languages are articulated into two levels which for convenience's sake I will call *signs* and *sounds*; the text's two levels I will term *functions* and *signs*.[2] The double articulation associated with language does not at first appear to the child, who in order to articulate language must fight the tendency to construe sounds as noises with immediate meaning. Only by rejecting a direct identification of the sound /o/ with the meaning 'surprise' can the child succeed in discovering a doubly articulated language. Likewise, the reader must resist the temptation to view language solely in terms of its linguistic meaning in order to articulate it with respect to textual meaning. It might be objected that the second articulation of language —sounds—constitutes a nonsignifying level, while the second articulation of the text—signs—is a signifying level. Such an objection is invalid, however, since the nonsignification of the second articulation of language holds only within the linguistic system. The phoneme /s/ does not signify in a linguistic system, but it may well, indeed had better, signify 'snake' to the weekend hiker. Likewise, the second articulation of the text may very well signify, but only at the level of language and not at that of the text. Conversely, not all noises prove to be significant at the level of language (though they may, like a grunt, have a clear sense at the level of phatic signification). So not every sign of a given text proves to be significant at the textual level (though it may have a clear sense at the linguistic level). On the other hand, it might be objected that the textual sign, or function, does not have the arbitrary nature characteristic of the linguistic sign. The musical film's typical relationship between dancing and happiness, for example, seems to be motivated by the frequency with which happy people dance. Yet we have only to witness the usage of dancing to signify 'frustration' or 'desire' or even 'insanity' (as in Zola's *L'Assommoir*) to recognize the limitations of this objection. Even when dancing does signify 'happiness' it is only because the society's texts have arbitrarily linked this activity with that meaning.

As will be readily apparent, this approach differs from that of other semiological analogies now current. First, my claim is not limited to the so-called "artistic" text, but to all secondary modeling systems, linguistic or visual, artistic or not. This does not make the category of art an indefensible one; it does mean, however, that the literary, artistic, or poetic nature of a text must be located somewhere other than in the text's ability to create a new, secondary language. A far more important difference between this and previous approaches grows out of the notion that the reader, like the child, does not necessarily know the text's language before beginning to read it. Most previous critics treat the text as a message rather than as a language. For these critics the text is the intersection of numerous codes, which the reader knows before entering the text. This reader, therefore, is not analogous to the child learning a new language but to the sophisticated researcher separating the various levels of a palimpsest, producing numerous separate texts each in a language the researcher already knows. Ambiguity exists only when separation is not possible. While I do not wish to suggest that texts lack intertextual, or precoded, meaning, I do suggest that the text's most radical and disconcerting method of making meaning is that which derives from its status as secondary modeling system. The experience of reading draws its special nature from the necessity of learning a new language in the course of reading. It is one thing to know the code and receive the message piecemeal; it is an entirely different affair when one must learn the language and construe a message during the same reception. This is the challenge which textual languages extend to us. It remains to be seen how the textual language carries its signification and according to what markers readers are expected to find their way.

A language's ability to make meaning depends on its ability to be commuted. From the point of view of the language learner, the operation of commutation lies at the heart of the arbitrary and doubly articulated nature of the linguistic sign. Only by performing the operation of commutation on the sounds which one hears is it possible to make a language one's own. There is of course a contradiction here, in that a language cannot be commuted unless it is already known, but the contradiction is in fact only apparent. The child tries out many hypothetical commutation operations before ultimately mastering the language. A mistake, whether at the level of sounds or signs, will go unrewarded by the community; that is, it will fail to produce the desired results in the auditors. Only by commuting the language properly, that is, with proper intuition of articulation and meaning alike, can the child obtain the reward of understanding that indicates the end of this particular part of the search. The linguistic community, therefore, or its substitute (such as a teacher or a self-correcting workbook) is the necessary transcendental level which grounds signification and the process of commutation along with it.

The text reveals its meaning in precisely the same fashion. Only through the reader's ability to commute the linguistic chain can the textual language be learned. This process is of course facilitated, as well as complicated, by the reader's prior knowledge of other textual languages, but for the moment I will assume a reader who has no prior knowledge of other textual languages. This reader, I have postulated, learns the textual language by a trial-and-error process of hypothetical commutation, but in order to perform this operation he or she must have commutable material. It is the function of what I will call *intratextual rewriting* to provide this material. It has often been remarked that artistic texts are particularly rich in repetitions, parallelisms, symmetry, and other recall devices. Other texts do not entirely lack such elements, but seem to use them more sparingly. What I call intratextual rewriting involves the reuse of material previously used in the same text. The simplest and most obvious example of intratextual rewriting is rhyme, which provides the model for all other instances, in that it includes a dissimilar context along with the repeated material (for example, *jump/dump*, where the *ump* is repeated, and *j/d* distinctive). This type of relationship can exist at any level in an infinite number of ways: a character enters a room holding a bottle, then later enters holding a gun; a Christian people are described as coveting a province which the pagans also covet; an object shown in a low-angle backlit shot is later shown in a high-angle front-lit shot; a musical theme is first played in one key, then in another; and so forth. Just as the process of commutation in language depends both on the presence in the language of such pairs and on the analyst's ability to draw the two halves of the pair together, so the process of intratextual commutation depends both on the text's capacity for introducing commutable pairs (through the process of intratextual rewriting) and on the reader's ability to bring them together. At this point a simple comparative example is in order.

Consider the English words *cut* and *cup*. If substituting a /p/ for the final /t/ of *cut* changes the meaning, then we can articulate the language, declaring /t/ and /p/ to be phonemes, that is, units of the second articulation. But how do we know if *cut* and *cup* have different meanings, that they are different words? We know by their use at a higher level, by the situations in which they occur, by the paradigms which can accommodate them. The process is of course circular, for in order to commute the language we must know the language, but to know the language is to have implicitly commuted it already. This circularity appears more obviously in the text, because our only method of deciding whether a difference in the second articulation level is significant is by analyzing on the spot the paradigms which will accommodate the first articulation syntagma.

I have belabored these rather obvious points only in order to set up a simple textual parallel. Let us now substitute words for the sounds of *cut* and *cup*. For the two shared phonemes I will put *to sing*; for the /t/ I will put *opera*; for the /p/ I will put *jazz*. In a film where the segment *to sing opera* is intratextually rewritten as *to sing jazz*, the textual language learner must commute the opera/jazz opposition just as the child implicitly commutes the t/p opposition of *cut/cup*. But the learner can commute the opera/jazz opposition if and only if the text ascribes different meanings to singing opera and singing jazz—that is, only if the text forbids substitution of one for the other in the same syntagm. Making this interdiction obvious may be the function of any number of secondary factors, for example, the woman who sings jazz gets the job or the man, while the woman who sings opera does not. Indeed, this is commonly the function of economic or romantic success in the Hollywood film, to *ground* the process of commutation in such a way that it remains entirely unambiguous, in much the same way that the rewards of the linguistic community operate for the child learning language. Now the opera/jazz system just described is a common one in the early films of Judy Garland. A style of music becomes a textual signifier only by virtue of being involved in a series of rewritten pairs permitting commutation of the two musical styles (usually involving parallel but quite different singing scenes). Demonstration of the nonidentity (that is, the commutability) of the two styles is provided by the results of the singing. Compare this to the situation in MGM's Jeanette MacDonald films, where musical style is not articulated for lack of a difference in the signification of diverse styles. For MacDonald the operative commutation opposes singers to nonsingers. Thus, the signification of a given textual sign is defined within the text by the paradigms with which it can be associated, but these paradigms can only be set up by intratextual rewriting. In a Judy Garland musical, the difference between *to sing swing* and *to sing jazz* is not articulated, but the difference between either of those activities and *to sing opera* is. By virtue of its opposition to swing and jazz, *to sing opera* will invariably fit into paradigms of unsociability (vs. friendliness), high art (vs. the people's art), tradition (vs. spontaneity), and failure (vs. success in love and on the job). In the Jeanette MacDonald film *to sing opera* fits into an entirely different set of paired paradigms, not by virtue of the opposition of opera to swing or jazz, but by virtue of the opposition between singing—any kind of singing—and not singing.

We can commute *cut/cup* because the two elements of a minimal pair enter into different sets of paradigms. Similarly, we can commute *to sing opera/to sing jazz* in the Garland film or *to sing/not to sing* in the Mac-Donald film because each *has* a different function and thus *constitutes* a different function—that is, a first articulation unit of the text. As this pair of examples clearly suggests, not every instance of intratextual rewriting will be commutable, a fact which lies at the root of much of the text's ambiguity. Only as the reader moves into the text will he or she be able to decide which rewritten elements to commute and which not. Some texts, however, go to great lengths to avoid such ambiguity. The familiar redundancy shared by myth and most popular texts makes the commutation process a far easier and earlier one. Griffith's Biograph films, for example, tend to be constructed in such a way that each new instance of intratextual rewriting repeats and reinforces the previous one, thus expanding an already existing paradigm rather than opening a new one. In such a situation it is a simple matter, even for the most unsophisticated of viewers, to reconstruct the textual language through a process of commutation which Griffith has done his best to make a trial-and-success one rather than trial-and-error.

At this point it is necessary to consider the relationship of intratextual rewriting to the creation of paradigms, for an understanding of this problem is essential to an appreciation of the difference between the text as a secondary modeling system possessing its own language and the text as a simple element of *parole* in the *langue* which provides its primary system. Now the notion that paradigmatic relations are *in absentia* has always been a fuzzy one, not in terms of its general meaning but in terms of the size of the field from which paradigmatically related terms are absent. At one point in *Langage et cinéma* Christian Metz (1971: 124) states that "a paradigm, by definition, is a class of elements of which only one figures in the text (or at a given point in the text)." Now there is a clear difference between these alternative claims. It is true that the other terms of a paradigm are not usually present within the same sentence, as are the terms of a syntagmatic relationship, yet the paradigm could not even exist if those other terms were not present within the language as a whole, a fact which leads Metz to rephrase his statement: if a syntagm implies contiguous copresence, a paradigm implies distant copresence (1971: 127). But how distant? In terms of a language we may conveniently say that syntagmatic relationships are in the *parole*, but paradigmatic relationships are in the *langue*. But what of a sentence like that of Genesis 27:11, "Esau is a hairy man and I am a smooth man"? Clearly this sentence, like myriad others, belongs to the level of *parole*, but by setting up parallelisms through intratextual rewriting, it highlights paradigmatic relationships, thus taking on the nature of *langue*.

Any *parole* which foregrounds *in praesentia* paradigmatic relationships is what I call a *text*. In one sense this comment is no more than a gloss on Roman Jakobson's (1960) oft-quoted but seldom understood notion that in poetry the paradigmatic axis is projected onto the syntagmatic axis, though I am applying this notion to any text and not just to the poetic or literary text. Indeed, it is most useful to locate the notion of intratextual rewriting in relationship to Jakobson's famous notion: in general we may say that intratextual rewriting is the method whereby the paradigmatic axis is projected onto the syntagmatic axis, or to be more accurate, the method whereby paradigmatic relationships are made to appear in a syntagmatic chain, thus transforming language into text.

Thus far I have for convenience's sake argued as if the text had only one source of meaning, its secondary modeling system or textual language meaning. Clearly, however, this is not the case. The text not only forms a new language; it also lies at the intersection of several preexisting languages. Only by reviewing the three major meaning-making methods and their interrelationship will we be in a position to understand the overall situation of textual meaning.

1. *Linguistic meaning.* This is the meaning derived from the text's primary language, be it French, photography, or any other sign system or combination of systems. No matter what else happens during the course of the text, this level of signification always remains available—though we shall later need to ask why it is that the latecomer is often more aware of linguistic meaning than the spectator who has been present from the beginning. Perhaps the most common error among individuals learning to read texts is the tendency to assume that linguistic meaning is the only type of meaning operative in the text.

2. *Intratextual meaning.* This is the type of meaning which grows out of intratextual rewriting; it is not present in language as such, but is created to a greater or lesser degree in every text. Intratextual meaning systems may be extremely simple, since not all of the linguistic signs present in a given text need be textualized; in a documentary film, for example, intratextual meaning may be relatively unimportant. On the other hand, the percentage of elements textualized serves as a primary indicator of the text's complexity *qua* text. In a doctrinaire realist novel like those of Duranty or Champfleury, few of the descriptive passages are textualized, but in *Madame Bovary* nearly every object appears to enter into a process of textualization. Whatever its extent, intratextual meaning is clearly distinguishable from other types of meaning; indeed it constitutes the basis for the third type.

3. *Intertextual meaning.* In *Eléments de sémiologie* Barthes (1964a: 130 ff.) claims that connotation is a system, yet he always assumes that

each connotation exists prior to the text in which it connotes, thus circumventing the necessity to describe the system by which a sign comes to connote. In "Rhétorique de l'image," Barthes (1964b: 48 ff.) constantly links the notion of connotation to that of *lexique*, as if some sort of connotation dictionary were a given of every language and culture. Before coming to the text, we know what any given sign might connote. But how did that knowledge come to us? And how did that sign come to connote in just that way? These are questions which Barthes never fully comes to terms with, but which the notion of intratextual meaning may illuminate. Suppose I have just seen the most recent Judy Garland movie, one of those in which *to sing jazz*, by opposition to *to sing opera*, becomes a textual function having a textual signification which I might tentatively summarize as the signified 'to be hep.' When I go to my next movie and hear a girl singing jazz, *to sing jazz* will still tend to carry the signification of 'to be hep,' in spite of the absence of the opera-singing which provided the original difference constitutive of the meaning of *to sing jazz*. It is this transfer of intratextual meaning to another text that I am terming intertextual meaning.

At this point it is important to consider various problems of intertextuality which might lead to some confusion. First, intratextual meaning derived from any text is susceptible of being transferred to any other text. The source for intertextual rewriting in the texts which we call artistic may thus be journalistic, historical, religious, or even mental. This is a problem which deserves more comment, but which I cannot develop here.[3] Second, continued use of the same or a similar textual language intertextually results in a code like those which we traditionally identify with generic types. In generically coded texts such as Hollywood genre films, a constant tension exists between what have been called *con*vention and *in*vention; this tension is none other than the tension between coded intertextual meaning and the text's never-ceasing ability to form its own language through intratextual rewriting. In a general way this tension between the text's various types of meaning is a major source of textual ambiguity, as is the conflict between a plurality of potential intertexts. No matter how simple and uncomplicated the text, however, it always remains the potential locus of these three types of meaning, superimposed and sharing peacefully or fighting violently over the text's structure and meaning.

It is instructive to see just how clearly the concept of intratextual rewriting helps to differentiate between these three types of meaning. If we may take the notion of intratextual rewriting to mean that in any given rewritten pair there is a "first writing" and a "rewriting," then the difference between linguistic, intratextual, and intertextual meanings will reside in the different ways in which they view each first writing and rewriting.

For linguistic meaning, there is no difference between first writing and rewriting; the fact that the same term may have previously been used makes no difference to the language itself. From the linguistic point of view, violence is violence, whether attributed to Cowboy or Indian. From the standpoint of intratextual meaning, however, that same violence becomes parametric to an opposition between Cowboy and Indian; the first writing is only a first writing, read at the linguistic level, but the rewriting carries the absence of the first writing along with it. From the point of view of intratextual meaning, Cowboy violence implies a paradigmatic relationship to Indian violence. The rewriting is thus read radically differently from the first writing; in fact, it retrospectively changes our reading of the first writing by inscribing it within a system. With intertextual meaning, the case is different still. Even the first writing is read as the rewriting of previous material. Intratextual meaning may thus be seen as balanced between linguistic and intertextual meaning. Linguistic meaning takes everything as first writing; intertextual meaning takes everything as rewriting. Only intratextual meaning maintains the balance, fully respecting the language formation capabilities of intratextual rewriting by distinguishing between the first writing and the subsequent rewriting.

Thus far I have indiscriminately mixed examples from linguistic and cinematic texts, without considering the specific problems which photographic primary systems pose for the semiotic analogy. Since Christian Metz in a well known essay (1964: 52-90) has supposedly put to rest for good the notion that cinema might be a language, it will be well to reconsider this problem. My conclusions differ from those of Metz because my argument differs from his at three major points:

1. *Level of analysis.* The question which Metz posed is this: is film—that is, the medium itself—a language? The answer he arrived at was inevitably no, because no medium can constitute a language prior to its systematization through the creation of individual texts. Instead of asking whether the film *medium* is a language I will inquire into the linguisticity of the film *text*.

2. *Arbitrariness of filmic signs.* In dealing with what he calls the denotative level, Metz (1968: 111-146) points out that there is little distance between the photographic signifier and signified; photography is a "message without a code," as Roland Barthes (1964b: 42) says. But this is at the level of primary modeling and not of secondary, or textual, meaning. In terms of secondary modeling, as we have seen in the musical style example, a primary sign—be it linguistic, musical, or photographic—can become the signifier of any textual signified desired. When he reaches the connotative level, Metz (1968: 112) insists on the partial motivation of the

signifier, but by motivation he always seems to mean nothing more than the sign's previous use in another text (for example, the use of the cross as a symbol of Christianity is motivated by the fact that Christ died on a cross). But this intertextual borrowing cannot be the same thing as motivation, or we would have to label every borrowed word within a language a motivated sign. Metz has confused motivation with intertextuality.

3. *Double articulation.* Again and again, Metz (1968: 72 ff., 117 ff.) sets up *montage* as a straw man in order to prove that the shot cannot be a basic unit of film, analogous to the second articulation or phonemic unit of language. He is of course perfectly right in this claim, because the shot is the basic unit not of the language itself, but of the apparatus creating the materials on which the language is based. As such the shot is perhaps analogous to the syllable, whose boundaries are created by the passage from an implosion to an explosion in the spoken chain, just as the boundary between shots is created by the passage from the operation of the camera to its stoppage. As Saussure (1959: 50) himself has pointed out, "Syllables are easier to identify than their sounds." The same is true of the second articulation of film. It is not the shot that produces this articulation, but the commutation inspired by intratextual rewriting. Many a background object in a film will never be commuted and thus must remain at the level of photographic (= linguistic) signification, whereas those objects that are commuted enter into functions having textual signification. Seen from this point of view, the process of viewing a text *is* the process of doubly articulating it. Metz's problem with double articulation goes back to the difference between his level of analysis and mine. Since he considers the medium rather than the individual film, he is constantly looking for stable units existing throughout the history of film; not finding them, he concludes that the double articulation characteristic of language does not exist in the cinema and therefore that cinema is not a language. The problem—and the conclusions—are entirely different once the question of double articulation is reinscribed into the problematics of textuality. Seen from this point of view, the double articulation changes from text to text (that is, from textual language to textual language), thus producing no stable units of the type sought by Metz. Though this rapid survey falls far short of being conclusive, it should show the extent to which the questions I am asking—and thus my conclusions—differ from Metz's concerns.

In conclusion, I should like to reflect briefly on the implications of the system I have so rapidly and incompletely outlined. There is a fascinating footnote in the published version of Saussure's *Cours* (1959: 126–127), in which the linguist affirms that "the mind naturally discards associations that becloud the intelligibility of discourse."[4] His claim is in every way supported not only by what we know about language, but also by the comments I have just made about textuality. When sounds become signs their sound value is all but discarded, for to play it up would "becloud the intelligibility" of language. In the same way, when signs become functions in a text, the sign value is at least temporarily submerged beneath the function's value as textual sign. This is why the latecomer often notices more linguistic details than the spectator who arrived on time, for the latter is under the spell of the text's textuality, of its ability to turn one thing into another. Indeed, we may in general say that whenever a unit of a lower order is integrated into a unit of a higher order (that is, whenever a language is formed), the lower order *phenomenon* is repressed by the higher order *structure*. This notion is particularly salient in Freud's famous *Fort! Da!* story, where, by mastering his mother's absence through the practice of intratextual rewriting, a child simultaneously represses that absence and grasps the formative principles of language. For Lacan this learning process signals the child's accession to the realm of the symbolic, a process which the reading of any text recapitulates.

In a more general way we may say that textual ideology is precisely the text's ability to close off the possibilities of language, to limit the reader/speaker to certain ways of modeling the world. Language itself does this to the world of sound. An untrained French speaker cannot distinguish between *the* and *ze* because the French language has not commuted the distinction. A similar process is constantly at work in the text, forcing us to validate, or commute, certain elements and rendering it impossible for us to commute others. By grounding the process of commutation, as the Hollywood narrative typically does with the help of an absolute sexual or ideological binary opposition, the text cuts off the play of language just as language cuts off the play of sound. At the outset I suggested that the text enjoys every property of language except grounding in a human speech community. We can now see that it is precisely this lack which permits the text to construct its own language system, its own supplementary meaning. But a supplement is never gained without a corresponding loss, in this case the repression of *language* by *text*.

But the fascinating thing about the text is that it is aware of this closing off of phenomenological play in favor of structured meaning. To begin with the most obvious example, rhyme foregrounds language's second articulation, thus highlighting the very sounds repressed by language's teleology of meaning. Paradoxically, though, it is only through rhyme and other forms of commutation that meaning was established to begin with. Intratextual rewriting does both simultaneously: it permits the commutation without which the text can have neither articulation nor signification, but by doing so it points back to the lower, linguistic level—the text's stuff rather than its meaning. It is this paradoxical position of the text which makes it self-focusing. Because the text contains its paradigms within the textual *parole*, it always already contains both the construction and deconstruction of its language. With an established language, articulation is automatic, invisible; only the linguist brings distant words and sounds together for purposes of commutation; that is, only the linguist need be concerned with language's linguisticity, but the text is the sum total of the new language, its only *parole* as well as the only place where the *langue* can be discovered. Unless the text contains its own commutability, its own intratextual rewriting, then it cannot become a language, whence the implicit reflexivity of every text (that is, reference to its creation out of language). The special property of the text, as incipient language, is thus to be doubly reflexive. At one and the same time the text foregrounds the process of structuring whereby language is turned into text *and* the process of repression whereby language is repressed by text. Both operations are initiated and controlled by the same technique of intratextual rewriting. It is this conflation of operations in the same material that creates the characteristic double bind whereby the text cannot make meaning without simultaneously repressing and revealing the elements which go into the making of that meaning. Because each text carries its own entire system, because it is a *parole* miming *langue* (or a *langue* miming *parole*), each text reveals both the creative and repressive functions characteristic of language as a whole. This is not all the text does, but it is the text's most characteristic activity: the revelation of a newly formed language through intratextual rewriting.

Notes

1. Throughout this essay, I will slightly modify Lotman's notion of *secondary modeling system*. For Lotman, "art can be described as a sort of secondary language, and the work of art as a text in that language" (1977: 10). By thus assuming that the secondary system *precedes* the text, Lotman raises an unanswerable question about the origins of the secondary system. Like Barthes, Lotman fails to consider the text's role not only in *expressing* a secondary system but also in *forming* that system. Instead of reserving the term *secondary modeling system* for a supratextual, originary level, I will apply it to individual texts on the assumption that the process of secondary modeling can be initiated only by actual texts and not by some imaginary supratextual model. This process is sketched out later in this essay.

2. I follow André Martinet (1966) in identifying the level of signs with the first articulation and the level of sounds with the second articulation.

By extension I will thus identify the text's functions and signs respectively with the first and second articulation of the text.

3. In particular, it is essential to consider recollected activity (childhood memories, social intercourse, ritual occurrences, and so forth) as a potential intertext of the linguistic or pictorial text. Conversely, it must be postulated that literary or artistic texts may serve as intertexts for human activity, that is, as models for the perception, recording, evaluation, projection, and recollection of physical or psychological events. Any theory of textuality must consider the possibility that events, like formal linguistic documents, may constitute texts. Establishing a semiotics of culture is a complicated problem, however, and cannot be given proper treatment in this essay.

4. Saussure's comment appears directly to contradict the Jakobsonian view of the poetic text as self-focusing. In the final pages of this essay, however, I will show why *every* text must be considered to exhibit both attributes.

CHAPTER 5

Inside Greimas's Square: Literary Characters and Cultural Constraints

BY NANCY ARMSTRONG

A. J. Greimas's description of the cultural codes governing the production and consumption of literary narrative resolves the major dilemma that has consistently subverted discussions of character in literature. Virtually all other approaches to the subject have foundered on attempts to explain what characters mean. Conventional readers have always seen characters in fiction as examples of social and psychological laws and thus have tended to confuse the meaning of a character with an ostensible referent in the world of human phenomena. Critics in the formalist tradition have side-stepped this problem by restricting their treatment of character to the level of the signifier, that is, to purely formal relationships within the text. But in doing so, the formalists have ignored the process by which fiction is produced for a reading public. After all, we tend to talk about characters the same way we talk about real human beings because authors have employed the same cultural codes in composing fiction as those used in ordinary descriptions of social experience. It is not surprising, consequently, that literary characters should appear to be both autonomous and referential. The fact remains that characters are primary units of signification for readers at all levels of sophistication.

Ironically, it is not the part of Greimas's work devoted specifically to literature—his book-length analysis (1976) of a Maupassant story, for example—that provides the most useful model for understanding character. In describing narrative syntax (1966a: 173-180; 1971), Greimas follows Propp and dismisses as "independent variables"[1] such stative features of character as appearance, disposition, or education. Greimas (1966a: 222) also denies character its integrity as a literary sign[2] in his semantic analyses where the descriptive terms composing character are levelled with the rest of the words in the text and reorganized in semantic categories. While such form/content divisions of the text have revolutionized the study of plot and theme, they have not advanced proportionately our understanding of character. The linguistic categories identified with Greimas's work on literary narrative simply do not correspond with the social and cultural expectations that readers bring with them to the reading of a text and that make the text's differences meaningful. In contrast with the limitations of his applied criticism, Greimas's more speculative description of the principles governing the possibilities for meaning of any cultural object offers an explanation both for the production of characters and for reader interest in the social and psychological laws apparently manifest there. It is unfortunate that because of his literary analyses—analyses with all of the limitations of formalism—his anthropological model has been largely ignored by literary criticism. For it is Greimas's approach to literature from a more anthropological perspective than a linguistic one that offers the best possibilities for new work on character.

Greimas prefaces the collection of his essays *Du Sens* (1970) by acknowledging that to the degree that meaning in a text is governed by the interpretive traditions of the reader, it cannot be induced from words. He does not concede to utter relativism, however. In the essay "The Interaction of Semiotic Constraints," Greimas and François Rastier (1968) identify the preconditions for the meaning of particular narratives. For purposes of intelligibility, they ask us to "imagine that the human mind, in order to achieve the construction of cultural objects, starts with simple elements and follows a complex course to which it must submit, as well as choices which it can make" (1968: 87). They argue for the operation of "deep structures" logically prior to the general rules organizing cultural materials into discursive forms, and hence prior to the rules governing manifestations in a given language or medium. These structures "define the fundamental mode of existence of an individual or society," according to Greimas and Rastier (1968: 87). In governing the semantic possibilities for both author and reading public, they constitute structures that are obligatory for all cultural communication.

By this reversal of his logical priorities for describing the production of meaning, Greimas avoids imposing linguistic categories on prelinguistic stages of discursive organization. This model consequently offers terms for the description of narrative that treat character, in both its active and stative features, as a meaningful unit. Second, the model attempts to contextualize the semantic universe of the specific text rather than approach it as an independent language system. The meaning of a literary narrative can be determined both deductively, from the rules determining what is meaningful for the culture in general, and inductively, from the specific grammar of the text. In other words, by seeing literary narrative as a manifestation of logically antecedent cultural codes, we allow literary texts

their communicative function and conduct literary analysis in terms that
avoid confusing characters with human phenomena but that can also describe more accurately the systems of meaning to which readers actually
respond.

Greimas first establishes a relationship between the formal sequence
described by Vladimir Propp in his *Morphology of the Folktale* and the
semantic dynamism of Lèvi-Strauss's concept of myth as a binary opposition that seeks symbolic resolution in the form of narrative. In "Narrative
Grammar: Units and Levels" (1971) Greimas contends that these two
models describe levels of narrative production paralleling the deep and surface structures of Chomsky's linguistic model. These two structures are related to one another as well as to the semantic universe shared by author
and reader by an "elementary structure of meaning." All meaning has the
same formal properties, according to Greimas. We conceive meaning as
two sets of binary oppositions which, when spatialized, form a conceptual
square. Once any unit of meaning (S_1) is conceived, we automatically conceive the absence of that meaning $(\bar{S}_1)$, as well as an opposing system of
meaning (S_2) that correspondingly implies its own absence $(\bar{S}_2)$.[3] Granted
that meaning per se independent of any particular text has the same formal properties as narrative, then the logical ground is established for describing the process by which general cultural assumptions are transformed
into particular literary texts. It is at least theoretically possible to describe
a particular narrative in terms of the semantic possibilities made available
to the author by the culture. These are the meaning systems that are abstracted in thematic studies, and those studies which define their terms
oppositionally to complete a conceptual square should seem least arbitrary
because they are intrinsically coherent.

The arbitrariness inevitably involved in designating semantic categories, however, does not disappear with the describing of a closed intertextual system and the assertion that it originates in the culture producing the
text. "The Interaction of Semiotic Constraints" (1968) is Greimas's most
concentrated effort to reduce the arbitrariness of semantic descriptions by
specifying those systems of meaning that regulate the semantic surfaces of
all narrative. "It is accepted," Greimas and Rastier say, "that human societies divide their semantic universes into two dimensions, Culture and Nature, the first defined by the contents they assume and with which they
invest themselves, the second by those which they reject" (1968: 93).
Next Greimas identifies primary semiotic structures "susceptible of interaction" with the structure of kinship described by Lévi-Strauss. Economic
and individual values constitute the possible semantic investments of this
system:

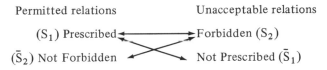

Permitted relations   Unacceptable relations

(S_1) Prescribed ⟷ Forbidden (S_2)

$(\bar{S}_2)$ Not Forbidden ⟷ Not Prescribed $(\bar{S}_1)$

Figure 5-1. Elementary kinship system.

In addition to social prescription and interdiction, sexual relationships may be valued as *profitable* and *unprofitable* and as *desired* and *feared*. Structurally congruent codes—communicating psychosexual, social, and economic values—interact according to a set of rules determining both choice (possible manifestations) and constraints (asemanticity) (Greimas and Rastier 1968: 91-103). These semiotic systems identify the fundamental categories in the organization of the culture, and presumably all meaningful statements will express one or more of these values. Furthermore, narrative will be generated by conflicts within the cultural experience of author and reader among these value systems in order to produce, as Lévi-Strauss describes it, a symbolic resolution to conflicts that cannot be resolved in real life (Lévi-Strauss 1963: 206-232).

The paradigm of the "fully developed" individual, formulated in rough correspondence to the rise of capitalism in England, offered a symbolic resolution for conflict among individual desire, economic necessity, and the demand for stable social relationships. The correlation of delayed gratification and economic gain with social respectability is surely a familiar one, and this reconciliation of the opposing value systems which Greimas identifies as the primary semiotic codes of a culture undoubtedly met problems posed by the interpretation of individual and social experience brought on by social change. So necessary was this cultural paradigm in making experience coherent that, unless we see the novels written during this period in relation to it, we are likely to misconstrue their meaning. In his study of the novel and society, K. Ludwig Pfieffer (1978: 52) argues that the complexity of the classic novel "does not traditionally generate indeterminacy":

> The method of bringing out the insufficiency of everyday paradigms or socially established ideologies, for instance, is, in most traditional novels, an indirect way of asserting more refined paradigms by denying the validity of crude life-world varieties. What may be maintained is that there is a historical process in which the comprehensiveness of literary paradigms is narrowed down, in which the range of paradigms is increasingly restricted. In other words: if it was the original func-

tion of myths to forge images of natural totality out of the diversity of life, then the unifying paradigms of novels may be termed "mythica analoga."[4]

While the great novels of the period inevitably present the social code as an oversimplification of social experience or a denial of the demands of the self, this was literature produced by the middle class for a middle class readership whose needs were served by the paradigm. Although authors refined, supplemented, or even undermined the veracity of that symbolic resolution to cultural conflict which the paradigm offered, this individual dimension of the text is intelligible only in so far as their novels observe the grammar of the cultural myth. The conjunction of the three contending semiotic systems specified by Greimas and evident in the social concept of the fully developed individual does in fact provide the literary paradigm of realistic characterization as formulated in the nineteenth-century novel. This kind of narrative has as its semantic intention the production of a "rounded" or "fully developed" character, in which contradictory values are reconciled with the unification of independently operating codes. According to the critical tradition, the characters of Jane Austen mark the beginning of nineteenth-century realism, and I turn to her novel *Pride and Prejudice* to demonstrate the usefulness of Greimas's cultural model as well as the problems that accompany the reduction of all semiotic experience to three specific codes.

The opening of Austen's novel explicitly states the intention of producing a symbolic conjunction of those semiotic systems identified by Greimas: "It is a truth universally acknowledged, that a single man in possession of a good fortune, must be in want of a wife." The coherence of interpersonal relationships and of the individual character hinges on the verification of this statement. At the novel's opening, the Bennet family is faced with economic ruin and a consequent decline in social position. The marriage of Jane and Bingley constitutes an alignment of social position (Jane is of genteel lineage) with the appropriate economic status (Bingley has a large fortune). Furthermore, this union is ostensibly the expression of spontaneous desire in both individuals, and the match thus promises a symbolic resolution of value systems contending within the culture. It promises to affirm the social rule with which the novel opens, but first it will lend a sentimental meaning to the statement's potentially ironic or purely economic message: Bingley, a man of good fortune, indeed seems to desire a wife from among the needy Bennet daughters. The socially approved match thus accommodates both economic necessity and individual desire.

After positing this ideal conjunction in the first phase of the novel, the Bingley marriage, and hence a symbolic conjunction of values, is postponed. The question arises as to whether such an ideal match is merely a matter of chance (first come, first serve) as the cynical characters claim, in which case the univocality of economic and sentimental messages becomes questionable. The novel proceeds to test the meaning of the initial social rule in terms of a second daughter for whom Bingley is eliminated as a possible match. We can say at this point that the union between Elizabeth and Darcy that comprises the central part of the narrative is a repetition of the ideal to persuade us that a character can indeed manifest both personal desire and economic profit within the social rules.

Desire asserts itself as an independent system of values in the character of Wickham. Wickham has all the amiable qualities of a Bingley but lacks comparable money and social position. But economic necessity throws the second sister together with the odious Mr. Collins, who has usurped both Wickham's social patron and the inheritance that ought to go to a Bennet. Since the oldest daughter is ineligible by virtue of her attachment to Bingley, social prescription designates Elizabeth, the second sister, as the appropriate mate for Collins, a man of good fortune and title. The social ritual of the dance pairs Elizabeth and Collins but excludes the desirable Wickham, and Elizabeth's manners provide no way of refusing Collins's invitation to dance. The social code is demonstrably inadequate for expressing personal desire. The prescribed match between Elizabeth and Collins thus generates a disjunction between those semiotic systems whose conjunction was affirmed in the ideal match, and the meaning of social rules seems consequently arbitrary:

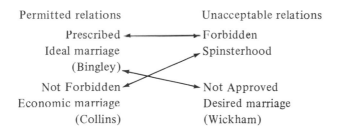

Permitted relations   Unacceptable relations

Prescribed ⟷ Forbidden
Ideal marriage   Spinsterhood
(Bingley)

Not Forbidden   Not Approved
Economic marriage   Desired marriage
(Collins)   (Wickham)

Figure 5-2. Incoherent social model.

In the second phase of the novel, the simple opposition of prescription and interdiction validated by the Jane-Bingley match is reversed in a system of meaning dominated by desire. This reversal opens the possibility of multiple modes of self definition, as well as the impossibility of incorporating the codes in one coherent social model. The narrative reaches a stalemate in which desire and social approval prove mutually obstructive, or semantically contradictory. A kind of paralysis sets in, and the narrative attempts to move beyond this impasse by developing more fully the range of possibilities beyond the simple binary or yes/no opposition. This brings to the surface the suppressed oppositions in a semantic square, corresponding, as Greimas formulates it, to the system of constraints and possibilities for manifestation in Lévi-Strauss's model kinship system:

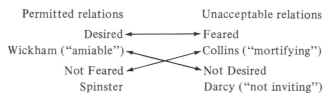

Figure 5-3. Psychosexual code.

The novel first entertains the possibility of negating Collins, who is marked "phobic" in terms of desire, and the negative alternative is clear. Elizabeth courts spinsterhood by refusing a man of good fortune in marriage. When the likes of Collins is socially prescribed, however, spinsterhood becomes a relatively positive alternative, not to be feared. Second, Darcy is brought within the realm of possibilities. In contrast to Collins, Darcy's manner is not a gross distortion of amiability that negates social and economic value. His snobbery is presented as the simple absence of that spontaneous desire which is presented as Wickham's amiability, and accordingly, Darcy is characterized as "not liked" or "not inviting," as distinguished from either "mortifying" or "amiable." But it is with the gradual emergence of the full set of economic relationships operating in the narrative that Darcy becomes the likely location for a conjunction of contending semiotic systems and hence the social model type affirmed by the novel.

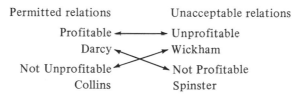

Figure 5-4. Economic code.

He is both acceptable and profitable, and these positive values are not negated by active antipathy. Conversely, Wickham's amiability comes to signify the charm of an adventurer, and marriage with him means both economic ruin and social ostracism. In the terms of the economic code as fully revealed, Collins is relatively unprofitable but certainly preferable to the wanton loss of social and economic status that is incurred by marriage to Wickham. Comparing the final set of social rules with that initially determining what characters mean makes it evident that the former—those prescriptions and interdictions that define the moral intelligence of the enlightened Elizabeth and the narrator's point of view as well—are produced by a conjunction of the code of desire with that of economic values:

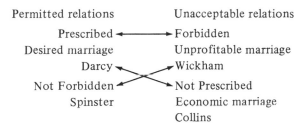

Figure 5-5. Ideal social code.

The production of a mediating structure that reconciles personal desire with economic necessity in a socially approved form constitutes the "education" or "development" of the protagonist. As she violates and then incorporates the three contending systems of meaning, this character emerges out of fragmentation and self-conflict into a complexly unified type. Elizabeth demonstrates Lydia's penchant for pleasure, as well as Charlotte's mercenary concern, and she also entertains the possibility of being a spinster before she achieves a social and economic station accommodating her personal desire. In this way, she incorporates all conflicting female roles and lends them coherence by means of the mediating concepts of "manners" and "judgment." It is this potential multiplicity that signifies the complete character, and this notion of completeness supersedes the simple obedience of the older sister as the positive middle-class model. In this novel, Austen transforms the passive heroine of Romance who adheres to the parental role model into one that is aggressive and complex, capable of change, and a permanent modification of the literary tradition. With her novels, literary character and the middle-class myth of the fully developed individual become mutually validating paradigms.

These paradigms serve to make increasingly complex individual and social experience coherent, so that the sense of multiplicity and freedom of choice is only one side of the narrative. At the end of Austen's novel, meaning in terms of a fixed system of social concepts is firmly attached to each character. We know "greater" from "less" in economic, social, and personal terms, and these hierarchies correspond to the moral values communicated by the novel. Austen's typology of character is unmistakable. Opposing terms are formulated and reformulated to produce a single mode of interpreting human behavior, one that adequately and accurately represents human worth. At the end of *Pride and Prejudice*, consequently, the reader has a sense of linguistic reform. Social status is conjoined with the appropriate intrinsic value in character, and arbitrariness is eliminated from the system of social relationships. The social rule which opens the novel is ironically reversible, saying something sentimental (that rich men desire good wives) but meaning an opposite, ruthlessly materialistic truth (that poor women must marry to survive). The narrative process restores a full and stable meaning to the rule by proving that initially disjunctive systems of meaning are in fact isomorphic.[5]

The correspondence of the semiotic possibilities specified by Greimas and Rastier to the semantic categories operating in such a classic novel as *Pride and Prejudice* provides evidence of a coherent social grammar that is neither literature nor social history per se but which, in Greimas's words (1970: 8), "commande le filtre culturel de notre perception du monde" ["determines the cultural filter of our perception of the world"] and also "sélectionne et arrange les épistémés qui 's'implicitent' dans les objets particuliers—tableaux, poèmes, récits—résultats d'enchevêtrements du signifiant" ["selects and arranges the hierarchy of meanings that are 'implied' in particular objects—paintings, poems, stories—as the results of various combinations of the signifier"] . Because these rules provide the most basic conditions for semiotic experience, however, they tend to be assumed rather than acknowledged in the interpretive process. The advantages of specifying the basic value systems we bring to a text and find verified there should be clear. Greimas's model leads us to the paradigm, modeled on a social grammar, which provides the reader with an idealized or shorthand text for organizing the surplus of signifiers in the classic novel. The difference between incomprehension and an appreciation of pluralism rides on our first recognizing what should be the obvious systems of meaning in operation. Furthermore, studies interested in the specific nature of a literary text, whether from a psychoanalytic, sociohistorical, or purely formal perspective, must abstract the author's personal paradigm from one serving the needs of the culture more generally. In the case of realistic characters, it is certainly necessary to understand them first of all not as representations of a psychological continuum but as a semantic operation serving to verify, modify, or dispute conventional resolutions to a cultural conflict, an operation which Greimas's model can explain. It is possible to determine the social or personal viewpoint expressed by the author's distinctive use of cultural codes only when the primary systems of meaning common to the culture are identified.

While the importance of such reductivism in making accurate critical statements about a text cannot be disputed, the specific terms of Greimas's model bear further examination. The coincidence of the three codes with the operative semantic categories in Austen's novel (and others of its kind) is truly remarkable, so remarkable in fact that it forces us to question the usefulness of these systems as a sufficient explanation of meaning. The kind of novel inaugurated by Jane Austen invariably operates in a dialectic with established norms in order to affirm the categories for self-realization shared by the culture. Greimas takes historical change into account when he cautions that the hierarchy of codes will vary like the definition of common sense from one culture to another.[6] On the basis of the literature he cites, however, we are led to suspect that Greimas relies chiefly on Balzac for verification of his theory, and if Balzac's novels are like Austen's in their conservative attachment to social norms, it is not surprising that we discover a correspondence between *Pride and Prejudice* and the metalanguage that Greimas develops for describing all cultural objects. Inasmuch as it operates in terms of clear distinctions between normalcy and deviance, the realistic novel will naturally be very accommodating to a model that roots intelligibility in the binary opposition of self and society but that, at the same time, asserts their essential isomorphism.

The adequacy of the model is clear in realistic fiction where literary language is semantically congruent with ordinary descriptions of human nature and behavior. A tradition of readers, furthermore, assures us that the opposition of love and money is one that can be induced from the semantic surface of the novel. Dorothy Van Ghent, for example, locates the genius of Austen in "her direct and oblique play with an inherited vocabulary that is materialistic in reference and that she forces—or blandishes or intrigues—into spiritual duties" (Van Ghent 1953: 111). But in much of literature the cultural terms cannot be taken literally and categorized according to their conventional meanings. To the degree that literature is an independent language, the correspondence between the functional categories of a cultural paradigm and those of the semantic surface of narrative will break down. As a case in point, in her study of binary oppositions in a poem by E. E. Cummings, Nomi Tamir-Ghez (1978: 240) follows a basically Greimasian method of discourse analysis but finds it necessary to modify the method according to Lotman's principle that the "poetic text creates its own system of synonyms and antonyms, which often reverses extra-textual semantic values." The reversal of the values of "life" and "death" which she discovers, furthermore, constitute an established literary code rather than the personal expression of the artist. She finds the use of literary codes that overturn or dissolve our ordinary conceptual oppositions to be characteristically modern. While perhaps less dominant in other literatures, these codes operate throughout literary history and in the nineteenth-century novel as well. I see no way, for example, of applying Greimas's semiotic model to *Alice in Wonderland*, because a coherent cultural paradigm is conspicuously absent there. Furthermore, we should consider, once we have successfully articulated a novel in terms of Greimas's three codes, whether we necessarily have the basis for a competent reading of texts that appear to observe the realistic schema.

Such a generically problematic work as Emily Brontë's *Wuthering Heights* can serve to clarify my point. When described in terms of Greimas's model, the novel seems to be a manifestation of the same cultural grammar and to require the same system of literary shorthand for a competent reading as that applied to Austen. In the first half of the novel, Heathcliff is marked "desirable" but "unprofitable," while in the second half, he is "profitable" but "feared." With Heathcliff's disappearance from the text, Hareton Earnshaw, the legitimate heir to the fictional "world," emerges as a socially approved reconciliation of the opposed anti-social excesses manifest in Heathcliff. If this were grounds for a competent reading of the novel, it would be easy to classify Brontë's narrative with Austen's, placing it squarely in the Great Tradition of nineteenth-century realism from which it is traditionally excluded. As in Austen, clearly positive and negative types emerge from muddy semantic waters as personal desire and economic necessity are resolved in a socially approved form.

But the reduction of the narrative to Greimas's three semiotic systems excludes too much of its semantic material. To account for this "extraneous" material, the critic Q. D. Leavis hypothesizes an earlier text that was begun, abandoned, and never excised from the finished manuscript. According to Leavis, it is up to the critic to finish what Brontë started and properly unify the novel. Yet other equally respectable readers base interpretation on the very semantic material that Leavis disregards.[7] In effect, they value a literary code that reverses the ordinary valences of cultural terms rather than one that affirms the middle-class paradigm. While Leavis reorganizes the surface in realistic terms according to the opposition of self and society, others conceive it as romance, which Northrop Frye identifies with the categories divine-human. From this perspective, the intrusion and elimination of Heathcliff in the dynastic succession of Earnshaws is not so much the testing and affirming of social categories as it is an undermining of their empirical base. Supernatural features and hyperbolic deeds are attributed to Heathcliff throughout the narrative, and at death he remains in the world of the narrative with his lover in the form of a ghost. We cannot say, therefore, that one paradigm or the other—the realistic or magical modes of organizing human experience—is actually more primary in generating the meaning of this narrative. While Greimas's codes adequately describe the common expectations we bring to such a novel, they falsify the text by rendering extraneous a philosophically and culturally hostile set of oppositions. Most readers do attempt to reduce the text in order to unify it, and most respond positively to Heathcliff in spite of his negative markings, bringing metaphysical rather than the normally materialistic categories to their reading of character. Recognition of both sets of possibilities is necessary for a literarily competent reading of the novel. In other words, Greimas's description of narrative as the interaction of semiotic constraints demonstrates not only the interdependence of literary and cultural codes, but also—by way of what is left out when the cultural model is imposed on literary language—the degree of independence of literary codes from those of the culture in general.

We must conclude that Greimas has reduced but not eliminated the arbitrariness involved in describing semantic categories.[8] His three specific value systems do not identify for purposes of literary criticism the meaningful categories for all cultural objects, for all narratives, and certainly not for all literature. While the limitations imposed by his terminology on the reading of such a novel as *Wuthering Heights* demonstrate that the semiotic systems at play in literature are too varied and complex to be so neatly specified, the three codes, by virtue of this specificity, do elucidate texts where intelligibility is rooted in middle-class norms, as well as the cultural context where realism is the privileged literary code. In describing such interdependent macro- and micro-universes of meaning, Greimas offers a way of seeing character as a location for the conjunction of codes and avoids the traditional confusion of meaning with some human phenomenon. The mutually verifying relationship between literary and social codes that identifies the language of literary character points us to the ideology maintained by realistic fiction and to the reader gratification it continues to generate, as well as to the nature of a modernist sensibility in fiction and criticism that turns away from this mode.

Notes

1. In his attempt to distinguish the invariable features of narrative, Propp (1971: 20) dismisses as "variables" such historical particulars as the

nomenclature and physical features of character, along with the elements of "style," and reduces the tale "to the functions of the *dramatis personae*." A story is generated whenever a specific sequence of functions is observed. Lévi-Strauss (1960: 139) points out that this model cannot account for a narrative's meaning, because Propp has emptied form of its original content and has then invested it with that of his own culture's terminology, his "heroes" and "villains" for example. While Greimas simplifies Propp's functions in order to demonstrate their conformity with the units of an elementary structure of meaning, and although he describes the agents and recipients of actions in such neutrally "scientific" terms as *actant* or *object*, the specific features of character remain in his model, as in Propp's, an "autonomous structure extraneous to the grammar of narrative *per se*" (Greimas 1971: 800).

2. The notion of the literary sign used here is based on Jurij Lotman's (1977: 22) description of the text as a secondary modeling system: ". . . a text is an integral sign and all the separate signs of the general linguistic text are reduced in the text to the level of elements of this sign." But, he continues, "while it constitutes *one* sign, a text simultaneously remains a text (a sequence of signs) in some natural language, and for that very reason maintains its division into words—the signs of a general linguistic system. A phenomenon thus arises which is characteristic for all art: a text is segmented into signs in different ways when different codes are applied" (p. 22). Since character constitutes a primary unit of signification for the novel reader, character should be considered as an integral sign when it comes to determining its meaning in a cultural context.

3. Greimas's "Narrative Grammar: Units and Levels" is an attempt to demonstrate that, if Propp's categories are reduced to irreversible syntagms, the models of narrative described by Propp and Lévi-Strauss will exhibit the same formal properties. When this has been accomplished, the way is paved for Greimas to describe plot as a transformation of Lévi-Strauss's binary oppositions.

4. Pfieffer establishes the basis for a comparative study of texts as the "relationships between configurations of reality manifest in literary and non-literary fictions" (1978: 45). He argues that the novel always refers to and depends for intelligibility upon cultural paradigms. Differences between novels are then perceived in terms of their differing relationships to the paradigm. Pfieffer borrows his definition of a paradigm from Kuhn and adapts it for purposes of literary analysis. His notion of "networks of shared commitments, beliefs, values, patterns of actions and the like, which meet problems posed by the interpretation of human environment, individual and social life" (1978: 45) and which also establish the interpretive possibilities for the novel, seems basically compatible with Lotman's concept of the text as a secondary modeling system and with the principles of secondary and tertiary language systems outlined in Barthes's semiology, as well as with Greimas's model of the general semiotic conditions

for all cultural objects. The Greimas model is both more limited and more useful than these other concepts to the degree that he systematizes and specifies the rules of the cultural paradigm.

5. Counter to the tendency that focuses on Austen's use of irony, we should regard the opening sentence of *Pride and Prejudice* not so much as an attack on social assumptions, but more as an overstatement of truth which for a while keeps us wondering: will this narrative produce an exception or simply affirm the norm? In its structure and content the sentence is generic, and the purpose of such sentences is "universalization" in reference to fields of experience outside the novel (Fowler 1977: 129–163). This is the very kind of statement that Barthes (1974: 205–206) identifies as the Voice of Science, and if we are to read the novel in its nineteenth-century terms, it is necessary to lend such statements the status of social belief rather than that of mere fiction.

6. In addition to the primary codes which determine the possible semantic investments of kinship relations, Greimas identifies the structure which determines the interaction of these codes. Specifically, this structure (which he calls an *epistemy*) determines the hierarchy of value systems in allowing or constraining manifestations. In Austen, for example, desire is an unlikely manifestation if it contradicts class lines, for this would make it both unprofitable and socially forbidden. In Defoe, Richardson, and Fielding, sexual liaisons across economic boundaries are presented by the violation of one class by another. They are conducted in an atmosphere of impending violence, if such desires are realized at all. That Austen's heroines bring social cohesion as they marry across similar boundaries implies a sociohistorical change from a homeostatic, class-oriented paradigm to one that is individualistic and evolutionary. Greimas and Rastier's (1968: 103) concept of a master code, determining the relative dominance and subordination of cultural codes, thus allows them to take "into account the historicity of the manifestations; its social component appears as *common sense*, implicit or not, which is an axiological and dialectical system immanent in all the semiotic structures of the society under consideration."

7. William Sale (Brontë 1972: 277–278) concludes his assessment of the novel's early reviews by saying that "the critics were finding it difficult to come to terms with a strangely difficult piece of fiction." The problems confronted by the novel's first readers are not resolved by more modern ones, as a cursory survey demonstrates. F. R. Leavis, for example, sees the novel as a "sport" undeserving of inclusion in *The Great Tradition* (p. 27). Q. D. Leavis (1972), in contrast, emphasizes Brontë's subordination of the fantastic to the realistic elements in the narrative. In locating the novel squarely within the tradition of realism, however, Q. D. Leavis finds it necessary to discount the emotional relationships of the first half and emphasize the second, where characters seem more bound by social and economic considerations. It is just this dual basis for coherence which allowed

Arnold Kettle (1960: 140) to say that Brontë's novel is "essentially the same kind of novel as *Oliver Twist*," after David Cecil had convincingly argued (1934: 148) that Brontë "stands outside the main current of nine-teenth-century fiction as markedly as Blake stands outside the main current of eighteenth-century poetry." Cecil concludes that *Wuthering Heights* was "never meant to be the same kind of novel as *Vanity Fair* or *David Copperfield*." Similarly, we find critics like Dorothy Van Ghent (1953: 153–170), J. Hillis Miller (1965: 157–211), and Leo Bersani (1969: 189–229) all placing Brontë in a Romantic tradition by emphasizing the metaphysical theme in her text. In contrast, a sociologically oriented critic like Terry Eagleton will privilege the social and economic codes which Brontë brings to play in her novel, and he finds it coherent in those social categories, not in the prevalent literary terms of her time.

8. Greimas is characteristically aware of the limitations of his models, and this essay would not be complete without reference to his own de-scription of the critical dilemma posed by the several levels at which mean-ing is encoded and thus susceptible to systematic analysis. In his "avant-propos" to *Maupassant* (1976), Greimas argues that the literary text may be described in various ways. Those terms with which we choose to invest the semantic square effectively place boundaries on the text in determin-ing the categories to be discovered there. Whether we choose a set of inde-pendently meaningful terms, those which denote some literary theme or code, or those which are generally meaningful outside the literary context as well as within it, the description we produce is necessarily hypothetical or incomplete.

CHAPTER 6
Semantic Oscillation: A Universal of Artistic Expression
BY ELEMÉR HANKISS

It is a puzzling fact, and it has been noted as such by generations of aestheticians, that the fundamental aesthetic phenomena have always been, and very probably can only be, defined through self-contradictory statements and paradoxes, such as: tragedy arouses fear and pity (Aristotle); it repels and attracts the spectator at the same time (M. Bodkin); the tragic hero is guiltlessly guilty (Aristotle, O. Ludwig); the work of art, or Beauty in general, is purposive without purpose, it inspires disinterested interest (Kant); it is timeless time and motionless motion (Lessing, Lipps); it is illusion and reality (Vaihinger, Lange); it is destructive and creative at once (Nietzsche); it is chaos and order, freedom and restriction simultaneously (Schiller); only by being impersonal can it become personal (T. S. Eliot); it is unity in variety, or multiplicity in uniformity (eighteenth-century thinkers); it is harmonious through dissonance, it is particular and general, abstract and concrete at the same time (Hegel, Lukács); it is concealing and disclosing reality (Carlyle, Heidegger); it gives complete satisfaction and, nevertheless, it leaves you unsatisfied (Santayana); it is obvious yet unspeakable (Goethe); it is meaningful and meaningless at the same time, it is a sign that means nothing but itself (Mukařovský), and so on.

Why all these self-contradictions? Why this compulsion to define aesthetic phenomena with paradoxes? This paper is another attempt, after some others (Richards 1925: 251–252; Langer 1953), to propose an answer to this question.

My answer can be summed up in the following proposition. The presence of these paradoxes and self-contradictions in aesthetic definitions is due to the fact that (1) *semantic oscillation* is a universal of aesthetic expression; and (2) aestheticians use these paradoxes and self-contradictions, and cannot help using them, because they are the only conceptual means of grasping the permanent oscillation between different levels of emotion, meaning, and value that underlies all sorts of literary and other artistic expression, ranging from popular poetry to the most sophisticated forms of contemporary literature.

In what follows, I am going to show that (1) there are two kinds of semantic oscillation; (2) following the increasing importance and intensity of the oscillating devices, there is a more or less continuous, linear transition between nonaesthetic everyday speech and aesthetically relevant poetic expression; (3) these oscillations are omnipresent in the field of aesthetic expression.

Horizontal and Vertical Oscillations

Repetitions (*figurae per repetitionem*) are the source of both "horizontal" and "vertical" oscillations (Hankiss 1971). When the reader's mind, decoding a written message, runs into a sign that it has the impression of having met earlier in the sequence, it is impelled to switch back to this earlier occurrence and will continue the decoding process only after having verified the identity or nonidentity of the two signs (repetitions are indicated in this essay by backward-pointing arrows):

$$x\ x\ x\ x\ x\ x\ x\ x\ x\ x\ A_1\ x\ x\ x\ x\ x\ x\ x\ x\ x\ x\ x\ x\ x\ x\ x\ A_2\ x\ x\ x\ x\ x\ x\ x\ x$$

This is what I have called *horizontal oscillation*. The same repetition may, however, elicit another oscillation as well. To illustrate, here are two rhyming half lines (these and other examples below are taken from Baudelaire's poetry):

$$A_1 \qquad\qquad\qquad\qquad\qquad A_2$$

Les sanglots, les ennuis   de ses affreuses nuits

("Réversibilité")

The decoding mind, arriving at A_2, flashes back to A_1, and verifies the identity of the two words or syllables. But, coming back to A_2 (and I apologize for this clumsy way of describing a subtle mental process), it realizes that something is wrong with this identity. And, in the course of a second flashback, it cannot help recognizing that the two words are iden-

tical only acoustically and have nothing to do with each other semantically. This is an annoying dilemma because the mind, in spite of many frus-
trating experiences, is stubborn enough to believe in an ordered semiotic
universe where the same signs ought to be obliged to mean always the
same things. While it is trying to solve the dilemma and is shuttling between the two words in question—this is what I have called *horizontal
oscillation*—another oscillation is set off as well. Yet this time, it is not
between two words in the message but between two ideas, two states of
mind: between the contradictory ideas of the *identity* and the *nonidentity*
of the two words. As these two ideas have no corresponding signs in the
message, the oscillation between them branches off, so to speak, from the
message, from the horizontal series of signs. So, for the sake of clear distinctions, I shall call this second type a *vertical oscillation* and shall symbo-
lize it by a vertical arrow: ↕. The two oscillations, horizontal and vertical,
elicited by the rhyming lines quoted above, can therefore be represented
in the following way:

A_1 A_2
ennuis   nuits

where the symbols = and ≠ stand for the ideas of identity and nonidentity
respectively. In the following example, on the other hand,

Dans les caveaux d'insondable tristesse

Où, seul avec la Nuit, maussade hôtesse,

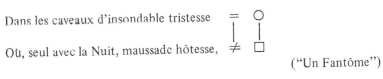

("Un Fantôme")

the horizontal repetition triggers vertical oscillations not only between the
ideas of identity and nonidentity but also between an abstract and a concrete noun—that is, between two different semantic "levels" (I am using
this term in order to remain within the framework of our system of horizontal and vertical axes). In the next quotation, the two levels of positive
and negative values respectively constitute the two poles of the second vertical oscillation:

Alors, ô ma beauté, dites à la vermine

Que j'ai gardé la forme et l'essence divine

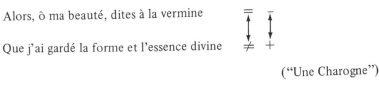

("Une Charogne")

Metaphors bring about particularly strong and rich vertical oscillations. In simple comparisons, however, horizontal oscillations prevail:

Mais la tristesse en moi monte comme la mer

In metaphors, on the other hand, where only the vehicle is encoded in the
message, the reader's mind has to search for the tenor outside the message,
outside the horizontal series of signs, by switching back and forth between
the vehicle and various possible tenors:

la tristesse?
le désespoir?
le souvenir?
la Mort?
? ? ? ?

Une mer monte en moi, ténebreuse et amère . . .

From Everyday Language to Poetic Expression

On another occasion, I tried to show that one of the main links between
everyday speech and poetry is provided by rhetoric, since to "rhetoricize"
a text means to implement a first reorganization of its pattern of signs,
while to "poeticize" it means to proceed to a reorganization of the second
degree. Or to put it more concretely though a bit crudely: a single repetition makes a phrase oratorical whereas a multiple repetition may render it
poetic. It is enough, for instance, to confront a simple everyday notion or
utterance with its own opposite, and one has already crossed the border
line between everyday speech and rhetoric:

Je veux et ne veux pas

This is already a rhetorical figure, an antithesis. If, however, the antithesis
is doubled—that is, if we cause the reader's mind to oscillate between two
pairs of opposites and if, in addition, we arrange these two antitheses in
the form of an isocolon balancing them with an equal number of syllables
—then this threefold or multiple oscillation may already have a poetic
effect and not only a rhetorical one:

Je veux et ne veux pas,   je m'emporte et je n'ose.

This happens to be one of the most famous lines of Corneille's *Cid*. An antithesis may also be turned into a poetic device by opposing in it logically incompatible notions (*oxymoron* is the name of this type of antithesis, so that the reader's mind, in trying to reconcile them but not succeeding, is forced to keep shuttling between them:

Je serai ton cercueil, aimable pestilence!

And this vibration between opposite poles may be still further increased by combining two oxymorons in a chiastic pattern:

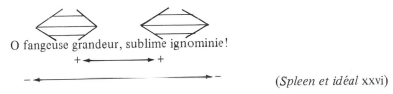

O fangeuse grandeur, sublime ignominie!

(*Spleen et idéal* xxvi)

The same transition from colloquial speech, through rhetorical figures, to poetic expression (by enriching the pattern of repetitions, or oscillations) could be illustrated with dozens of examples. (For further examples see Hankiss 1971.)

Comic expression, being itself an aesthetic quality, is another way of structuring language that mediates between everyday speech and poetic expression. It can be shown that at the source of both poetic and comic experience there is a sudden shift between two semantic or axiological levels. Let us reconsider, first, one or two of the poetic figures we have just cited. Shifts between levels will be symbolized by broken arrows:

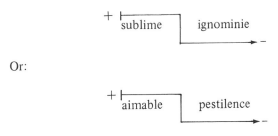

The same kind of sudden shift from positive to negative values takes place in one of the most typical sorts of puns. For example:

Cannibal Boy to His Dad: "But I don't *like* my grandma . . . "
Cannibal Dad to Son: "Shut up and keep eating."

Besides the unexpected and grotesque change in the meaning of the word *like*, there is here, too, a sudden change in the word's value; in the first line, it has a definitely positive connotation, yet in the second, it flashes over to the realm of horridly negative values:

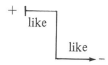

There is, however, an important difference between the comic and the poetic patterns, just as there is a difference between rhetorical and poetic devices. Puns and jokes and gags elicit, as a rule, only a single switching over between two semantic or axiological levels; once we have realized the real meaning of *like* in the pun quoted above, we cannot and do not switch back, in the context of the pun, to its first, positive meaning. Poetic figures, on the other hand, elicit in our minds not only a single switching over but a prolonged oscillation between the two poles:

Both meanings and both the positive and negative values are kept alive in our minds. It is this very oscillation that becomes the source of aesthetic experience. In this respect, the comic repatterning of a text may be considered, just as its rhetorical rearrangement, as a link between nonaesthetic everyday speech, on the one hand, and aesthetically relevant poetic expression, on the other.

Comic devices also work the other way around; they secure a passage from the field of poetry back into everyday reality. They are, for instance, the antagonists of poetic metaphors. The poet, devising a metaphor, transfers the vehicle (the signifier) from its conventionally fixed tenor (the signified) to a new tenor, which usually has only a vague denotation and is rich in connotations. In the following example from Yeats, vehicles appear between quotation marks, tenors in block letters:

But one man loved the *pilgrim* soul in you

("When You Are Old")

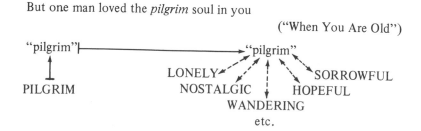

Puns, practical jokes, and cartoon gags, on the other hand, are fond of making this transfer of meaning in the opposite direction. Freud quotes, after Heine, the following joke:

> This lady is like Venus of Milo. She, too, is very old, her teeth are all gone, and she, too, has yellowish spots on her skin.

The transfer of meaning, in this case, can be schematized in the following way:

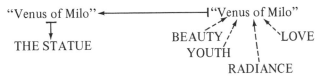

This reversal of the metaphor (that is, taking it in its literal sense by reducing it to the original, nonmetaphoric meaning of the vehicle) is one of the favorite patterns of animated cartoon gags, which show people "sitting on pins and needles," "having their hearts in their mouths," "losing their heads," and so on—in the literal sense of these idioms.

Oscillation as an Essential Factor of Literary Expression

In another essay (Hankiss 1971), I have shown the presence of oscillating devices in every literary genre, from the simplest folk song to the most sophisticated theatre of the absurd in our own age. Let me offer several examples.

Folk Poetry

Mobility and immobility frequently act as the two poles of a vertical oscillation, as in the type of repetition called *anadiplosis* or *epiploche*, which is found in a number of Hungarian folk ballads:

> Ma fille, ô ma fille! dans mon jardin fleuri
>
> De mon premier essaim la fin rayon de miel,
>
> Du fin rayon de miel la cire jaunissante,
>
> De sa cire dorée la fumée rampant au sol,
>
> La fumée rampant au sol et la flamme montant au ciel . . .

Reading gathers momentum here and stops short intermittently, bringing about in this way an alternating chain of mobility/immobility experiences. This oscillation is often reinforced by a syncopated repetition of words ("Père, o père chéri") which is called *epizeuxis* or *geminatio cum interiectione* and which is found in erudite literature as well (Lausberg 1960). The presence and importance of repetitions (and of oscillations generated by them) in folk poetry is such a well-known and obvious fact, however, that it would be superfluous to give further examples here. (See Steinitz 1934; Jolles 1956; Jakobson 1960; Žirmunskij 1964.) And the same goes for poetry in general.

Poetry

Here are two stanzas from Baudelaire's "Confession"—and similar stanzas, poems, lines could be quoted indefinitely from classical, modern, and contemporary poetry—in which a complex network of repetitions dazzles the reader with a firework of oscillations.

> Tout à coup, au milieu de l'intimité libre
>   Eclose à la pâle clarté,
> De vous, riche et sonore instrument où ne vibre
>   Que la radieuse gaîté,
>
> De vous, claire et joyeuse ainsi qu'une fanfare
>   Dans le matin étincelant,
> Une note plaintive, une note bizarre
>   S'échappa, tout en chancelant . . .

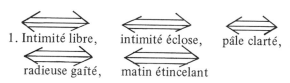

1. Intimité libre,   intimité éclose,   pâle clarté,
   radieuse gaîté,   matin étincelant

All these are metaphors in which an abstract noun and a concrete adjective are yoked together, thus setting off an oscillation between the levels of abstract notions and concrete objects, and triggering at the same time a chain reaction of oscillations between various poles of association. The pattern of these tracks of association blazed by the metaphor *intimité éclose*, for instance, could be sketched in the following rudimentary way:

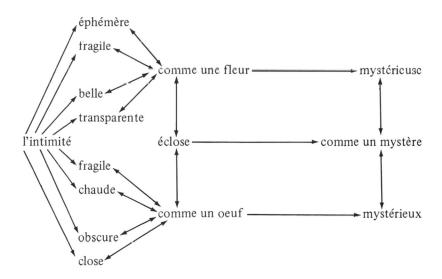

Let us turn to another example:

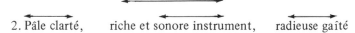

2. Pâle clarté, riche et sonore instrument, radieuse gaîté

These are inversions, consisting of a crossover between the noun and the adjective which raises the meaning of the latter from the level of causal denotations to that of symbolically and emotionally rich connotations.

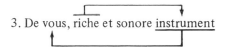

3. De vous, riche et sonore instrument

This is a double metaphor, *instrument* being the metaphor of *vous* 'you', while *riche* in its turn is the metaphorical attribute of *instrument*, suggesting something like "rich in harmonies, in beauty, in joy, in life." A similar double metaphor is to be found in lines 3 and 4:

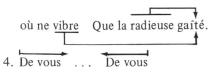

où ne vibre Que la radieuse gaîté.

4. De vous ... De vous

This is an *anaphora*, in which the same word is repeated at the beginning of two lines.

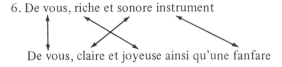

5. Vous   . . .   ainsi qu'une fanfare

This is a comparison.

6. De vous, riche et sonore instrument

De vous, claire et joyeuse ainsi qu'une fanfare

This is an *exargasia*, that is, a repetition of synonymous sentences.

7. "De vous, claire et joyeuse ainsi qu'une fanfare" is a complex pattern of metaphors eliciting oscillations between the levels of concrete and abstract meanings. If the two adjectives are referred to *vous* (the lady), then *claire* becomes a metaphor, whereas *joyeuse* preserves its original, concrete meaning. If, on the contrary, they are connected with *fanfare*, then *claire* turns out to be a synaesthesis, and *joyeuse* a metaphor:

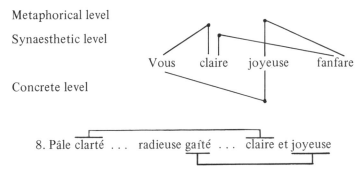

Metaphorical level

Synaesthetic level

Vous   claire   joyeuse   fanfare

Concrete level

8. Pâle clarté   . . .   radieuse gaîté   . . .   claire et joyeuse

This is a *polyptoton* combined with another polyptoton—like *synonymy*, that is, the repetition of the same notion in different forms, in this case linking abstract nouns (*clarté, gaîté*) with concrete adjectives (*claire, joyeuse*).

Let us stop here, as the purpose of this essay is not to give a thoroughgoing interpretation of Baudelaire's "Confession" but only to show the repetitive and oscillatory devices in his poetry and in poetry as a whole. (For further examples see Hankiss 1971.)

Fiction

It is easy to demonstrate that stylistic and poetic devices generating various kinds of oscillations play an important part even in the most matter-of-fact prose works. We have to confine ourselves, however, to only a few examples. Some recent investigations have proved, for instance, that a peculiar kind of oscillation between positive and negative poles of value is one of the basic mechanisms of literary expression. Starting from Propp's famous morphology of Russian fairy tales (Propp 1958), Meletinskij and his associates succeeded in describing folk tales as chains of alternating positive and negative episodes or "functions" (Meletinskij et al. 1969). Another study discovered different kinds of "micro-oscillations" in the style and structure of the novel (Hankiss 1971). A kind of oscillation between positive and negative values can be observed, for instance, in the descriptive passages of novels; or, to put it more precisely, in the descriptions of their protagonists. Balzac, for instance, describes Eugénie Grandet, one of his famous heroines, in the following way (1961: 72–73). Positive and negative value judgments will be marked + and –; conjunctions indicating a manifest swing in the balance of values will be italicized:

$$\overset{-}{\text{Elle avait une tête}} \overset{-}{\text{énorme, le front masculin }} \textit{mais } \overset{+}{\text{délicat du }} \overset{+}{\text{Jupiter}}$$

$$\overset{?}{\text{de Phidias. . . . Les traits de son visage }} \overset{-}{\text{rond, jadis frais et }} \overset{+}{\text{rose, avaient}}$$

$$\overset{-}{\text{été grossis par une petite vérole assez }} \overset{+}{\text{clémente pour n'y point }} \overset{+}{\text{laisser}}$$

$$\overset{-}{\text{de traces, }} \textit{mais } \text{qui avait détruit le velouté de la peau, } \textit{néanmoins } \text{si}$$

$$\overset{+}{\text{douce }} \text{et } \overset{+}{\text{si fine que. . . . Son nez était un }} \overset{+}{\text{peu trop fort, }} \textit{mais } \overset{-}{\text{il}}$$

$$\overset{+}{\text{s'harmonisait avec une }} \overset{+}{\text{bouche d'un rouge de minium. . . .}}$$

This oscillation between two poles can be discovered in almost all the novels, or let us rather say that different types of this oscillation are to be found in novels belonging to various literary periods and movements. In the romantic novels of a Scott, a Dumas, or a Victor Hugo, for instance, the descriptions of the favorite heroines oscillate, as a rule, not between a positive and a negative pole, but between two positive poles. In Thackeray's *Vanity Fair*, Amelia is described through a series of bivalent value judgments; in the novels of Proust, descriptions gradually shift from positive to negative values and vice versa:

Balzac: + – + – + – + – +

Scott: + + + + + + + +

Thackeray: (+ –)(+ –)(+ –)(+ –)

Proust: + + + (+ –)(– +)– – –

Especially strong oscillations can usually be observed in the concluding lines, paragraphs, and pages of novels. Value oscillations present throughout the novels are, as a rule, amplified and intensified in these concluding passages (see Hankiss 1975). Here, for instance, is the closing passage of *The Good Soldier* by Ford Madox Ford. The story is rather well known. Edward, the "good soldier," is in love with his stepdaughter, Nancy. But he wants to spare her from himself, so he sends her off to India. At the very end of the novel he gets a telegram from the girl, reads it, hands it to his friend (the narrator of the novel), takes a pen-knife from his pocket, and says:

> "So long, old man, I must have a bit of rest, you know."
> I did not know what to say. I wanted to say "God bless you," for I also am a sentimentalist. But I thought that perhaps that would not be quite English good form, so I trotted off with the telegram to Leonora. She was quite pleased with it. (1951: 256)

With these words the novel ends. But the reader already knows what Edward read in the telegram: "Safe Brindisi. Having rattling good time. Nancy." This piece of news, taken in the ordinary, everyday sense—good news—amounts to a positive (+) value. For Edward, however, it is the straw that breaks the camel's back; it is the worst possible news for him (−), and the reader knows that as soon as his friend leaves him he will commit suicide, a negative (−) value. He kills himself in despair, at the very moment when his wife is inside reading the telegram and "is happy about it"; thus here we have a value contrast (− ←→ +).

We know that the girl, as soon as she hears of Edward's death, goes insane, clearly a (−) value. The narrator, who was Edward's best friend and who hopelessly loves the girl, loses both of them, a (−) value, but he faithfully nurses the girl afterward, a (+) value. Leonora, Edward's widow, easily and tastelessly finds herself a new husband and lives happily ever after, a (−) value, at least from a moral point of view. And all these values of contrasting prefix do not follow one another sequentially; they are not drawn apart in time. They are evoked almost simultaneously by the very last words of the novel and elicit, in this way, a rich, oxymoron-like oscillation in the reader's mind.

Similar oscillations can be detected in most major novels, though the type and intensity of these oscillations vary according to the writer and the literary period. In cheap, trashy novels, on the contrary, oscillations of this sort are usually weak or nonexistent.

Drama

In dramatic works, oscillations between different poles or levels of meaning are still much more important and explicit. Dramatic criticism typically claims, for instance, that tragic experience is an ambiguous state of mind wavering between pleasure and pain, pity and fear, the demoniac and the ideal, life and death, and so on. This oscillation in the dramatic experience can be empirically demonstrated. In a study done some years ago, for instance, I registered the number of positive and negative interactions (verbal utterances, gestures, and acts expressing sympathy and antipathy) in a handful of tragedies taken from various literary periods, and charted the fluctuation of the "sociometric" value of these tragedies, that is, the changing balance of positive and negative human relations (Hankiss 1973). Figure 6-1 shows the patterns of five of these tragedies. As can be clearly seen, these tragedies, as far as their sociometric oscillation is concerned, belong to three different types.

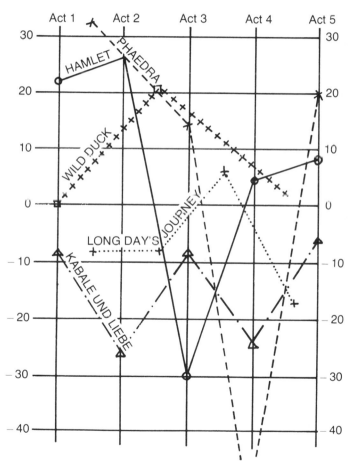

Figure 6-1. Patterns of five tragedies.

The two early tragedies, Shakespeare's *Hamlet* and Racine's *Phaedra*, start with a strong predominance of positive human relationships; later, in the third and fourth acts, respectively, the heroes of the plays, and the spectators with them, are precipitated into the realm of negative human relations; then in the last act(s), they veer about and struggle their way back to a more positive level. This final tipping of the balance of human relationships to the positive side is likely to contribute to the creation of cathartic effect at the closure of these plays.

In Schiller's *Kabale und Liebe* there is a continuous (romantic? melo-dramatic?) fluctuation between more or less negative levels of human re-lationships.

The graphs of the two modern plays, Ibsen's *Wild Duck* and O'Neill's *Long Day's Journey into Night*, are the exact reverse of those of the two earlier plays. They start at a low positive level of human relationships, they reach a climax (rather than a low-water mark) in the middle part of the play, then change their direction and slope downward in the last act(s), eliciting in this way an anticathartic rather than a cathartic effect in the spectators.

Beside these and various other kinds of "macro-oscillations," there is in all these plays a very rich "micro-oscillation," similar to that observed in lyrical poetry and fiction. By way of illustration let us briefly analyze a short passage in the first scene of the third act of *Hamlet*, where Hamlet attacks Ophelia and accuses her and the whole world of corruption and dishonesty. It is a more or less common experience of spectators that here he is right with respect to the environing world (+ impulse), but is only partly right in relation to Ophelia (+ – impulses); we protest, at the same time, against his brutality (– impulse) and feel that he is destroying some-thing valuable in Ophelia (– impulse); but we sympathize with him, never-theless, because we are pervaded by his tragic despair and because we have definitely sided with him in his struggle against Claudius (+ impulse). On the other hand, we generally sympathize with Ophelia (+ impulse), but at this moment we reprobate her for cheating and betraying Hamlet (– impulse), even if involuntarily. But the fact that her punishment is out of all proportion to the offense causes us to take pity on her (+ impulse), and so on. (For further analysis of this scene and its "impulse pattern" see Hankiss 1970.)

Oscillation and the Communication Model of Poetic Experience

Oscillations can be examined and classified, however, not only according to literary genres but also according to the constitutive factors, or "functions," of verbal communication as defined by Jakobson (Jakobson 1960: 350–358). It can be shown that oscillatory devices are at work not only in the *Poetic* and *Emotive* functions, where their presence is obvious, but probably in all other functions as well—in the *Phatic* and *Conative* functions, for instance, or even in the *Metalingual* function, where their presence seems, at first sight, unlikely.

The Phatic Function

Jakobson defines this function in the following way: "There are messages primarily serving to establish, to prolong, or to discontinue communication, to check whether the channel works . . . , to attract the attention of the interlocutor or to confirm his continued attention. . . . " And he adds that the working of this function "may be displayed by a profuse exchange of ritualized formulas, by entire dialogues with the mere purport of prolonging communication" (Jakobson 1960: 355). Now, it can be shown that some of the formulas serving to establish aesthetic communication are very rich in oscillatory devices; their function is not only to establish communication but also to trigger, from the very beginning of communication, oscillations that will echo throughout the communication process. In the stereotyped openings of Hungarian folktales, for instance, there is an *epizeuxis*-like rocking, seesawing word repetition; the storyteller begins the story, draws back for a moment, starts afresh, and goes on with the story uninterrupted:

| $\longrightarrow$ | $\longleftarrow$ | | $\longrightarrow$ |

There was — or maybe there wasn't — once upon a time, then, there was . . .

These repetitive beginnings elicit, however, something more important than a movement/immobility oscillation: they also set off a vertical oscillation between the experience of reality and illusion and between existence and nonexistence, and this by constructing a chain of contradictory affirmations (+) and negations (−):

  $\qquad$ + $\qquad\qquad$ − $\qquad\qquad$ +
Once upon a time there was, or wasn't, on the other side of seventy

  $\qquad\qquad$ + $\qquad\quad$ − $\qquad\qquad$ + $\qquad\quad$ −
countries, on this side of the other side, on the other side of this side,

  +
once upon a time there was . . .

And examples of this kind could be multiplied.

The Conative Function

In an earlier paper I sought an answer to the question of how poets reach their readers and found that only a negligible minority of lyrical poems are addressed, at least directly and explicitly, to the reader (Hankiss 1972). The overwhelming majority of poems, at least European lyrical poems written since the Renaissance, are addressed, directly and explicitly, not to the reader but to somebody or something else, or they are not addressed to anybody or anything at all, and they ignore, or pretend to ignore, the existence of the reader. That is to say, if we designate the poet by the symbol A, the somebody or something addressed in the poem by the symbol B, and the reader of the poem by the symbol R, then we cannot yet fix the reader's place in the communication model of the poem:

$$A \longmapsto\!\!\!\longrightarrow B$$

$$R \quad ?$$

The poet, however, cannot do without readers and consequently strives to help them enter the communication circuit. The question is, how? Most often by leaving factor B "open," that is, by not specifying too strictly the identity of the addressee and thus allowing the reader to identify with the person or thing being addressed.

The reader has two other ways to enter the communication circle: he or she can "plug in" not only at pole B but also at pole A of the circuit, that is, become a substitute for the *addresser*—in this case, the poet. It is a matter of common experience that, when one is listening to a poem for the first time, one automatically assumes the position of the addressee, but when one begins to feel the poem congenial, when one rereads it or memorizes it, sooner or later—sometimes already when reading the first words or lines of the poem—there is a click, a sudden metamorphosis, and without even noticing the change, one goes on reading the poem as one's own experience, one's own confession or message to the world. It might even be ascertained that, in the majority of cases, the meaning of the poem is wholly realized by the reader only after this crossover has taken place, that is, after the reader has changed from addressee into addresser.

This metamorphosis of the reader entails, however, an important change in the meaning of the poem, for the meaning (M) of linguistic signs and messages is different at the input and at the output of the communication channel: they do not mean exactly the same for those who use them as addressers and for those who receive them as addressees. So the reader of the poem—who is, or may be, simultaneously the addresser and the addressee of the poetic message—will grasp *two meanings of the poem* ($M_a + M_b$) at the same time. This is a special semantic phenomenon (eliciting a kind of oscillation between the two meanings), as in everyday speech M_a and M_b mutually exclude each other or at least seldom occur together.

The reader's third possibility for taking part in a communication process is not to plug in either at the addressee's or at the addresser's pole but just to stand by, look on, and listen to what the addresser (the poet) is saying to the fictitious addressee. Here the spectator is listening, nay, eavesdropping, at the theatre, or the reader of fiction is "secretly" watching what is going on in the novel. This tapping, or intercepting, of the communication process is probably the most important channel of poetic information. And in this third process, a third meaning of the poem (M_c) comes into being: the meaning the poem has for somebody who intercepts and watches the communication process from outside.

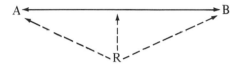

In intense poetic experience all the three semantic aspects are likely to be present, and the reader, continuously switching back and forth among them, understands the poem as addresser (M_a), addressee (M_b), and outside observer (M_c) all at the same time. This three-channel communication between the poet and the reader   not to be found in real life, where one is either addresser, or addressee, or outside observer of the communication process—and the semantic oscillation triggered off by it is, in my opinion, one of the most important criteria of poetic communication.

The Metalingual Function

Jakobson describes this function in the following way: "Whenever the addresser and/or the addressee need to check up whether they use the same code, speech is focused on the CODE: it performs a METALIN-GUAL (i.e. glossing) function" (Jakobson 1960: 356). I shall use the term in a broader sense and shall call it a metalingual act whenever "object language," due to some outside interference or even "sabotage," breaks up and, as a result, derails the communication process, exposing itself and its own inner mechanisms to the outside observer. As Jakobson states, this metalanguage "is not only a necessary scientific tool utilized by logicians and linguists" and not only plays an important role "in our everyday language" (Jakobson 1960: 356), but it also has an aesthetic function. One of the main sources of comic expression lies in the process of breaking up the conventionally tight relationship between objects and signs, disclosing in this way one of the basic structural elements of language. And jokes, punch lines, and cartoon film gags go even further than this; they break one of the strongest linguistic taboos safeguarding the strict separation of the world of signs from the world of objects, and they start shuttling back and forth between these two realms. In a Hungarian animated cartoon, for instance, the teenage master detective in pursuit of a criminal in the street collides with an advertising post which bears the painted sign of Santa Claus (here we are in the realm of signs). Afterward, he emerges on the other side of the post wearing a Santa Claus outfit (here we have switched to the realm of objects), still running, while his own blue-striped shirt (an object) suddenly appears on the advertisement in the place of the Santa Claus outfit (that is, in the realm of signs). An even more daring scene from another cartoon series, eliciting an even more dazzling oscillation between the realm of signs and that of objects, is the escape of a convict wearing a striped prisoner's jacket that resembles the white stripes painted on the street for a pedestrian crosswalk. In order to fool his pursuers, he suddenly lies down on the striped crosswalk and literally becomes one with it, to the point that cars and trucks can even drive over him without hurting him. With the danger passed, he quietly gets up and walks away. By doing so he changes from object into sign, and from sign right back into object. We are treated to an even weirder semiotic extravaganza in another Hungarian trick film in which a painter draws the portrait of a man. The resulting picture, however, is a terrible distortion and does not resemble the customer at all. When the latter objects and points out how this is no picture of him at all, the painter starts to beat him until, bruised and tattered, black and blue, he actually looks like his distorted carica-ture. What we have here is not a sign representing the object, but the object (the customer) representing the sign (the portrait). This is an actual "metalingual" oscillation.

I am not the first, and certainly not the last, to point out the presence of these oscillatory devices in literary works and to stress their importance in the generation of artistic experience. Goethe remarked that tragedy elicits a "wavering and unstable" state of mind in the spectator. Friedrich Schlegel spoke of "the charming symmetry of contradictions, the marvel-lous eternal alternation of enthusiasm and irony" as the main source of poetic inspiration (Schlegel 1882: 2: 361-362). Poetic expression "oscil-lates" between conceptual and musical expression according to Henri Delacroix (Delacroix 1927: 412) and between sound and meaning, in the wording of Valéry (1958); Heinrich Lausberg discovered "oscillations" in rhetorical figures (Lausberg 1960: 1: 332). "Vacillation," "oscillation," "oscillating systems" are key words in I. A. Richards's theory of litera-ture (Richards 1925: 251 ff.). Even Georg Lukács refers to the "wavering," "fluttering," "fluctuating" character of aesthetic experience (Lukács 1965: 1: 696, 697; 2: 22, 137, 175, 189, 208).

My own studies have confirmed their findings and have shown that in literary works every stylistic and poetic device   rhymes and metaphors, parallelisms and inversions, epic and dramatic structures, syntactic and semantic patterns—serves to create and perpetuate an intense oscillation between different levels of meaning, emotion, and value—an oscillation that is probably an aesthetic universal and one of the main sources of aesthetic experience.

CHAPTER 7
The Literary Artifact
BY MIROSLAV ČERVENKA

The concept of the work of art as not only a complex texture, a structure of signs, but also a "single" coherent and integral sign affords an important starting point for a general theory of art. It opens the way for solving such basic problems as the relation of the work of art to extra-artistic reality, to the personalities of the author and the recipient, and to the structure of society and culture. However, these opportunities for explaining the relations of an artwork to its external contexts have to be buttressed with a further clarification of the problems concerning the internal structure of this proposed work-sign in the individual branches of the arts.

The Prague School, which remains the inspirational basis for this line of inquiry, did not sufficiently explain the relation between their thesis of the artwork as a single integral sign on the one hand and their analysis of the work as a many-sided semiotic process on the other. Some uncertainty as a result has developed around the concept of the aesthetic object. Mukařovský, who has clarified the complexity of the semantic structure of the literary work better than anybody else, stated in his treatment of the semiotic character of the work of art (1934a) that the locus of an "aesthetic object" (that is, the meaning of an artistic sign) is the collective consciousness; but this is in evident contradiction to the complexity of semiotic processes connected with the work. Therefore I have preferred the view, in accordance with tradition (Christiansen 1909) and also with some other statements by Mukařovský himself (Mukařovský 1936: 52) that the locus of the aesthetic object in all its complexity can only be the consciousness of the perceiving subject (Červenka 1973: 157; 1978: 167). This again is just an opinion and needs further elaboration in light of the problems handled more easily by Mukařovský's original thesis.[1]

In the following pages I should like to add a few ideas concerning the other pole of the literary work conceived as an integral sign, the *signifier* or *artifact*. It would not be correct to understand these remarks as a continued attack against Mukařovský's theory of the artistic sign. Mukařovský was not concerned with a static conceptual scheme but with the possibilities implied in a certain epistemological standpoint; in his methodology, concepts are used as instruments, and their meanings change according to what other concepts they are opposed to at a given moment. So, for example, the quality of "thingness" (*věcnost*) was sometimes attributed (1934a) to the artifact (that is, the sensorily perceptible signifier of the artistic sign) as an opposite to nonmaterial meaning, whereas in other places (1943) "thingness" was connected with the "unintentional" elements of the artistic work, which were identified with the very opposite of semioticity. In Mukařovský, concepts function simply as conveniences, allowing him to stress whatever aspect of the problem is needed in developing his theory and to leave other aspects unexplained. In this way some contradictions appear which give the whole system a nondefinitive character; at the same time, however, they often lead to the posing of new problems. Our task now is not to systematize or close anything—to mummify it—but rather to try to carry on in the same way. This is not to say, of course, that we should not endeavor to clarify some points which have become especially unclear. For instance, it seems that a certain looseness and tentativeness in relation to ontological problems enabled Mukařovský to treat whole clusters of questions in an almost metaphorical way; at present, such a tentativeness would not do. That is why my attention has been directed toward the artifact.

The concept of the artwork as a single integral sign was developed by Mukařovský almost exclusively within the framework of his general theory of art. At the same time, he clarified the specificity of the literary work most penetratingly through another conceptual key, the category of material (1940: 84). The material of literature is linguistic signs, characterized first of all by the fact that they are not only preformed but also generally known and used in the extra-artistic sphere.

To some extent this genetic independence, and especially the inherent discreteness of the linguistic signs constituting messages unfolding in time (Jakobson 1967), makes it difficult, especially in a literary work, to integrate the individual sign elements into a coherent, unified work-sign. We are clearly faced with a different situation than that of a visual work, where the individual partial signifiers and their appurtenant denotations and connotations interpenetrate in such a way that it is very difficult, to say the least, to distinguish them (except in some special cases). Also, from the linguistic point of view, there arise difficulties once we try to enlarge the category of the sign so as to embrace hierarchically higher units than the word, or better, naming. (Cf. Stempel's introductory remarks to Červenka 1978: 29; Stempel's important critical thoughts on the structuralist explication of the artwork as a coherent sign have been one of the incentives for my present attempt at tackling the theme of the artifact.)

Under what conditions do lexical units higher than the word become integral signs in the extraliterary sphere? The simplest example of such a process are idiomatic phrases like "to take to one's heels" (*vzít nohy na ramena*). It means the same as "to run away" (with some additional connotations), and the path from the signifier (sound) to the translatable meaning is quite short, perhaps not even requiring a decomposition into individual signs (except, of course, when jokes play on the literal meaning of individual words). The same can be said about magical formulas or more complex linguistic formations. Whatever pains are taken by the justice of the peace in addressing an engaged couple, many participants of the wedding will receive the sounds coming from his mouth as the signifier of one performative meaning: "I am marrying you." Otruba (1970) has analyzed Czech journalistic texts of the second half of the nineteenth century which defended the authenticity of seemingly ancient Czech manuscripts; he came to the conclusion that despite all their individual variations, these often long-winded statements have practically no denotation, and their connotative meaning is identical in all cases—part of the repetitive ritual of public national- and self-purgation. The common feature of these linguistic formations is a low degree of complexity and repetitiveness in the meaning conveyed, which is known to all participants of the communication in advance. Even in the case of a literary work one cannot deny that the same or similar processes are functioning in the fusion of the individual signs into a single work-sign. However, there is no doubt that for literature, the heart of the matter lies elsewhere.

The question is whether the constitution of the artwork as an integral sign is not based on exactly opposite processes. I trust that it is not necessary to discuss here in detail what has been formulated many times elsewhere. Under the domination of the aesthetic function new signs are constituted in an artistic text which are based on a multiplex exploitation of the same "substance" simultaneously organized in a number of signifiers. Their gradually arising meanings produce complex semantic relations, articulating the continuum of extralinguistic experience in different ways. Thus, the interpenetration of meanings, each of which has a discrete character of its own, gives rise to a complex, unique, continuous meaning. In this simultaneous process of integrating elements into several contexts, an important role is played by signs that are preformed not in the extra-literary sphere but in literature itself (rhythm, composition, genres, and characteristic features of individual artistic periods and styles) or ad hoc within the individual text. Even features of nonartistic linguistic formations applied outside the corresponding communicational circle and situation participate in this semantic process. Meanings constituted in this fashion are, of course, hierarchically ordered and can be abstractly divided into parts to which we attribute corresponding signifiers. However, all this does nothing to alter the fact that these parts are mutually interconnected (in a more complex way than words in common utterances) and therefore tend toward integration and the formation of a single work-sign.

This is a short summary of what has been elaborated in more detail in other papers (Janković 1967; Červenka 1978), and is based on Mukařovský's general and concrete analyses of the semantic structure of the literary work. However, it is not in accord with his definition of the artifact as the signifier of the work-sign.

In Mukařovský's study "Art as a Semiotic Fact" (1934a: 85), the basic conception of which was never modified by the author, the artifact[2] is characterized by two features: first, that it is the "thing representing the work of art in the sensory world" and, second, that "it functions as an external symbol (the *signifiant* according to Saussure's terminology)." Just as the analogy with linguistic meaning had led Mukařovský to locate the aesthetic object in the collective consciousness, the analogy with the linguistic signifier allowed him to claim that the vehicle of meaning in the work of art has a sensory nature.

However, do both these qualities ("to be a thing" and "to be a signifier") have the same extension in the literary work? If it were so, the sphere of the signifier would constitute only the lowest stratum of the artwork, the "sound" component of its verbal level. All the rest would become a loosely defined aesthetic object functioning as the meaning of the work-sign. In interpreting the artwork as an integral sign the danger arises that the impoverished, reduced signifier will not be able to bear the semantic complexity and dynamism of the aesthetic object, which is here for the moment mechanistically conceived as something "consisting of what the subjective states of consciousness evoked in the members of a certain collectivity have in common" (1934a: 85). The work-sign is limited to the collocation of sensorily perceptible sounds and the collectively acceptable scheme of meaning. All the intermediate levels, in which the unique semantic activity takes place, are somehow lost in this conception.

Perhaps you will permit me a small digression at this point to recall Morris's definition of the artistic work-sign. It represents to my mind a mirror-image of Mukařovský's concept. If, according to Morris (1939–1940), the designatum of the artwork is a value, then the sphere of the signified is limited to the thinnest upper stratum, the highest level of the semantic hierarchy; all the rest is shifted to the realm of the signifier which represents this value iconically. The danger of ignoring the complexity of the artwork in both cases is equally great.

My proposed solution for the artwork considered as an integral sign is to broaden both the category of the signifier vis-à-vis Mukařovský and the category of the signified vis-à-vis Morris. This means, returning to Mukařovský, that we shall credit the quality of "being a signifier" with a larger extension in the literary work than the quality which I now describe tentatively as "being a thing" (I shall define it more precisely later on). Naturally I assume that those parts of the work that appear as signifieds vis-à-vis the lower levels appear as signifiers vis-à-vis the higher levels.

Any meaning or complex of meanings is subjected to this process in one way or another (or better, in several ways at the same time) during the constitution of the aesthetic object, as long as this constitution takes place under the domination of the aesthetic function. (When some other function prevails, the process of transformation of signifieds into signifiers is blocked at a certain stage.) Meanings fuse into groups that are able to function as signifiers of signs of a higher order. This integration proceeds along several axes which correspond to the various semiotic systems functioning in the constitution of the aesthetic object: the thematic line, the line of metaphorical, allegorical, or symbolic meaning, the line constituting the semantic complex of the persona (where the meanings of all the other levels become signifiers of specific indexical signs), and the line of connotated meanings signified by stylistic (artistic or extra-artistic) formations (Červenka and Jankovič 1976). Further there is the line of "gestalts" which are also constituted (as in the case of composition or genre) out of meanings and complexes of meanings placed high in the hierarchy (for example, thematic complexes).

If one were to list all the types and directions of these transformations in all their dynamics, one would be obliged to present a whole theory of the semantic structure of the artwork, including poetics. This is certainly not my present task. I merely want to explain the thesis that, besides sensorily perceptible elements and their relations, the sphere of the signifier incorporates virtually the whole artwork (not as one whole, to be sure, but in the form of individual structures constituted within the work). The only exception to this is the highest level of the total meaning which, of course, being signified by all the parts, does not signify anything at all within that framework. This semiotic process functions during the constitution of the aesthetic object and merges with some aspects of this constitution, as should be expected of immaterial signifiers in the constant process of becoming. The aspects of the aesthetic object concerned are those closest to the intersubjective regulatory structures (the *Regelstrukturen* of Husserl) represented by the linguistic, literary, and cultural codes of the given collectivity.

While thereby including almost the whole artwork in the sphere of the signifier, we should not forget that the components of this signifier are, in all but the elementary "thing" level, created by meanings (and their complexes); consequently, they belong with equal right to the sphere of the signified of the integral work-sign. Therefore it is necessary to effect a similar revision in Morris's model, which places the signified only at the highest level of the work, as a designated "value." Then the whole work, with the exception of the aforementioned "material" level, would at the same time be included in the sphere of the signified.

Thus the scheme of a literary work as an integral sign can be represented—with great simplification and an awareness that many substantial aspects are omitted—as follows:

The lowest field represents the "sound" or "material" level of the work, whereas the highest field represents the level of its overall meaning. What is between represents—very imperfectly—the individual levels of the semantic process. On every level signifieds turn into signifiers of signs on one of the levels higher up.

This figure will of course suggest Ingarden's discussion (1931) of the stratified, heterogenous structure of the literary work. Without denying Ingarden's inspiration, I must stress the fact that it is exactly the imperfection of this figure that makes it so reminiscent of his concept. First of all, my figure does not express the multiple interconnections between the individual strata of the work and its total meaning. I have tried to suggest this by the enumeration of different axes along which individual signifieds are grouped into the signifiers of signs of higher orders. Nor does the figure show the fact that in any stratum signs can be constituted which immediately participate in the constitution of the overall meaning of the work, without needing the mediation of any "higher" stratum (here the use of quotation marks is fully justified). One instance of such an immediate contact has been insightfully analyzed by Mukařovský in his study of poetic designation (1938). A proper graphic representation of all these processes lies beyond the capacities of my visual imagination. Such a representation would make the scheme of all intermediate strata much more confusing, diversified, and dramatic, changing the static oblongs into a cluster of connecting lines constantly shifting and striking out in all directions.

In conclusion, one might say that the complexity of an artwork, including the interconnection of its different parts and strata, need not be a hindrance in our conceiving the work as an integral sign. On the contrary, it can facilitate such a concept.

With the essential difference between the extension of the attributes of the artifact stated, the category of the artifact should be reserved for only those components of the work that are characterized by their "thingness." (Without this feature, the difference between the artifact and the aesthetic object would be obliterated; this difference, despite all its relativity, must be systematically maintained in any theory of literature.) It follows from what I have said that these components of the artwork have only one relation to the opposition of signified/signifier: they are the only unsignified and hence "primary" signifiers within the framework of a particular complex sign. However, as one can easily imagine, even this primary characteristic of the artifact is not quite so easy to grasp. What in fact is this "thingness" of the literary artifact?

While Mukařovský continued to consider the artifact as the "work-thing" in his studies of general aesthetics, in passages dealing with the artifact in literature he abandoned this impractical term as unsuitable for the temporal arts; in this case he speaks of the "material" aspect of the artwork, that is, what is sensorily perceptible in it. The quotation marks surrounding this term express Mukařovský's general reservations toward the metaphysics of epistemological realism, for in the same context (1944: 196) he characterizes reality as such in exactly the same way: "'material' reality, i.e., that perceived through the senses (to which the literary artifact belongs as much as the artifact of sculpture). . . . " Here he explicitly obliterates the ontological differences between the artifact in literature and in other fields of art and, moreover, between the artistic artifact and sensorily perceptible reality in general.

However, four years earlier, Mukařovský had written his study "On Poetic Language," where he analyzed the specificity of the literary artifact much more profoundly (without actually using the word "artifact"). I shall be referring to this study repeatedly; here I merely want to juxtapose the above quotation, placing the literary artifact in "material" reality, to an opposite view of Mukařovský's, which stresses the specificity of verbal "material": "Unlike the materials of sculpture and painting, language has a semiotic character and for that reason a relative independence from sensory perception. Poetry does not, therefore, appeal directly to any human sense (if, of course, we disregard its sound realization, which from the artistic viewpoint is the subject of a special art, recitation), but indirectly to all of them" (1940: 84).

In quoting this my aim is not to expose the inconsistencies in Mukařovský's views; rather I should like to mark the extreme positions between which the concept of the sensory nature of the literary artifact can fluctuate. To give up the view that verbal art appeals to one definite human sense (at least at the point where semiotic processes begin) is obviously to make an exaggerated and unnecessary sacrifice for the sake of distinguishing literature from the other arts. The thesis of an indirect appeal to all the senses is certainly valid in a discussion of the semiotic material of verbal art, but it adds nothing to our picture of the nature of the artifact. This indirect appeal can be made only by "images" based on the meanings of words and sentences, that is, only in the sphere of the aesthetic object.

As a matter of fact, Mukařovský himself, in "On Poetic Language" and a number of other articles (such as 1934b), has richly characterized this appeal of verbal art to one particular sense, hearing. The perceptibility of the artifact consists for him in its sound, even if it is a perceptibility of a specific type and ontic order. As can be seen from the previous quotation, the literary artifact for Mukařovský is independent of its realization in concrete sounds. Here he follows Jakobson's studies of verse (as summarized in 1960: 365). The artifact of a literary work and the artifact of recitation are two different things (Jakobson's categories of *verse instance* and *delivery instance*).

However, before we go into the phonic nature of the literary artifact, it is necessary to realize that concentrating on sounds as the sensory sphere that forms the basis of a literary artifact is a deliberate choice out of several possibilities. Another alternative is to give the second possible substance of speech, visual graphic signals, the same status as sounds. This alternative could lean toward the views of Hjelmslev which, though somewhat discredited today by Jakobson's criticism (summary in Jakobson and Halle 1956: 474), are still attractive to literary critics. It is not beside the point to note that the Prague School included simultaneously an original theory of written language, connected with the name of Josef Vachek (1942), which demonstrated in a most useful way the independent functions and stylistic features of written speech. Although this approach fully appreciated the importance of the phonic level of poetic language, it was not far in some of its theoretical generalizations from the notion of two equivalent substances.

The attractiveness of this notion for literary scholars and also for non-specialists consists in the fact that the sensorily perceptible "thing" with which we come in contact in perceiving literary works is a written (printed) record, at least in our cultural area. One can easily object that the artifact of a literary work remains the same in all graphic and typo-graphic forms as well as in the innumerable copies multiplied by mechan-ical means. Such an objection, however, can be met on the basis of the theory of equivalence of written and auditory speech: the succession of *graphemes* as types is preserved within the framework of various and equivalent tokens. The abstract graphic scheme, setting the norm for indi-vidual realizations, can be seen from this point of view as assuming the same position as the abstract sound scheme which is the basis of different realizations of the artifact in the form of the sounding voice. The visual work of applied "book art" (or manuscript art) is a parallel to the work of recitation. (Further discussion could raise the question of whether literary works are incorporated in recitation to the same degree as in works of book art; the unequal measure of these two incorporations seems to be beyond doubt: in most cases the graphic layout is only an external "dress," as against the recitative performance, which takes the sound level of the literary work for its norm and basic component. This question, however, must be left aside at present.)

A more promising approach toward the hierarchy of auditory and visual impulses (and an attitude more suitable for theoreticians of art) can be summed up in the question: which side, the auditory or the visual, is more likely to generate independent signs with an active function in the semiotic structure of the artwork? What I have in mind, of course, are not the standard signs that constitute the elementary level of verbal meanings, but the "superfluous" organization, by means of which the sensorily per-ceptible aspect of a work is incorporated in its semiotic process, not as a prerequisite for the immediately higher level but as a source of indepen-dent activity and semantic energy. In this case the priority of sound over written speech is unquestionable. Without enumerating all the means dis-cussed in books of poetics, it is evident that only a few of these means can be ascribed to the graphic representation of the text (such as the acrostic). Euphonic structures, for example, are composed of phonemes not graph-emes: the opposition of front versus back vowels, which is frequently the basis of euphonic structures, has no equivalent in the appearance of the corresponding graphemes (the grapheme *e* is more similar to *o* than to *i*).

Those who argue that independent artistic signs exist that are graph-emic in their essence draw support from three different areas. First, they point to cases in which graphic signs with phonic equivalents serve merely to supplement punctuation as signals of sound qualities that are usually not expressed by graphemes, that is, as means of division and emphasis (such as marking the boundaries of verses and stanzas or stressing important words by capital letters). Second, graphic design may play a completely independent role inexpressible through sounds; by virtue of this fact, however, the given work becomes a synthesis of two artistic branches, i.e., literature and the visual arts (as in the case of concrete poetry, or in cases of schematized "images" of materialized language objects of the external world, such as newspapers or tables with inscriptions like those in Čapek's *War with the Newts*). It is only in the third case that graphic signs play an independent role in the constitution of the literary artifact. Most frequently, this role concerns higher levels of composition, as when different types of letters mark the difference between contemporaneous and retrospective narrative, or between description and interior monologue; or when the hierarchy of compositional breaks is marked by the size of spaces and headline letters, and so on. With the growing importance of these means, the artifact of a literary work can assume, in certain cases, a mixed auditory-visual nature.[3]

The main argument for the equivalence between graphic signs and sounds, however, starts from the premise that, at least in some branches of literature, the sensorily perceptible substance is artistically neutral. According to a common view, poetry makes use of sound structures but in prose we pass directly through graphic signs to the meanings of words. Here, then, independent signs based on an intense organization of sensory stimuli are obliterated and the artifact is given a purely ancillary position, or is even argued out of existence. The decisive argument seems to be that prose is not read aloud by readers and that its "silent" perception does not call forth internal sound images. The first part of the argument does not even need answering, whereas the latter requires concrete psycholinguistic research. Whatever the result, however, the fact remains that even the silent reading of a prose text has as an indispensable component schemes of "intonemes"[4] that are phonic signifiers of the syntactic organization, topic-comment articulation, and so forth. In this respect, no artistic prose can remain amorphous and without stylistic organization. Therefore, phonic structure has an independent artistic function even in prose. When we recognize the considerable asymmetry between means of intonation and their graphic equivalents (the "homonymity" of graphic expression, or more often nonexpression, of various semicadences; the "synonymity" of such means as full stop and semicolon), it becomes apparent that this active role cannot be played, under any circumstances, by graphic signs.

The decisive reason for emphasizing the phonic nature of the artifact in literature becomes clear finally when we concentrate more closely on the graphic representation of utterances. Graphic representation reflects

in all its essential features one aspect of the appearance of linguistic formations which, despite all its abstractness, is directly linked to their phonic
nature. This is, of course, the successivity of linguistic signs, which follows
from their phonic nature and which, on the other hand, mechanically stip-
ulates the graphic representation of the speech. We speak about successivity, not about linearity, which was proved by Jakobson (1939a: passim,
esp. 304) to be an inadequate characterization of speech, and even more so
of the literary work, which is formed by simultaneous structures with
various independent meanings. There I must disagree with Vachek's view
(1942: 243) that written speech makes use of the second dimension of the
printed page. The division into lines is only a technical means for placing
one infinite "line," in which the temporal succession of the utterance is
realized. The advantages ascribed to it by Vachek—that is, the possibility of
changing the tempo of perception or of returning against the stream of the
unidirectional time of the utterance—do not follow, in fact, from the use
of the other dimension but from the fixation of speech. Even though this
fixation allows us to go back and repeat the reading, it does not alter the
given succession of the elements of the utterance. Even if we return, in
reading, to some passage of the text, we are well aware of the fact that this
passage comes "before" the passage we had to skip in our movement
"backwards."

It is necessary to stress that the absolute domination of the successive
over the simultaneous in a literary work (argued in detail in Jakobson
1963a, 1967) is limifed to its lowest level; on the higher levels we can observe side by side with successive segments parts functioning simultaneously. All successive elements of an artwork, be they perceptible to the senses
or not, are integrated in the process of perception according to Husserl's
principles of the constitution of temporal objects discussed by Mukařovský (1940; see Steiner and Steiner 1976). This process is, of course, complicated by the structural and hierarchical relations between the elements;
Mukařovský's model consciously leaves this out of consideration but it is
properly included by Jakobson (1963a: 337) in his remark about "the
transposition of the successive event into the synchronic structure." En-
grossing as all these problems arc, thcy arc not relevant for the specific
discussion of the artifact, and so I shall leave them aside for the present.

The successivity of elements is the minimal and omnipresent expression of the phonic nature of the literary artifact. On the highest level of
abstraction, successivity can be correlated to pure auditoriness as such.
At the opposite pole is the maximal concreteness of the sensory perception of the literary artifact as represented by the sounds of speech in their
fullness. As we have seen, this is reached only when the literary work becomes part of another artwork, recitation. Recitation, of course, is already

an (objectified) concretization of the literary work. Consequently, the artifact of recitation contains a number of components which are not part of the literary artifact; it is the result of many choices which need not be made in the process of constituting the latter. Without these components and choices the sound of concrete speech is impossible.

The artifact of a literary work stands somewhere between these extreme poles; it approaches the one or the other pole according to a given genre, style, and cultural tradition. Mukařovský in the study discussed above provided a general formulation of this position, even though he stated that poetry did not appeal directly to any human sense (1940: 84). When characterizing the material of literature, that is, language, as a system of signs functioning in the broad areas of social intercourse and preformed for this purpose, he recognized its semiotic character expressed in the form of the sound itself: sound in language is turned from a "natural phenomenon" into a phenomenon of culture and "comes from the speech organs already formed" to fulfil the function of the signifier in the language sign.

In this connection, Mukařovský repeatedly referred to phonology, which at the time of his study had passed through two decades of turbulent development in the Prague Linguistic Circle. By defining the ontological status of the phoneme, phonology supplied all the prerequisites for solving the problem of the literary artifact. The phoneme, a "bundle" of distinctive features, is more abstract than the speech sound, but it cannot be separated from concrete sound absolutely (a criticism of "external" approaches to the relation between the phoneme and the speech sound was summed up by Jakobson and Halle 1956). Exactly at the time when Mukařovský was writing his study "On Poetic Language," Jakobson, then already exiled from occupied Czechoslovakia, stated: "Le phonème n'est ni identique au son ni extérieur par rapport au son, mais il est nécessairement présent dans le son, il lui demeure inhérent et superposé: c'est *l'invariant dans les variations*" ["The phoneme is neither identical to the sound nor external to it, but rather is necessarily present in the sound, being both inherent in it and superimposed upon it: it is *the invariant in the variations*"] (1939b: 315; Jakobson's emphasis).

For our purposes we can perhaps presuppose that this formulation is applicable *mutatis mutandis*, to intonation patterns insofar as they are parts of the linguistic system. Conceived in this way, phonemes (and intonemes) become the building blocks of the literary artifact. They are phonic schemes undetermined in all their sensorily perceptible features but inseparable from their phonic content. Thus, although the nature of the literary artifact is schematic, it is a scheme of sounds and not of anything else.

The creator of an artwork chooses phonemes from an intersubjective system in which the continuum of possible sounds is already obligatorily divided into a finite number of syncretic elements. This system emerges in the consciousness of the participants of communication as a part of their linguistic "set" (*Einstellung*) as soon as the communication takes place. It becomes one of the regulatory structures[5] which influence the perception of the communicated text. Under the pressure of this structure shades of voice which are not essential to the constitution of phonemes (and intonemes) are evaluated as irrelevant (but see later the restriction concerning tempo and timbre; there exist, too, coded intonemes bearing emotional signifieds), so that various phonically different uses of the same speech sound appear as tokens of the same phoneme.

As the relative stability of this system is usually greater than the other systems controlling the perception of the artwork, the perceiver enters into contact with a succession of phonic schemes which are fairly close to the succession intended by the author of the work. If we disregard long-term historical changes in the phonological system, a change in any element of this succession is evaluated as an interference in literary communication. (Consider the principles of textual criticism and editorial practice concerned with the preservation of the artifact conceived in this way.)

As demonstrated by Prague School phonology, culminating in Jakobson's theory of distinctive features, neither the system as a whole nor any of its elements represents a mere totality of abstract oppositions neutral to sound qualities. On the contrary, it is only on the basis of its phonic nature that a phoneme takes its place in the system and enters into relations with other phonemes (for example, into pairs of marked and unmarked members).

Nevertheless, as I have already said, the phoneme is not identical to a sound as it is actually uttered and perceived. Some obligatory qualities of the sound, as it is produced by the organs of speech and perceived by the ear, remain outside the properties defining the phoneme (although this does not mean that the phoneme is defined only by distinctive features); other qualities are marked not as a nondimensional point of the sound continuum but as an "abscissa" or little "surface" marking the boundaries of the possible dispersion. The phonic nature of the literary artifact remains, in this respect, as indefinite as the phonic nature of its elementary components. This obviously applies to most cases of the individual perception of the literary artifact. The phonic nature is always present in the perception of an artwork as a schematic invariant of *possible* sounds. As a matter of fact, this is not true only for so-called silent reading; even when perceiving an actually recited artifact one can focus on its schematic nature if one perceives solely the literary component of the recited work or if the recitation is taken as mere information about the literary text without artistic aims. In such cases, the perceiver would be capable of disregarding the phonic qualities presented by the recitation; but this does not mean that the perceiver would concentrate only on the "content," since he or she would also perceive the phonic schemes that are its bearers.

My argument is fully in accord with the intentions of Mukařovský, who—influenced as he was not only by phonology but also by the prestructuralist research of his predecessor Zich (1918) and his polemics with Sievers's *Schallanalyse*—repeatedly insisted on a careful differentiation of "the sound qualities given in the text itself from those which depend on the reciter's decision" (Mukařovský 1940: 92). Nevertheless, he regarded —again rightly, I believe—even some nonphonological parts of the utterance as components of the phonic level of the work. In doing so, he had in mind not so much such matters as Czech stress (which, in spite of its nonphonological character, that is, its inability to differentiate among linguistic forms of higher levels, does have a systemic nature). Rather he was referring to phenomena which in the Saussurian terminology of his day were said to be determined by the norms of *parole*. For example, he discussed in detail the many possible semantic functions in a literary work that may be played by *timbre* (voice coloring). According to him, the means by which timbre is implicitly provided in the text is the emotional shading of the content; timbre is deautomatized especially in dialogue, where it is subjected to frequent changes.

The norms of *parole* discussed by Mukařovský can be classified today as pragmatic agents connected with the participants in the communication and the given situation. In the case of literary communication, in which these agents remain indistinct and their influence upon the form of the communication is limited, their functional equivalent (at least from the viewpoint of the partial properties of the text, such as the character of its timbre) is the reality represented in the literary work, especially by literary characters and the lyrical subject. This again accords with the examples given by Mukařovský ("emotional shading," "dialogue"). These semiotic complexes are, of course, themselves based on the phonic level of the work which provides signifiers for semantic elements that constitute these represented realities within the semantic structure of the work. Consequently, timbre (and, *mutatis mutandis*, tempo, which is also discussed by Mukařovský in this connection) exists within the phonic stratum of the artwork only as a result of the reverse effect of the thematic components on this phonic stratum. This fact, of course, does not prevent us from considering timbre and similar phenomena including some nonsystemic components of intonation as parts of the literary artifact. I do not mean obligatory parts: they enter the frame of an artifact only in cases where they are specially foregrounded by certain qualities of the work.

Mukařovský's careful differentiation between components given by the text and those that are not leads us to the last question that I wish to pose in this essay. How are we to understand this "givenness," and what is the content of this category in the case of the literary artifact? In his study of art as a semiotic fact Mukařovský defined the work-thing as "open to the perception of all without any reservation" (1934a: 85). But the fact that each experience with an artwork begins with the artifact as the most elementary level should not evoke the illusion that the artifact simply "is there," serving automatically as the source of stimuli for the reader's perception, which can remain quite passive on this level. After all, such a claim does not hold even for the perception of the objects of common experience; so much the less does it hold for the perception of linguistic objects and their phonic level, a perception which, as we have seen, is based on the actualization of the regulatory structure, that is, the phonological system. And in the case of the literary artifact, we must add further regulating structures, like metrical rules, which also pertain to the sound stratum of the work.

The degree of immediate accessibility, of the "givenness" of an element of the work, depends on the degree of simplicity, conventionality, and economy of energy of the activity necessary for the transfer of this element from the potentiality of the text to the actuality of the reader's perception and understanding (though this actuality is incomplete, as we have just seen in the case of the literary artifact as a sound structure). It is clear that this transfer is not limited to the mere connecting of signifieds to signifiers, since it includes complex operations of integration. It would be erroneous to assume that numerous structures in the sphere of the phonic literary artifact are not "given" in this difficult, energy-expensive way. The constitution of numerous sound structures, such as euphony or rhythm, requires a knowledge of relevant codes and traditions and the ability to find the common denominator of varied sound phenomena and to notice and integrate elements and configurations which are hidden from our attention behind other more conspicuous phenomena from higher strata of the work. The active role of the aesthetic function is the point of departure for our effort at constituting such qualities of the message, which could not fully reach the sphere of existence without this "aimless" attention directed toward the message itself.

If, then, we began this essay with the thesis that the characteristics "to be a signifier" and "to be sensorily perceptible" do not have the same extension in the case of the literary artwork, we must now make a further differentiation: the extension of the category "sensorily perceptible" is different from the extension of "givenness." Moreover, the latter is defined only relatively; that is, it is dependent on the amount of a receiver's energy demanded. The "immediacy" of the "givenness" of certain sound configurations in the framework of the artifact can be lower than the "immediacy" of the connection of a signified with its signifier in the framework of the aesthetic object. An activity of the perceiver is presupposed on both sides; it depends on the relation between standardization and strangeness, this relation deciding whether the perceiving and understanding of the element or complex of elements will be smooth or will need a more intensive use of effort and experience.

Thus, even in moments when the whole problem of the mode of existence of an artwork is apparently simplified by our adopting a serious theoretical standpoint (for instance, the conception of the artwork as a single, integral sign), the complexity of a work of art and its components must be systematically taken into account. It is apparent even in the most elementary structures on the level of the literary artifact.

Notes

1. For example, what, in fact, is the object of the semiotic analysis of a literary work? Some suggestions seem to be offered by the different modes of existence of the aesthetic object. Such a differentiation was suggested by Mukařovský (1936: 52), when he contrasted the "independent" aesthetic value inherent in the artifact, which has "only a *potential* character," with the "*actual*" value of the aesthetic object (my emphasis). However, I am not interested in values but in the opposition of potentiality and actuality. Scholarly analysis is concerned with the *possibility* of the meaning of an artwork in its duration and metamorphoses. It is clear that this pair, actual/potential, is something quite different from the opposition of *verbal meaning* and *significance* which was developed by Hirsch in his well-known book (1967); *verbal meaning* is more static and less complex than possible meaning.

2. Incidentally, Mukařovský did not use the term *artifact* in this text; he only speaks of a *work-thing*; but it is evident that he has in mind what he elsewhere calls the artifact.

3. It seems that in cultures strongly oriented toward written signs, for example, especially in classic Chinese culture, the situation is completely different; here the artifact has, in a full sense, a graphic nature, and verbal art assumes a somewhat different place than in the European tradition.

4. I use this term for the sake of brevity, being aware of the fact that the status of the units of intonation (each of which is a sign with its own individual signifier) and phonemes (which distinguish pure "otherness,"

the difference of one word from another) is considerably different in the semiotics of language (Jakobson 1939a: 289). This difference, however, is not essential to our present discussion.

5. The relation between phonology and Husserl's theory of intersubjectivity is discussed in Holenstein 1975.

CHAPTER 8

Typography, Rhymes, and Linguistic Structures in Poetry
BY NICOLAS RUWET

In its written or printed form, a poem looks like a sequence of lines (word sequences) of unequal length (in terms of words or letters), surrounded by wider margins than is usual in prose. The first word in each line traditionally has its first letter capitalized—whether or not it begins a sentence, whether or not it is a proper name. The width of the left margin is generally uniform, though the beginnings of some lines may be indented, often at regular intervals. Finally, some groups of lines are frequently separated by blanks; the occurrence of blanks often obeys a systematic principle (a blank every three lines, every four lines, and so on).

In linguistic terms, however, a poem is differentiated from a text in prose by being subject to a dual type of structuration. On the one hand it is in principle (see Ruwet 1975a) subject to the various grammatical and intersentential constraints which determine the well-formedness of a connected discourse. On the other hand (see Jakobson 1960; Ruwet 1975a, 1979), it is characterized, at the "superficial" (that is, phonetic, phonological, morphological, or surface syntactic) levels of representation by the recurrence of certain features which determine relations of equivalence (i.e., identity and contrast) between various points in the sequence of the text; within a given tradition, some of these equivalence relations are codified according to specific rules (meter, rhyme, etc.).

Thus, one may ask what kind of relation—if any—exists between the special typographical features of written poetry and its special linguistic features. One hypothesis which might seem natural at first sight is the following: the special typography of poetry would reflect or graphically express the linguistic properties which differentiate a poem from a prose text. According to an extreme form of this hypothesis, there would be a one-to-one relationship between the typographical features of a poem and codified equivalences (those which are defined by the rules of versification).

It seems obvious that there is some truth to this hypothesis, even in its extreme form. For instance, the division of the text into units (lines) which are metrically equivalent; in the same vein, the regular setting off of the beginnings of certain lines seems to correspond to the alternation of longer and shorter (in terms of syllables or feet) metrical units; finally, the systematic recurrence of blanks seems to correspond to more complex equivalence relations, those which define stanzas. I think, however, that this hypothesis is too simplistic; in its extreme form, it is inadequate and must be rejected, for the relation between the typography and the linguistic structure of a poem is more complex. This paper will be devoted to an attempt to clarify this relation, at least in part. But before going on, some preliminary remarks are in order.

One should not lose sight of the opposite and equally extreme hypothesis: that there is no systematic relationship between the typography of poems and the equivalence relations (especially the coded ones) which define a poem at the linguistic level; typography would constitute a level of representation in its own right and would create between the elements of the text certain particular types of relations (some being equivalence relations). A poem would then be subjected to three different kinds of constraints—grammatical (in the broad sense), poetical,[1] and typographical.

I will not deal directly with this second hypothesis; in its extreme form, especially if we are concerned with "traditional" poetry, it also seems to me to be untenable. The mere existence of Mallarmé's *Un Coup de dés* or of Apollinaire's *Calligrammes*, however, shows that it cannot be simply dismissed. Even in the case of "traditional" poetry it contains a grain of truth. It may also be the case that some typographical features are purely conventional, arbitrary, and structurally irrelevant.[2]

I will limit myself to a consideration of "traditional" French poetry, to the kind which obeys more or less strict rules of versification. I will leave aside, for the time being, the special problems that might be posed by a great part of modern poetry which, while having discarded the rules of versification, still contains special typographical features, some of which are familiar and some of which are new. Several lines of investigation might be pursued in this domain. Given a poem written in "free verse" and obeying no known rule of versification, one might raise several questions: does the typography function as an autonomous level, suggesting for instance relationships of meaning between some parts of the text through purely graphic means? Or does it reflect noncodified equivalence relations (such as assonances, alliterations, syntactic parallelisms)? Or does it work only as a kind of camouflage, disguising ordinary prose in verse thanks to the typographical habits of the reader? I suspect that all three cases would be found, as well as an indefinite number of intermediary types.

I will take for granted that the division into successive lines does reflect the division of the text into metrical units (verse); I will also take for granted that the setting off of the beginnings of lines reflects the alternation of different meters. This seems obvious, but maybe some oversimplification is lurking here; I will, however, leave this aside.[3]

I will limit myself to one aspect of the problem. What, among the linguistic features of a poem, are those which correspond to the systematic alternations of sequences of lines and blanks? I will ignore all cases where the occurrence of blanks is irregular: one can assume, provisionally, that the function of the blanks in this case is the same as it is in prose: they delimit paragraphs, which signal the main logical articulations of the text.

The problem thus circumscribed amounts to trying to clarify the content of the notion *stanza*. In ordinary usage this word seems to be ambiguous; a stanzaic poem would be a text in verse which at the same time is subject to a peculiar type of organization in terms of rhyme or meter and is represented graphically by systematic alternations of sequences of lines and blanks (but see note 2).

One example will suffice to suggest that the relation between a linguistic stanza and a graphic stanza is no simple matter. According to one tradition, a regular (French) sonnet is built on one meter (the alexandrine); thus, among the codified principles, only rhyme would apparently play a role in justifying a division into stanzas. Typographically, a sonnet has the following shape: four lines—one blank—four lines—one blank—three lines—one blank—three lines; hence, the distinction between quatrains and tercets. On the other hand, the rhyme scheme is the following: *ABBAABBACCDEFDE* (I am leaving aside for the time being the distinction between masculine and feminine rhymes). This scheme would apparently justify a division into four stanzas, two quatrains of framed, identical rhymes, one distich of plain rhymes, and one quatrain of crossed rhymes. There is thus no direct correspondence between the linguistic structure and the graphic representation of the last six lines. In fact, the division of the first eight lines into quatrains is equally arbitrary; one could as well—given that they are built on two rhymes—consider them as constituting an eight-line strophe (*huitain*), of which the second part is the mirror image of the first. In brief, given the rhyme structure, several different ways of dividing the poem by means of blanks are possible, the traditional way being one of the least obvious.

Before going on, it might be useful to have a graphic means of representing the rhyme structure of a poem that would be completely distinct from the usual typographical conventions. Only then would one be in a position to compare the latter with precision to at least the aspects of the linguistic structure which have to do with rhyme. So I will propose the following notation, which is more or less derived from the so-called "finite state" linguistic model (see Chomsky 1957; Ruwet 1967b). It is a purely descriptive notation which does not claim yet to give a "generative grammar" of rhyme systems within French poetry.

The rhyme structure of a poem will be represented by a graph using two kinds of elements, labelled boxes and arrows linking the boxes. The arrows are numbered from 1 to n; loops (arrows linking a box to itself) are permitted. Each box is meant to represent a sound sequence[4] which, in each line, is relevant to the rhyme (in traditional terms, the last pronounced vowel plus, as the case may be, one or more consonants and/or a "mute" e). For particular poems, each box thus contains the representation of a specific sequence of sounds (given in traditional orthography and/or phonetic-phonological transcription),[5] or, in the case of general schemes, a capital letter, $A, B, C, \ldots, N$. Each box thus represents a *state* of the poem, and each arrow represents a *transition* between two states. We distinguish an *initial state* (A) and a *final state* (N), which may be identical. The number of lines in a poem being finite, each arrow is numbered to prevent the infinite recursion which the presence of loops would otherwise allow; an arrow numbered i will thus represent the transition from the ith line to the $i + 1^{th}$ line.[6]

As the alternation of feminine and masculine rhymes plays an important role in French versification, it is necessary for our notation to account for it. We will make use of a binary feature $\pm F$ (where, by convention, $+F$ = feminine rhyme, $-F$ = masculine rhyme) and the "alpha" notation (see Chomsky and Halle 1968), where aF represents a variable on $+F$ and $-F$. When general schemes are represented, each box will contain, following a capital letter and within parentheses, either aF or $-aF$. This is to be interpreted in the following way: if aF takes the value $+F$ (feminine rhyme), then $-aF$ necessarily has the value $-F$ (masculine rhyme); if aF has the value $-F$, then $-aF$ has the value $+F$.

A few examples will serve as illustration. Figure 8-1 represents a certain number of well-known general schemes: (a) plain rhymes; (b) crossed rhymes; (c) framed rhymes; (d) *terza rima*, which is used in Dante's *Divina Commedia* and in several poems by Verlaine; (e) and (f) two different types of six-line stanzas (*sizains*);[7] and (g) the so-called regular sonnet.

If we examine Figure 8-1, we are led to several observations.

1. In all examples, the distribution of feminine versus masculine rhymes follows a systematic principle quite independent of the differences between schemes. It is thus possible to factor out this principle, which will work as a general constraint on French versification, independently of the choice of any specific rhyme scheme. This constraint can be stated as fol-

lows: *Given two states* I *and* J, *which are linked by a transition, and where* I $\neq$ J, *if* I *is* aF, *then* J *is* $-$aF. Once this constraint is stated, we can get rid of the features $\pm F$ in the notation of schemes. This constraint accounts among other things for the fact that, traditionally, in a poem made of quatrains on crossed rhymes, the order of feminine and masculine rhymes is the same in all quatrains, while in a poem made of quatrains on framed rhymes, the order of feminine and masculine rhymes is reversed from one quatrain to the next. Sometimes, however, this constraint is violated in some particular poems;[8] these exceptions will be treated as instances of the "marked" case.

2. In all examples of Figure 8-1, each rhyme is repeated at least once, which corresponds to the traditional idea that, for rhymes to be present, certain sequences of sounds must be repeated. Our notation would indeed allow certain rhymes to appear only once, as in the scheme illustrated in Figure 8-2. It is thus necessary to state a second general constraint: *Each state must be the point of departure and/or arrival of at least two transitions.* This constraint will rule out as ill-formed the scheme in Figure 8-2, where states *B* and *D* do not satisfy it. Like the preceding one, this constraint is sometimes violated. Figure 8-2 represents the rhyme scheme of Verlaine's *Romances sans paroles* III (Pléiade, p. 122).[9]

3. In most examples from Figure 8-1, there are recurring cases of a unique transition between two different states. See, for instance, the arrows numbered 2, 4, 6, 8 in Figure 8-1a; 4, 8 in Figure 8-1b; 4, 8, 12 in Figure 8-1c; 2, 6, 8 in Figure 8-1e; 6, 12 in Figure 8-1f.

4. In most examples, a regular recurrence of certain patterns is visible; a graph can be decomposed into subgraphs which are identical in terms of the number of states and the number and type of transitions; each subgraph is linked to the next one by a unique transition. This suggests that one might account for this regularity by means of a more compact notation; see Figure 8-3. The notation in Figure 8-3 must be read in the following way. Each graph in parentheses corresponds to a recurring subgraph. The numbering of the arrows counts only within one subgraph; the index subscript to the parentheses represents the number of occurrences within a poem of the rhyme pattern corresponding to one subgraph; each subgraph is, by convention, linked to another subgraph by a unique transition.

The reader will have noticed that we have not yet made any appeal to the notion of stanza. Starting from observations 3 and 4, one might suggest several different systematic principles which could be used to define the notion of stanza exclusively in terms of rhyme. Having done this, one could come back to typography and determine whether the hypothesis of a correspondence between linguistic strophe and typographic strophe holds or not.

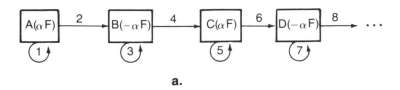

a.

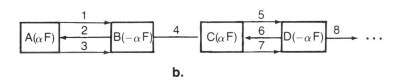

b.

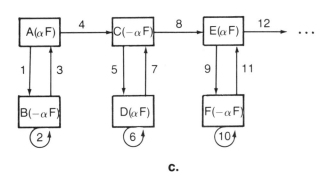

c.

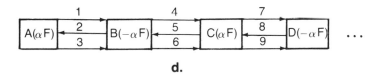

d.

Figure 8–1. Rhyme schemes: *a*, plain rhymes; *b*, crossed rhymes; *c*, framed rhymes; *d*, *terza rima*; *e*, *sizains* (first type); *f*, *sizains* (second type); *g*, regular sonnet.

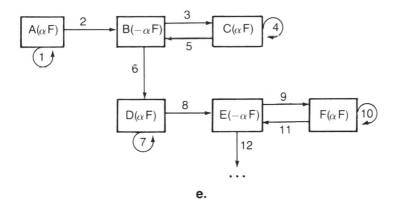

e.

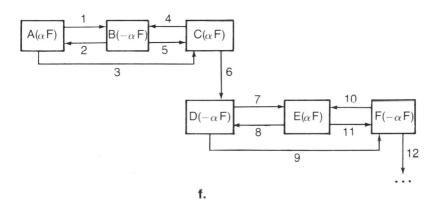

f.

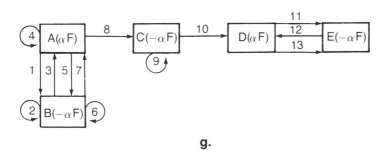

g.

Principle a: A blank corresponds to any unique transition between two different states (see observation 3).

Principle b: A blank corresponds to a transition between two subgraphs as defined by the notation in Figure 8-3 (see observation 4).

Principle c: As in *b*, a blank corresponds to a transition between two subgraphs, under the condition that no unique transition can occur between two different states within one and the same subgraph (this combines observations 3 and 4).

What are the consequences of applying these principles, as regards the definition of the stanza and as regards typography?

According to principle *a*, and supposing that each passage from one stanza to another is marked by a blank, one would have blanks every two lines in Figure 8-1a; every four lines in Figure 8-1b and c; every six lines in Figure 8-1f; after two lines, four lines, two lines, four lines, and so on, in Figure 8-1e; after the first eight lines and after the next two in Figure 8-1g; and there would be no blanks in Figure 8-1d.

According to principle *b*, one would have blanks every two lines in Figure 8-1a, every four lines in Figure 8-1b and c, every six lines in Figure 8-1e and f, and no blanks in Figure 8-1d or g.

According to principle *c*, there would be blanks every two lines in Figure 8-1a, every four lines in Figure 8-1b and c, every six lines in Figure 8-1f, and no blanks in Figure 8-1d, e, or g.

These three principles thus make different predictions. They agree only on Figure 8-1a, b, c, and f, where each of them gives the same definition of the stanza and predicts the occurrence of blanks at the same places, and on Figure 8-1d, where, for all three, the notion of stanza is not defined and the occurrence of blanks is excluded.

When these results are compared with current typographical usage, it is clear that the correspondence is far from perfect. Only crossed-rhymed quatrains, such as Figure 8-1b, or framed-rhymed quatrains, such as Figure 8-1c,[10] and the kind of *sizain* exemplified in Figure 8-1f—which by the way is far less common than the type exemplified by Figure 8-1e—do not raise any problem: in those cases there is a real correspondence between the linguistic strophe and the typographical strophe. Otherwise, there are divergences. The hypothesis of a strict correspondence between linguistic strophe and typographical strophe is both too strong and too weak. On the one hand, whether taken together or separately, our principles predict the occurrence of blanks where none is found; on the other hand, they predict there should be no blanks where blanks are found.

Let us leave aside the cases where the predictions made by these three principles are different. None of them predicts the traditional typography for the sonnet. As principle *b* is the only one to make the correct predic-

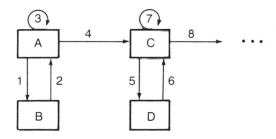

Figure 8-2. Rhyme scheme of *Romances sans paroles* **III.**

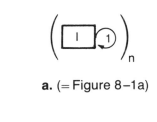

a. (= Figure 8–1a)

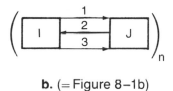

b. (= Figure 8–1b)

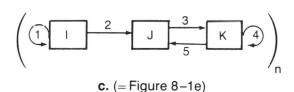

c. (= Figure 8–1e)

Figure 8-3. Rhyme schemes: a more compact notation.

tion in the case of Figure 8-1e, one might be tempted to prefer it and choose it alone for a definition of the linguistic strophe.

In any case, our three principles all predict that a plain-rhymed poem, Figure 8-1a, should be represented by a series of distichs separated by blanks. This happens sometimes—for instance, in Verlaine's "Colloque sentimental" (*Fêtes galantes*, Pléiade, p. 97)—but it is quite exceptional; usually, a plain-rhymed poem presents no systematic occurrence of blanks.

Conversely, none of our principles predicts the systematic occurrence of blanks in the *terza rima*, Figure 8-1d; in other words, they do not define a linguistic stanza as far as the *terza rima* is concerned. A poem built on this scheme, however, usually appears in its written form as a sequence of tercets separated by blanks and ending on an isolated line (see Verlaine, *La Bonne Chanson* XX, "Les Coquillages" in *Fêtes galantes*, etc.; also Mallarmé, "Le Guignon" and "Aumône"). But if all the tercets have something in common (all have two identical rhymes surrounding a different one), no tercet in itself is sufficient to express the regularity shown by Figure 8-1d. The division into n tercets plus one line indeed expresses the fact that a *terza rima* poem necessarily comprises a total number of lines which is a multiple of 3 plus 1; but, according to our principles, no special privilege should be bestowed on the last line. An inherent limitation of typography shows up here: its units—lines and blanks—do not directly correspond to the units which define rhyme systems, that is, states and transitions. Typography, as it were, tries to express by its own means, in a necessarily distorted way, the regularity typical of the *terza rima*: there are no loops, and there are three transitions between two successive states.

I will now deal more succinctly with the contribution of metrical variations to the definition of the linguistic stanza. As has been done for rhyme, one must first examine metrical schemes independently of the other factors involved.[11] The possibilities for structuration are apparently more limited than is the case for rhyme, as it is seldom the case that more than two different meters are involved in one poem.[12] Given two meters, several types of combinations are possible: regular alternation, whether simple ($xyxyxy$ . . .), double ($xxyyxxyyxxyy$ . . .), triple ($xxxyyyxxxyyy$ . . . , etc.), mirror-image ($xyyx\,xyyx\,xyyx$ . . . , $xxyyxx\,xxyyxx$ . . . , etc.), mirror-image around a center ($xxyxx\,xxyxx\,xxyxx$ . . . , $xyxyx\,xyxyx\,xyxyx$ . . . , $xyyyx\,xyyyx\,xyyyx$ . . . , etc.), uneven distribution ($xxy\,xxy\,xxy$ . . . , $xxxy\,xxxy\,xxxy$ . . . , $xxyx\,xxyx\,xxyx$ . . . , $xxxyx\,xxxyx\,xxxyx$ . . . , etc.).

Combining rhyme schemes and metrical variations may, according to the case, give different results, as regards the definition of the linguistic stanza as well as the typography. Here are some examples. Simple alternation combined with plain rhymes does not modify the problem (distichs vs. no blanks); combined with crossed rhymes, it creates something of a tension (quatrains vs. distichs); with framed rhymes, it reinforces the internal structure of the stanza. Multiple alternation gives different results according to the type of rhyme scheme with which it is combined. In Malherbe's "Plainte pour une absence" (Garnier-Flammarion, p. 121), the triple alternation (8, 8, 8, 12, 12, 12), combined with the rhyme scheme of Figure 8-1e (*AABCCB*), defines a type of strophe and suppresses the type of ambiguity left by the rhymes. But let us imagine a case of quadruple alternation (*xxxxyyyyxxxxyyyy*) combined with crossed or framed rhymes; would it define a certain type of *huitain* (eight-line stanza) or the alternation of two kinds of quatrains? I imagine that these two different results would be realized typographically (for a similar, though more complex case, see Baudelaire's "Le Jet d'eau"). Generally speaking, mirror-image (whether with or without a center) and uneven distribution define types of stanzas which can corroborate or modify the types defined by the rhymes;[13] they are often reflected in the typography. One very striking case is the combination of uneven distribution with plain rhymes: in Verlaine's "A Clymène" (*Fêtes galantes*, Pléiade, p. 92), which is built on plain rhymes, hexasyllabic rhymes are regularly followed by one tetrasyllabic line (*xxxy xxxy xxxy* . . .) which defines a type of quatrain reflected by the distribution of blanks every four lines. Uneven distribution is also a means of suppressing the ambiguity we found in the definition of the *sizain* of the type shown in Figure 8-1e: in Verlaine's "Chanson d'automne" (*Poèmes saturniens*, Pléiade, p. 56), two tetrasyllabic lines are regularly followed by one trisyllabic line. Curiously, in the case of *terza rima*, poets do not seem to have exploited the means offered by metric variations (for instance *xxy xxy xxy* . . . *x*, or *xyx xyx xyx* . . . *x*) so as to individualize the tercets and the last line, thus justifying the typography.[14]

The problem of the relationships between the linguistic stanza (or the absence of a definable linguistic stanza) and the typographical stanza is complicated when one goes beyond general schemes and considers the usage of particular poets. For instance, a poet will make use of different typographies for poems built on the same linguistic stanza or will have recourse to the same typography for poems built on different linguistic stanzas.

We saw that Verlaine, in "Colloque sentimental" and elsewhere, presents plain-rhyme poems in distichs, thus falling back on the linguistic definition. However, in "Spleen" (*Romances sans paroles*, Pléiade, p. 135) he uses distichs for what are, from the linguistic point of view, crossed-rhymed quatrains made of octosyllabic lines; neither rhyme nor meter justifies this choice of typography.

Another poem by Verlaine, "Le Faune" (*Fêtes galantes*, Pléiade, p. 91) comprises eight octosyllabic lines built on two crossed rhymes (*-uite, -rins*); graphically, the poem is divided into two quatrains separated by a blank, while, according to our criteria, it is one eight-line stanza (*huitain*). "L'ombre des arbres . . . " (*Romances sans paroles*, "Ariettes oubliées" IX, Pléiade, p. 126) comprises eight lines built on plain rhymes, with a simple alternation of two meters (twelve and seven syllables); it is graphically divided into two quatrains: our principles would favor a division into four distichs, and the usual typography would have no blank at all.

Verlaine again makes use of one and the same typography—four tercets separated by blanks—in three twelve-line poems without metrical variation: "Un Dahlia" (*Poèmes saturniens*, Pléiade, p. 65), "Fantoches" (*Fêtes galantes*, Pléiade, p. 90), and "Cythère" (ibid.). In none of these cases does a tercet correspond to a linguistic stanza according to our criteria. The scheme of "Fantoches" is that of Figure 8-1e. The graphs corresponding to the three poems are very different, as shown in Figure 8-4.[15]

Thus, typography masks differences. The scheme found in "Fantoches" (which is generally graphically represented by *sizains*—see note 7) corresponds to an "open" form; it can be indefinitely reiterated. Those found in "Un Dahlia" and "Cythère" correspond to two "closed" forms, which could only be reiterated as wholes (and would, then, define two types of twelve-line stanzas): in "Un Dahlia" we have a case of mirror-image around a center.[16]

One is thus led to wonder whether the choice of a special typography which has no justification in rhyme or in meter, or in the usual typographical conventions, is not to be explained in terms of other features of the poem; these features would be structural too, but they would not depend on the principles of versification, and could vary from one poem to another.

It is true that various authors of versification treatises (for instance, Mazaleyrat 1974) tell us that a stanza should correspond to a meaning unit; however, this notion is too vague to be useful. Once more, it is necessary to distinguish clearly between levels while approaching a text; after having considered rhyme and meter, we thus turn to syntax, beginning with the most superficial aspect, the division of the text in terms of constituents, especially sentences.[17]

Let us look again at Verlaine's poems. The division into sentences gives certain clues. "L'ombre des arbres . . . " is made of two complex sentences, which correspond to the two typographical quatrains. In "Un Dahlia" and "Cythère" the four tercets each correspond to one sentence. "Les

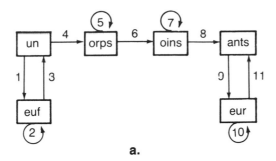

a.

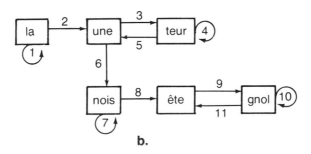

b.

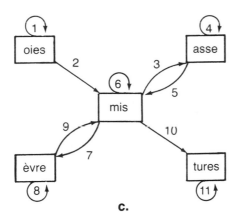

c.

Figure 8-4. **Rhyme schemes of three poems by Verlaine:** *a*, "Un Dahlia"; *b*, "Fantoches"; *c*, "Cythère."

Coquillages" (*Fêtes galantes*, Pléiade, p. 87) is a thirteen-line poem in *terza rima*; it comprises five sentences, the first four corresponding to the tercets and the last one to the final line. In "Chanson d'automne," each *sizain* corresponds to one complex sentence; the syntactic link between the first two lines (built on plain rhymes) and the next four (built on framed rhymes) is especially close ($_2$"Des violons $_3$De l'automne," $_8$". . . quand $_9$Sonne l'heure," $_{14}$"Au vent mauvais $_{15}$Qui m'emporte"). "En bateau" (*Fêtes galantes*, Pléiade, p. 90) comprises fifteen octosyllabic lines grouped in five tercets, with a rhyme scheme *AAABBBCCC* . . . ; each tercet corresponds to a complex sentence (the first two and the last two each comprise two conjoined clauses, the conjunction *et* occurring just before the end of the second line in the first two and at the very beginning of the second line in the last two).

Elsewhere, the correspondence between sentence and typographic stanza is not so perfect, but some regularities are still recognizable. In "Colloque sentimental," the typographic distichs correspond either to sentences (the first three and the last one), or to pairs of sentences constituting short dialogues (question/answer or exclamation/comment). In *La Bonne Chanson* XVII (Pléiade, p. 112), a nineteen-line poem in *terza rima*, all the tercets correspond to sentences, except the fourth one, which can be interpreted as a question/answer pair, and the sixth one, which constitutes a sentence together with the last line. In "Fantoches," each of the first two tercets corresponds to a sentence. The other two constitute together one complex sentence; however, each tercet contains a human noun phrase corresponding more or less closely to the first line ($_1$"Scaramouche et Pulcinella," $_4$"l'excellent docteur $_5$Bolonais," $_7$". . . sa fille, piquant minois," $_{10}$". . . son beau pirate espagnol"); the second and fourth noun phrases are strictly parallel from a syntactic point of view, even if one takes into account the word subclasses (*le/son, excellent/beau, docteur/ pirate, bolonais/espagnol*). In "Spleen," among six distichs, the first four correspond to sentences, and the last two constitute a complex sentence (see below).

The typographic stanza, when it is not defined by versification, tends thus to correspond to a syntactic unit, especially at the beginning of a poem. It is as if, once the reader has become accustomed to this association between stanza and syntactic unit, the poet is allowed more freedom.

Apparently more complex cases can be accounted for along similar lines. *La Bonne Chanson* VI (Pléiade, p. 105) comprises eighteen tetrasyllabic lines in the rhyme scheme *ABABCC*—which would justify a division into typographical *sizains*, or rather an alternation between crossed-rhymed quatrains and plain-rhymed distichs—cf. Figure 8-1e, of whose scheme this could be considered a variant. The typography is the following: five lines—a blank—one line—a blank—five lines—a blank—one line, etc. The key to this is to be found in the syntax (and semantics) of the piece. Each five-line group is followed by points of suspension and corresponds to two sentences in the first case, one in the other two; in fact, each five line group contains two clauses, the second one being a relative clause in the last two groups. The three isolated lines, though discontinuous, and in spite of the punctuation (a period following each line), constitute a "meaning unit"—as a matter of fact, one sentence, some elements being partially repeated ($_6$"O bien-aimée . . . $_{12}$Rêvons, c'est l'heure . . . $_{18}$C'est l'heure exquise"). The five-line groups are related two-by-two by syntactic parallelisms; see especially the beginnings of groups I and II ($_1$"La lune . . . Luit . . . "/$_7$"L'étang reflète . . . ") and the end of groups II and III ($_{10-11}$"Du saule noir Où le vent pleure"/$_{19-20}$"Du firmament que l'astre irise").

Even in such a small sample, however, the correspondence between the typographic stanza and the sentence is not general. For instance, "Le Faune" comprises only one complex sentence, with four degrees of embedding; the main clause covers the first two lines, and the blank separates an antecedent ($_4$"ces instants sereins") embedded within a gerund ($_5$"Présageant . . . "), which itself modifies the main subject ($_1$"Un vieux faune . . . "), from a relative clause which covers the whole second quatrain ($_5$"Qui m'ont conduit . . . ").

It is thus not possible to rest content with such sketchy syntactic observations. If one wants to justify the choice of a special typography, one will be led to deal with subtler details of structure, such as syntactic parallelisms (some have already been noticed) or special aspects of the rhymes which are not predicted by traditional versification. One will be led by degrees to undertake as complete an analysis as possible of the poems, in which of course the semantic aspect will be taken into account. Even then, it may be the case that some aspects of the typography will remain unaccounted for and may be considered arbitrary.

I will not try here to give anything like a complete analysis of a poem; I will limit myself to a few fragmentary analyses, dealing mainly with rhymes and syntactic parallelisms. It will also be shown that the notation proposed above is capable, at least in some cases, of throwing light on some aspects of the rhyme system of a poem which are not provided for by the traditional rules of versification.

Let us come back to "Le Faune," whose typography has until now resisted all our efforts at explanation. Two features at least justify the division into quatrains. (1) Lines 3–4 and 7–8 present rather complex cases of parallelisms in which both the syntax and prosody play a role: in both cases, there is an enjambment between two related constituents ("une suite/₄Mauvaise à ces instants sereins"//₇ ". . . la fuite/₈Tournoie au son des tambourins"); lines 4 and 8 are both divided, syntactically, into one disyllabic word and one hexasyllabic prepositional phrase (whose head is *à* in both cases). (2) Line 5, the first line of the second quatrain, is singled out by the preceding blank; its internal structure is quite special: this is the only case in the whole poem of a strict syntactic-semantic parallelism between the two parts of the line. Moreover, both parts have the same number of syllables (₅"Qui m'ont conduit et t'ont conduite"); this way of presenting the two protagonists as independent is unexpected: one would rather expect something like ". . . ces instants sereins qui nous ont conduits [ensemble] . . . jusqu'à cette heure . . . "

In "Cythère" two additional features at least justify the division into tercets. The third line in each stanza begins with a verb, preceded or not by a clitic (₃"Qu'éventent . . . "/₆"Se mêle . . . "/"Communique . . . "/₁₂"Nous préservent . . . "). The first and the third tercets present "weak" enjambments between the second and the third lines (₂"nos joies/₃Qu'éventent . . . "//₈"sa lèvre/₉Communique . . . "); the second and the fourth tercets present "strong" enjambments between the first and the second line (₄"grâce/₅Au vent léger . . . "//₁₀"Hormis/₁₁La faim"); this feature suggests something like a "crossed" relation between the four stanzas.

We have already seen that the syntactic divisions correspond to the division into distichs in the case of "Colloque sentimental." Moreover, the third distich is in large measure a repetition of the first, and the last one repeats some elements of the second. If one were to characterize "Colloque sentimental" as a poem solely in plain rhymes, one would not do justice to its peculiar rhyme structure, which is represented in Figure 8-5. The division into distichs, while not exactly reflecting this kind of "closed" structure, probably makes the reader more sensitive to it than would the traditional, blankless typography.

The division of "Spleen" into distichs, as we have seen, clashes with the rhyme scheme; it corresponds only imperfectly to the syntactic division into sentences. But there are complex syntactic parallelisms between the distichs, involving both identities and contrasts. Let us begin with the first four distichs (I, II, III, IV), each of which constitutes a complex sentence.

I and III, taken together, contrast with II and IV, once more suggesting a crossed structure, this time between distichs rather than lines. Within this massive contrast, one finds internal contrasts between I and III, and II and IV.

I and III, in the imperfect tense and third person, display a syntactic parallelism between their two lines (this parallelism is stricter in I than in

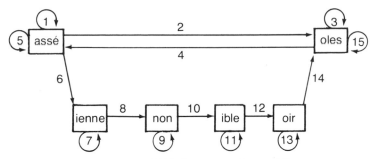

Figure 8-5. Rhyme scheme of "Colloque sentimental."

III); the clauses, which are conjoined, are all predicative, and the rhyming words are all adjectives. I and III present something like a natural landscape—in I particular plants ("discrete" objects), in III a general horizon ("the elements"). There are contrasts between plural (I) and singular (III), presence (I) vs. ellipsis (III) of the copula, and between different adjectival modifiers (*toutes/tout* in I, *trop* in III).[18]

II and IV, in the present tense, introduce the two protagonists (first and second persons): the rhyming words in each case are a verb and a noun, in that order;[19] the complex sentences, containing detached or parenthetical subordinate elements (both of which contain a clause) and lexically full verbs (*craindre, renaître*), contrast with the conjoined predicative clauses in I and III. Neither in II nor in IV is there any internal parallelism between the two lines; there are syntactic parallelisms between the two distichs taken as wholes, but they are much less clear than those of I and III; there is a partial parallelism, combined with contrasts, between ᵢᵢ"tous mes désespoirs" and ᵢᵥ"Quelque fuite atroce de vous" (quantifiers: *tous, quelque*: possessives: *mes, de vous*; this enhances the cause-and-effect relationship between *fuite atroce* and *désespoirs*). Some other contrasts between II and IV: the subject-verb order is inverted in II, normal in IV; the second person is *tu* in II, *vous* in IV; the relative order of the protagonists is reversed—*tu*, the subject in the first line in II vs. *vous*, a noun complement (possessive) in the second line in IV; *mes*, a possessive in the second line in II vs. *je*, the subject in the first line in IV.

Consider now the last two distichs (V and VI). One would expect a correspondence between V and I-III, between VI and II-IV; there are some traces left of this proportion: in V, the rhyming words are adjectives; in VI, as in II and IV, the quantifier *tout* occurs (notice that each time, it occurs under a different shape: *tous, toujours, tout*);[20] *tout* (VI) and *quelque* (IV) contrast (they are the only indefinite quantifiers, and they both occur at the beginning of the second line in the distich); *vous* occurs both in IV and VI as a complement of the preposition *de* at about the end of the second line in a stylistically marked context (*fuite atroce de vous* is almost ungrammatical; *fors de vous* is archaic).

However, in V and VI, we observe a sort of general redistribution of the relations presented before. One single sentence in the present tense (the imperfect has disappeared) combines features both from I-III and II-IV; as in I-III, it is predicative (*je suis las*) but its predicate (*las*) is transitive (like *craindre* in IV); adjectives comparable to those of I-III occur, but they are attributive (*feuille vernie, luisant buis, campagne infinie*), vs. predicative in I-III; the sentence is composed of conjoined clauses, with ellipsis, as in III. Elements corresponding to those in I and IV are directly related in V (*je*, the subject); elements equivalent to those in III and II or IV are directly related in VI. The contrast between the protagonists, characteristic of IV, is maintained, but it is distributed between both distichs (V "je suis las," VI "de vous, hélas," more or less in the same prosodic positions). The first four distichs make a clear distinction between the natural background and the protagonists, themselves contrasted; in V-VI we have, on one side, *je*, and on the other side everything else, which includes *vous*, itself contrasted to the natural background.

The division into distichs is thus justified in the case of I-IV. It creates something of an ambiguity in the case of V-VI.

I shall end this section with some remarks on a thirteen-line poem in *terza rima*,[21] "J'allais par des chemins perfides" (*La Bonne Chanson* XX, Pléiade, p. 114).

The first three tercets (I, II, III) each comprise two sentences (S_1, S_2), the first one covering the first two lines and the second covering the third line. The last four lines (that is, the fourth tercet IV and the final line, which is typographically isolated) are divided into two sentences, each covering two lines.

Tercets I, II, III present clear cases of parallelisms. S_1 each time is in the imperfect tense, S_2 in the *passé simple*. Of the two protagonists, S_1 is centered on *je*, S_2 on *vous*. *Je* is each time presented in a different way, directly in the subject of S_1 in I ($_1$*J'allais* . . .), in the third person in the object in III ($_8$ . . . *le voyageur*), in a purely implicit way in II; in S_2 *je* is presented directly in I (*mes guides*) and even more so in III (*me dit*), but it does not occur at all in II (compare "furent *mes* guides"/"fut *le* matin"). *Vous* is each time presented in the same way by means of synecdoches in the subject at the beginning of the third line in each distich (*Vos chères mains, Votre regard, Votre voix*). The syntactic structure of S_2 is exactly the same in I and in II. In S_1, the verb always occurs at the beginning of a line, the first in I (*J'allais*) and the second in II (*Luisait*) and III (*N'encourageait*); the subject is each time accompanied by some sort of appositive element ($_2$*Douloureusement incertain,* $_4$*Si pâle à l'horizon lointain,* $_7$*Si-non son pas sonore*); the first line each time ends on a prepositional phrase with the structure of preposition/determiner/noun/adjective (*par des che-mins perfides, à l'horizon lointain, sinon son pas sonore*).

The first sentence (the first two lines) in IV is in many respects paral-lel to S_1 in I-III: the subject relates to *je*, the verb is in the imperfect tense at the beginning of the second line (*Pleurait*); there are appositives on the subject (*mon sombre coeur, seul*); there occurs, though at the end of the second line, a prepositional phrase whose internal structure is very similar to that of the prepositional phrases in I-III (*sur la triste voie*); the syntac-tic structure of this sentence is especially close to that of S_1 in I ("J'allais ... incertain par des chemins perfides"/"Mon coeur ... pleurait seul sur la triste voie"). One would thus be tempted to see in the last two lines an equivalent to or a transformation of S_2.

In fact, the last four lines taken together enter into complex relation-ships with I-III. In I-III *je* was presented by various means and *vous* ex-clusively by means of synecdoches. In IV, *vous* does not occur at all, *je* is presented in the form of a (repeated) synecdoche (*Mon coeur ...*) parallel to those of *vous* in I-III; finally *nous* (that is, *je* plus *vous*) occurs in the last line, while the *passé composé* replaces the *passé simple* ($_{13}$*nous a ré-unis*). The superiority relation between *vous* and *je*, marked especially by the *tutoiement* in line 9 (*Marche encore!*), disappears.

In I-III, especially in I and II, there is a clear syntactic contrast be-tween S_1 and S_2. The contrast is less clear in the last four lines where the second sentence presents features which relate it to S_1. The sentence ends on a prepositional phrase (*dans la joie*) which is analogous to those of S_1, though lacking an adjective (this is joy pure and simple, contrasted to the *chemins perfides, triste voie,* etc.). The appositive on the subject (*L'amour, délicieux vainqueur*) reminds one of those found in S_1, especially *Doulou-reusement incertain* in I (there is some phonic similarity [*doul. . . /dél* . . .] as well as morphological kinship: an adjective or adverb derived from an abstract noun by means of the same suffix, -*eux*; the functional rela-tionship between the two terms—determiner and head—is the same, cf. the possible *incertitude douloureuse, délicieusement vainqueur*). The sen-tence is transitive, has a nonhuman, bisyllabic subject at the beginning of the line, which itself is followed by an appositive between pauses and by a verb (preceded by a clitic) at the beginning of the following line. All these features point to a resemblance with S_1 in IV.

The relations between the beginning and the end of the poem are somewhat similar to those which we found in "Spleen." The division into tercets is well justified in the case of I-III; as regards the end, where the main syntactic-semantic division occurs just before the last two lines, the typographical isolation of the last line would seem to lack justification. However, most of the new elements introduced, which contrast with all the rest of the poem, are concentrated in the last line: the presence of *nous* and the *passé composé*, and the absence of an adjective modifying *joie*.

To conclude, I will make two general comments. The first one is theoretical. While it is rather easy to define the typographical stanza as a group of lines set off by blanks (but see note 2) whenever the recurrence of blanks obeys some systematic principle, the definition of the linguistic stanza becomes problematic. In fact, the stanza, as opposed to meter and rhyme, is not a primitive concept of poetic theory. One does not need it in order to define any kind of rhyme scheme: the notation and the two constraints suggested in observations 1 and 2 above will suffice. The reader must have noticed that the constraint accounting for the distribution of feminine and masculine rhymes does not mention the stanza. Let us imagine, on the contrary, a situation in which the versification imposes schemes like those in either of the following sets: [22]

1. AbbA CddC EffE ... (*)
   aBBa cDDc eFFe ... (*)
   AbAb CdCd EfEf ...
   aBaB cDcD eFeF ...
   AAbAAb DDeFFe ...
   aaBBccB ddEffE ...

2. AbbA cDDc EffE ...
   aBBa CddC eFFe ...
   AbAb cDcD EfEf ... (*)
   aBaB CdCd eFeF ... (*)
   AAbCCd ddEffE ... (*)
   aaBccB DDeFFe ... (*)

To define these distributions, one would need the notion of the stanza. To account for the first set, one would have the principle: *All stanzas have the same distribution of the features +F and -F*; to account for the second set, one would have: *The distribution of the features +F and -F is reversed from one stanza to the next*. A priori, such principles appear plausible; no logical necessity excludes a versification which would obey them. The fact is, however, that they do not play any role in traditional French versification, for which the constraint of observation 2, which does not mention the stanza, is adequate. Let us not forget, moreover, that there are rhyme schemes such as that of the *terza rima*, which never define a linguistic stanza, even derivatively.

My second comment is methodological; it applies in fact to the study of poetry in general and is not limited to the relations between typography and linguistic structures. It is always necessary—whether one tackles some general problem or analyzes one particular poem—that one carefully distinguish, at least at the start, the different levels of analysis (meter, rhyme, phonetics/phonology, morphology, syntax, semantics, etc.). Only then, after one has determined the structures that are relevant to each level (rhyme schemes, metrical variations, syntactic parallelisms, noncoded phonetic equivalences, etc.), will one be in a position to deal with the more or less complex interrelations between elements or structures pertaining to different levels.

Among other things, this rule of method implies that one should never take for granted or consider as a basic given the division of a poem into typographic stanzas. The latter may very often reflect, more or less clearly, some linguistic regularities. However, if we make it our starting point and begin to look systematically for equivalence relations whether of identity or contrast between the different stanzas grouped or opposed in various ways (odd stanzas vs. even stanzas, central stanzas vs. peripheral stanzas, etc.), we run the risk of getting a distorted view of the structure of a poem; secondary features may be given undue importance at the expense of more relevant ones. In practice of course, and especially while writing down the final version of an analysis, one may find it more expedient to mix observations pertaining to different levels, but the general rule of method should never be lost sight of.

One last word on the relations between typography and linguistic structures. As we have seen, these relations are complex. Nothing in the linguistic structures corresponds to the main division between compact typography with no systematic use of blanks—in principle reserved for plain-rhyme poems—and more spaced typography—making no distinction between rhyme schemes which do not define stanzas (such as the *terza rima*) and those which do so, though derivatively. The justifications one may find for the choice of such and such a typography are heterogeneous. It sometimes happens that even an elaborate linguistic analysis, making use of observations on all levels (semantics included), leaves unexplained some aspects of the typography, which only the force of traditional conventions can account for. This often happens in the case of the sonnet. For at least two of the sonnets of Baudelaire of which I have published an analysis, "La Géante" and "Je te donne ces vers . . . ,"[23] I have been unable to find any significant feature which might justify the division of the last six lines into two tercets.

Thus, neither of the two extreme hypotheses on the relations between linguistic structures and typography which we considered at the outset has proved to be correct. In some respects, which should be made more precise, the relation between typography and the linguistic structures of poetry seems to be similar, on the one hand, to the relation which exists between traditional orthography and the linguistic structure of a language and, on the other hand, to that which exists between musical notation and musical language. Musical notation as well as orthography do reflect structural features, but there are omissions and distortions, which are due partly to their practical function, partly to the special constraints to which they are subject—for instance, in the case of typography, the need to represent in two dimensions multidimensional aspects of structure—and partly to the force of more or less arbitrary conventions.[24]

Appendix

Un Dahlia (*Poèmes saturniens*)

Courtisane au sein dur, à l'oeil opaque et brun
S'ouvrant avec lenteur comme celui d'un boeuf,
Ton grand torse reluit ainsi qu'un marbre neuf.

Fleur grasse et riche, autour de toi ne flotte aucun
Arome, et la beauté sereine de ton corps
Déroule, mate, ses impeccables accords.

Tu ne sens même pas la chair, ce goût qu'au moins
Exhalent celles-là qui vont fanant les foins,
Et tu trônes, Idole insensible à l'encens.

—Ainsi le Dahlia, roi vêtu de splendeur,
Elève sans orgueil sa tête sans odeur,
Irritant au milieu des jasmins agaçants!

Fantoches (*Fêtes galantes*)

Scaramouche et Pulcinella
Qu'un mauvais dessein rassembla
Gesticulent, noirs sous la lune,

Cependant que l'excellent docteur
Bolonais cueille avec lenteur
Des simples parmi l'herbe brune.

Lors sa fille, piquant minois,
Sous la charmille, en tapinois,
Se glisse demi-nue, en quête

De son beau pirate espagnol
Dont un langoureux rossignol
Clame la détresse à tue-tête.

Cythère (*Fêtes galantes*)

Un pavillon à claires-voies
Abrite doucement nos joies
Qu'éventent des rosiers amis;

L'odeur des roses, faible, grâce
Au vent léger d'été qui passe,
Se mêle aux parfums qu'elle a mis;

Comme ses yeux l'avaient promis,
Son courage est grand et sa lèvre
Communique une exquise fièvre;

Et l'Amour comblant tout, hormis
La faim, sorbets et confitures
Nous préservent des courbatures.

Le Faune (*Fêtes galantes*)

Un vieux faune de terre cuite
Rit au centre des boulingrins,
Présageant sans doute une suite
Mauvaise à ces instants sereins

Qui m'ont conduit et t'ont conduite,
Mélancoliques pèlerins,
Jusqu'à cette heure dont la fuite
Tournoie au son des tambourins.

La Bonne Chanson VI

La lune blanche
Luit dans les bois;
De chaque branche
Part une voix
Sous la ramée . . .

O bien-aimée.

L'étang reflète,
Profond miroir,
La silhouette
Du saule noir
Où le vent pleure . . .

Rêvons, c'est l'heure.

Un vaste et tendre
Apaisement
Semble descendre
De firmament
Que l'astre irise . . .

C'est l'heure exquise.

Ariettes oubliées IX (*Romances sans paroles*)

L'ombre des arbres dans la rivière embrumée
    Meurt comme de la fumée,
Tandis qu'en l'air parmi les ramures réelles,
    Se plaignent les tourterelles.
Combien, ô voyageur, ce paysage blême
    Te mira blême toi-même,
Et que tristes pleuraient dans les hautes feuillées
    Tes espérances noyées!

Colloque sentimental (*Fêtes galantes*)

Dans le vieux parc solitaire et glacé,
Deux formes ont tout à l'heure passé.

Leurs yeux sont morts et leurs lèvres sont molles,
Et l'on entend à peine leurs paroles.

Dans le vieux parc solitaire et glacé,
Deux spectres ont évoqué le passé.

—Te souvient-il de notre extase ancienne?
—Pourquoi voulez-vous donc qu'il m'en souvienne?

—Ton coeur bat-il toujours à mon seul nom?
Toujours vois-tu mon âme en rêve?—Non.

—Ah! les beaux jours de bonheur indicible
Où nous joignions nos bouches!—C'est possible.

—Qu'il était bleu, le ciel, et grand, l'espoir!
—L'espoir a fui, vaincu, vers le ciel noir.

Tels ils marchaient dans les avoines folles,
Et la nuit seule entendit leurs paroles.

Spleen (*Romances sans paroles*)

Les roses étaient toutes rouges,
Et les lierres étaient tout noirs.

Chère, pour peu que tu te bouges,
Renaissent tous mes désespoirs.

Le ciel était trop bleu, trop tendre.
La mei tiop veite et l'aii tiop doux.

Je crains toujours,—ce qu'est d'attendre!
Quelque fuite atroce de vous.

Du houx à la feuille vernie
Et du luisant buis je suis las.

Et de la campagne infinie
Et de tout, fors de vous, hélas!

La Bonne Chanson XX

J'allais par des chemins perfides,
Douloureusement incertain.
Vos chères mains furent mes guides.

Si pâle à l'horizon lointain
Luisait un faible espoir d'aurore;
Votre regard fut le matin.

Nul bruit, sinon son pas sonore,
N'encourageait le voyageur
Votre voix me dit: "Marche encore!"

Mon coeur craintif, mon sombre coeur
Pleurait, seul, sui la tiiste voie;
L'amour, délicieux vainqueur,

Nous a réunis dans la joie.

Notes

I would like to thank all those who, by their remarks, criticisms, and encouragements, helped me to improve the content of this article: the students in my course on poetics at the University of Paris-Vincennes, the participants of the Summer Seminar in Linguistics at Tunis (July 1978), and the participants of the International Conference on the Semiotics of Art at Ann Arbor. Special thanks are due to Benoît de Cornulier, who read the French version of this paper, and to Wendy Steiner, who edited the English version. The French version has appeared in a special issue of the *Revue d'Esthétique* (1-2: 1979) devoted to rhetoric, under the editorship of the Groupe *mu*. Most of the poems by Verlaine discussed in the text will be found in the Appendix; they are quoted from the *Oeuvres poéti-*

ques complètes, edited by Y.-G. La Dautec (Paris: Gallimard, Bibliothèque de la Pléiade, 1954).

1. By this rather unhappy term (but I have found no better one), I mean all the principles which govern equivalence relations, whether coded or not.

2. From one period or tradition to another, typographical principles may vary. Compare, for instance, the typography of Du Bellay's "Si nostre vie . . . " and that of Baudelaire's "Les Chats" as they are both reproduced in Jakobson 1973: 319, 401. Du Bellay's sonnet has no blanks, and it is the setting off of the beginnings of certain lines which marks the beginning of stanzas. These variations, I think, have no bearing on the general point I want to make here. In what follows, I will limit myself to current French typography.

3. In French metrics one must distinguish two types of verse (see Cornulier 1977): simple (from one to eight syllables), without any systematic internal structure, and compound (four syllables plus six syllables, six plus six, etc.), the linking between the two subparts being subject to definite rules (which define the caesura). In theory, if one does not take rhyme into account, a written text, made up of n "long" lines, could correspond to a poem of $2n$ simple verses; conversely, a written text, made up of $2n$ "short" lines, could correspond to a poem of n compound verses. For instance, Baudelaire's "La Mort des Amants," which is written in decasyllabic lines (see Ruwet 1975b), could be viewed as a poem in pentasyllabic verses; in fact, the second quatrain presents framed rhymes at the hemistich (on the fifth syllable): $_5$*envi*, $_6$*seront*, $_7$*réfléchiront*, $_8$*esprits*. On the other hand, Verlaine's "Le ciel est, par-dessus le toit . . . " (*Sagesse*, Pléiade, p. 184) shows an alternation of long (octosyllabic) and short (tetrasyllabic) lines; it could be read as if it were made of alexandrines, obeying the constraints which, according to Cornulier (forthcoming), define this meter in the work of Verlaine.

4. This is a simplification; I am leaving aside the question of *rime pour l'oeil* (eye rhyme).

5. See note 4. For practical reasons, in what follows I will make use of only an orthographical representation, which will create some minor distortions.

6. Some interesting theoretical questions might be raised which I will not deal with. Why, for instance, are schemes such as *ABBA ABBBA ABBBBA ABBBBBA* . . . excluded in general? (They would justify a freer use of loops.)

7. Type e is to be found in Malherbe, "Prière pour le Roy allant en Limozin," and in Verlaine, "Bruxelles II" (*Romances sans paroles*, Pléiade, p. 129). Type f is found in *Sagesse* I, XX (Pléiade, p. 163).

8. See, for instance, Verlaine, *Romances sans paroles*, II (framed rhymes, all feminine), IV (crossed rhymes, all feminine), IX (plain rhymes, all feminine). Baudelaire's "Au lecteur" is, if I am not mistaken, the only

piece in *Les Fleurs du mal* which, made up of framed rhymes, never reverses the order of feminine and masculine rhymes from one quatrain to another. On this constraint, see also the concluding section of this article.

9. Notice that, given the principles stated below, the stanza is defined for this poem.

10. In the case of framed-rhyme quatrains, typography does not account for the systematic inversion of the respective order of feminine and masculine rhymes, which is a consequence of the constraint stated in observation 1 above.

11. One could invent a notation for the distribution of meters, more or less similar to the one proposed for rhymes; or one could complicate the latter and integrate into it metrical variations; several ways of dealing with this come to mind, which I will not consider here. In what follows, x and y are variables on the number of syllables in a line.

12. One finds in the work of Malherbe one case of an extraordinary combination of several meters: the *chanson* "Chère beauté, que mon ame ravie . . . " (*Oeuvres poétiques*, Garnier-Flammarion, p. 124) consists of *sizains*, with the following meters: 10, 9, 7, 10, 8, 11 (in terms of syllables). See also "A la reine mère du roy pendant sa régence" (ibid., p. 69), whose quatrains present the distribution 10, 8, 10, 6. The key to the understanding of the meter of the former poem is to be found in the music for which it was written.

13. Or contradict them. All sorts of theoretical possibilities, once more, could be imagined. Suppose we have a twelve-line poem, with the rhyme scheme *ABBACDDCEFFE* and the metrical scheme *xxyxxyxxyxxy*; a consideration of the rhymes alone would suggest quatrains, a consideration of the meter, tercets; the combination of rhyme and meter defines one complex twelve line stanza.

14. All of Verlaine's and Mallarmé's poems written in *terza rima* use only one meter. According to Benoît de Cornulier (personal communication), there are cases of what I am thinking of in Martinon's compilation (Martinon 1912).

15. In "Cythère," if the rhyme takes into account the penultimate syllable, one falls back on scheme e: $_3$ . . . *amis*/ $_6$ . . . *a mis*/ $_9$ . . . *promis*/ $_{12}$ . . . *hormis.*

16. The mirror-image structure is corroborated by phonic equivalences: *un/ants, euf/eur.*

17. I am leaving aside, generally, the distinctions (period vs. semicolon) created by punctuation.

18. Line 1 would deserve long commentary. "Les roses étaient toutes rouges" is in principle ambiguous, meaning either "all the roses were red" or "the roses were completely red"; in isolation, the first reading would be the more natural one: normally, a rose is either completely red, or completely white, or the like, and it does not change its color (compare "ses joues étaient toutes rouges"—"his cheeks were all/completely red"). How-

ever no reader seems to perceive this reading, except on reflection; this I take to be an effect of the parallelism between line 1 and line 2, whose interpretation is unambiguous; apparently, there is something like a retroactive effect of the interpretation of line 2 on the interpretation of line 1. I will not try here to determine the very subtle semantic results of this parallelism.

19. There are some variations: finite verb vs. infinitive, lexically full noun vs. (strong form) pronoun.

20. *Toutes* and *tout* in I have a different function; see note 18.

21. The structure of this poem should be compared to that of "Les Coquillages" (see above); the relation between the typographically isolated last line and the rest of the poem is markedly different in the two cases.

22. For convenience, I am using here the traditional notation, where capital letters refer to masculine rhymes and lowercase letters to feminine rhymes (according to Cornulier, Martinon 1912 does just the opposite). The parenthetical asterisks (*) signal schemes which are "ungrammatical," or rather, marked, according to traditional French versification. See note 8.

23. Besides, none of these sonnets is "regular" according to traditional canons. See Ruwet 1972, Chapters 9, 10.

24. On orthography and its relation to linguistic structures, see, for instance, Chomsky and Halle 1968. For an example of a "mixing of levels" within musical notation, see Ruwet 1972, Chapter 5.

CHAPTER 9
Toward a Semiotics of Music
BY HENRY ORLOV

It is not possible to determine when music was first thought of as a language. In many primitive societies and in many civilizations of the past, including that of medieval Western Europe, music was worshipped as a language of divine revelation. The eighteenth-century doctrine of affects (*Affektenlehre*) claimed that music was the language of passions and emotions, as had Plato and the thinkers of the ancient Orient earlier on. For Beethoven music was the language of a higher wisdom, and for the Romantics, the language of beauty and poetic truth, to mention only a few definitions.

Various hypotheses about the origins of music have connected it with, or derived it from, the intonations of excited speech, nonverbal voice signals, or significant inflections of the voice in the tonal languages. A widely accepted notion maintains that both natural language and music, alone of all the arts, involve sound unfolding in time, and that both have the human voice as their common source. Finally, music, like natural language, developed a system of writing—musical notation.

The intuition that language and music developed along parallel lines remains true, though imprecise, in light of the modern concepts of structuralism and semiotics. Without doubt, music lies within their reach, because it is a kind of communication which has both organization and significance. Moreover, music may seem the most appropriate and gratifying object for these new approaches, because it is the purest system of abstract relationships presented in concrete form, and the most immediate expression of meaning.

Yet at this point one has to be cautious, for the first stumbling block lies right where the road seems to be open and unobstructed. That music may be described in semiotic terms does not necessarily mean that the terminology and theory of semiotics will help us to understand music better. As such attempts have shown, music stubbornly and defiantly conceals even what is already known, and turns out to be a very difficult object to deal with.

From a semiotic viewpoint, music, like other arts, myths, and culture generally, is a "secondary modeling system" (Lotman 1977) based on the primary modeling system, which is natural language. Or so we are told—without, however, being offered proof or evidence that such a subordination is an essential one and not merely an occasional, superficial or technical involvement of natural language elements in musical creation and perception.

According to another proposition, the work of art, including the musical one, is considered a sign or a structure of signs, chiefly of the type called *iconic*, the iconic sign being defined as that which has a similarity to, and shares some properties with, the object it denotes. With regard to the plastic arts, where the similarity is perceived by the eye, the proposition may be deemed appropriate, while with regard to music it looks dubious, to say the least. For the similarity between the music in some illustrative passages of programmatic pieces and the audible phenomena of the world is by no means characteristic of music in general. Thus the still unanswered question of what music's object is, which semiotics should clarify, becomes even more obscure.

The purpose of these remarks is not to deny the applicability of semiotics to music. It is rather to suggest that semiotics as a descriptive analytical method must be further refined and adjusted if it is to become a useful and productive approach to the peculiarly complex system of music. Similar adjustments may eventually be required by other arts, too, for it seems somewhat improbable that a concept formed on the basis of linguistics should have an immediate explanatory power outside of its original boundaries.

One has to distinguish clearly between semiotics as a self-sufficient theory of communication systems and as a metatheoretical extension of linguistics, between its two aspects still bound together by an umbilical cord. Hence, the first step one has to make is to reconsider the proposition that music is a superstructure supported by and subordinate to natural language. This postulate, which comes as a result of speculation, is clearly premature and constraining.

We do not know whether music indeed has its origins in human speech. We do know, however, that the historical development of music has in no way been determined by that of language. And this fact gives us a right to treat them as intrinsically independent branches of evolution, even though both stem from the human voice, both aim at communication, and both are interconnected in innumerable ways.

Language and music should be seen, therefore, as two autonomous and mutually complementary domains, each of which has its own sets of patterns and values, field of competence, and view of reality. We can describe one in terms of the other, and the two expressions—"the language of music" and "the music of language"—are perfectly legitimate. These expressions correspond to two different attitudes of the observer and point to two different aspects in each of the objects so described. Roughly, the first is the attitude of analytical rationality, which aims at logical understanding of relationships and discursive explanation. The second is the attitude of syncretic, all-inclusive sensitivity, which values the qualitative fullness of the contemplated material phenomenon living in time. In both domains, "language" refers to abstract structures and functions, while "music" stands for the concrete experience of the unique, sensed reality of sound in process. And this is where the dividing line lies.

To assume a priori that music as sound, like natural speech, is a text generated by certain models, whatever truth there may be to it, is not enough. Those unknown models have to be reconstructed from the respective text and not hypostatized in the image and after the likeness of another kind of model only because the latter is known better. The thing we have lost and are looking for does not necessarily lie in the best-lit place.

To speak of language and music respectively as primary and secondary systems for modeling reality is to cover rather than to uncover an essential difference between them. For what these models reflect is not reality itself, of which no immediate knowledge or experience is possible, but different modes and patterns by which human beings apprehend and handle reality. These models and patterns are culturally determined and hence relative. But still more important is that they realize and channel different human powers and propensities.

Natural language reflects and determines the way human beings cope with reality intellectually, developing a stock of abstract signs (vocabulary) and abstract structures (grammar) which replace all the particular realities and relations that people single out and deem noteworthy in light of their culture. Thus, language functions as a filter, a quantifier, permitting only those facets of reality to enter the mind that it can denote.

Words are abstract conventional signs. They have nothing in common with what they denote, and this gives natural language the freedom of reflecting the world without being tied to it. In this detachment, language gains an enormous *discoursive* power but loses whatever *presentational* capacity it might originally have had. Words fail to present the difference between blue and green to the blind or to the daltonic, and, as everyone knows, all the attempts to "translate" music into words invariably appear awkward, crude, and inadequate. For there is neither transition nor similarity between the two modeling systems, one of which is discrete, linear, and abstract while the other is continuous, multidimensional, and sensuously concrete.

This incongruity can only be understood as an outcome of diverging evolution. Language developed, selected, and accumulated its elements—phonemes, letters, words, morphemes, sentence structures, etc.—which constitute finite sets of standard units—structural, signifying, and functional. Each of these elements is the invariant of a certain class of realities and allows for an unlimited number of particular realizations. Linguistically, the identity of an utterance does not depend on the way it is pronounced, on the quality of the voice, pitch, speed, and loudness; a letter is recognizable as the same letter in all kinds of print, handwriting, shape, and substance; a word refers to all and each of the things which have, or may be given, the same name. The elements of language are of a generic nature.

The elements of music are of a different, singular nature. It is within the scope of music theory only, which projects music into the system of language, that these elements appear to be standard units, such as seven diatonic or twelve chromatic tones in the octave, basic note values, their fractions and multiples, typified chords and harmonic progressions, and the like. And it is in the notation only, which is the musical counterpart of written language, that music appears to consist of discrete elements organized in linear chains.

Musically, the tones are unique elements of an infinite set. Even those tones that have the same name and hold the same position are not identical and differ in their presentational value if they differ in at least one of several other characteristics. A popular saying holds that "the tone makes music," and indeed so do the timbre, the loudness, the duration, the manner and the coloring of sound production, and, especially, the continuity of sound—the "curve" of its ephemeral life from birth until disappearance. Each single tone is contemplated and experienced by the listener as an inimitable multidimensional object, a piece of reality itself alive and rich with all sorts of meaning.

As distinct from the evolution of language and speech, the concreteness of sound material became one of the most important lines in the genesis of music. It makes a great difference whether the sound has the quality of a male, female, or child's voice, each of whose individual peculiarities is significant as well. Faculties and features of the human voice have developed tremendously in various cultures so that an immense variety of styles, manners, and techniques of singing has been created. Similarly the treasury of sonorities has been constantly enriched throughout history by the invention and improvement of musical instruments, which now number in the thousands, and by the development of various techniques of playing them. Vocal and instrumental palettes offer the musician a virtually unlimited choice of sonorities that may be combined in innumerable ways so that every instant of musical sound, let alone the entire piece, becomes for the listener not a reference to, but the direct source of, a rich multifarious sensuous experience.

It may seem that we have arrived at a point of agreement with the assumption earlier described as dubious, that to discuss the presentational power of musical sound is, in fact, to confirm and amplify its iconic nature. Yet such a conclusion would be a hasty one, for the situation is rather controversial and does not allow for a simple yes or no. In some respects musical sound does conform to the concept of iconic sign, while in others it does not.

The sound may be viewed as an iconic sign because what it is valued for is not *in* it but, as it were, *behind* it. The qualities we experience as the sound's meaning are not confined to its acoustical properties, and their modalities go far beyond the auditory. Language itself is witness to this fact. The nouns, verbs, and adjectives with which we describe our experience of musical sounds form a huge vocabulary in which I know only one word—"loud"—that refers to the audible quality proper, all the others referring to something else. The sounds and sound textures are felt to be light or dark, bright or dull, hot or cold, sharp or blunt, rich or hollow, hard or soft, solid or transparent, smooth or rough, rigid or pliable, sweet or tart, fragrant or insipid, and so on, with all intermediate shades and all sorts of mixtures. Music theory itself has to speak about high and low tones; intervals and scales; melodic leaps, curves, and arcs; density of harmony; and various kinds of motion. It also discusses musical form in quasi-geometrical terms.

To consider all these as the significates of the iconic signs of music is tempting yet wrong; in fact, musical sound meets the definition neither of sign nor of the icon. As a sign, the sound would have to have a recognizable identity and to stand for an extraneous reality, which it obviously does not. It is unique and, in this sense, unidentifiable, and it stands for nothing but itself, referring to nothing but its own experienced reality. As an icon, the sound would have to resemble in a way, be similar to, what it signifies —to represent its significate, as blue represents the color of the sky, a sculpture the shapes of the body, and a crossed bent arrow the prohibited direction of turn. Needless to say, this type of relation does not apply to the materiality of musical sound and to the diverse feelings it provides for. It certainly does not share in and does not "look like" the properties of the above-mentioned optical, chromatic, spatial, tactile, muscular-motor, let alone gustatory and olfactory images which it seems to project in the listener.

What relates the sound to its experienced qualities? Or, in other words, why is it experienced as it is? This is a question which needs special attention and cannot be discussed here in detail. At any rate, it cannot be answered by referring to the phenomena of association and synesthesia, though both may contribute to the effect. The correlations between sound and its meaning are neither fully biologically determined, nor must they depend entirely on the whims of individual experiences. The safest assumption is to see them as cultural patterns learned by individuals in the cultural environment. Suffice it to mention that the most important dimension of Western music that is described in terms of high and low tones is equally alien to little children in the West and to the Africans who, as Alan Merriam witnesses, found his question about high and low tones "silly," preferring to speak instead of "weak" and "strong" or "small" and "big" sounds (Merriam 1964: 96-97).

Thus, relations between the signifier and the significate in music are mediated by a cultural convention rather than based on immediately felt resemblance or shared properties. From this point of view, signs characteristic of music act in an abstract rather than iconic manner. However, one can apply the concept of the abstract sign to music only tentatively and reluctantly.

In any abstract sign system—in natural languages as well as in the specialized languages of science—the sign cannot function properly before its significate is defined clearly and unambiguously. Words have immense self-explanatory possibilities; they are definable through other words, and so are symbols used in mathematics, physics, chemistry, and so on. In music, on the other hand, and in art generally, the possibilities of verbal definition are limited to a few technical generalities. No self-explanation or intrasystemic translation is possible here, and the sign is the only means to point at and reveal its content. This follows quite logically from what was said earlier about the uniqueness of both sound and sense in the elements of music.

If music is to be considered a sign system, then it is a very strange one: an icon which has nothing in common with the object it presents; an abstract language which does not allow for a prior definition of its alphabet and vocabulary, and operates with an indefinite, virtually infinite number of unique elements; a text which cannot be decomposed into standard interchangeable items.

These discrepancies can be reconciled if music is approached in terms of semiotics but without its preconceptions. Music is an icon on the surface, by appearance; it is perceived as an icon. The icon is peculiar, however, since it does not and cannot resemble the object it presents, which is ideal and unattainable to the senses. Therefore, what appears as the icon on the surface acts, behind the surface, as an abstract sign—a symbol, but a special kind of symbol which is unique and otherwise undefinable.

The reason for this strangeness is that the reality so symbolized is that of preverbal experience—the reality of immediate mental, emotional, and sensuous life in the human being. As Donald Ferguson puts it: "Music is in its fullest function a definition of experience" (Ferguson 1960: 17). The way it defines experience, the type of relation between the musical signifier and significate, is akin to that of an ideogram. Music can be said to be the audible ideogram of experience. This is so far the nearest conceivable approximation that can be made to it in terms of semiotics.

As a matter of fact, music can function in many different ways. It can act as a signal, an emotional symptom, a pictorial image, a regular abstract sign denoting a thought, even as a huge composite symbol referring to an entire concept. However important in particular musical styles, and however convenient they may be for semiotics to tackle, all these functions belong to the periphery rather than to the essence; they constitute the fore rather than the core of a musical system of communication.

Another kind of snare for the semiotic approach to music is the hidden, often unrealized assumptions received through the back door from music theory and aesthetics. Relying on particular metadescriptions, which themselves should have to be critically examined, and developing its theory on the basis of other theories, musical semiotics runs the risk of replacing its object, getting lost in sheer speculation, and diverging from its proper course—which is to proceed from and rely fully on only the primary reality of the text, that is, music as sound.

CHAPTER 10
Two Views of Musical Semiotics
BY ALLAN R. KEILER

Some Trends in Current Musical Semiotics

Comparisons between language and music are not hard to find in most periods of musical scholarship. Indeed analogies of this kind occur already in
the earliest periods of Sanskrit literature. Some of these earliest concerns
with language and music reflect the Indian scholars' particular attitude toward universals. One anonymous manuscript, for example, "explains the
formation of musical sounds on the basis of the *Maheshvara Sūtra-s*, an
esoteric arrangement of syllabic sounds, which Nandikeshvara also ac-
cepts as the philosophical basis of the Sanskrit language and, in fact, all
language."[1] Vedic, unlike classical Sanskrit, was a tone language, and
Indian theorists also reflected on the relationships that might exist between these features of Sanskrit and properties of scale patterns. Later
works, such as Bharata's treatise on dramaturgy, discussed music as part of
"the harmonious combination of concept, speech, expression and music,
both vocal and instrumental" (Chaitanya 1962: 22). To take another
period closer to us both in time and tradition, and one, in fact, hardly
examined sufficiently, the eighteenth century in Franco-German Western
music theory affords a rich example of discussions and theories concerned
with points of contact between language and music. The relation often
drawn between musical phrase structure and the hierarchical levels of language discourse has been pointed out often enough. Not so well known,
and even more closely related to current thinking about language structure
and use, are the aesthetic doctrines of such theorists as Sulzer, Koch, and
Johann Mattheson.[2] These discussions, devoted as they are to such problems as the relation of word and music, or language and musical creativity,
should have an immediate semiotic pertinence.

We would surely look back on many of these attempts to compare
music with language as superficial and even misguided. The point of such
comparisons, after all, was not to raise questions in one area from the

vantage point of the other. The role of linguistics as a model for other disciplines, by virtue of either substance or method, is a more recent development. And now that linguistics has become the dominating force of semiological studies, it might be expected that the long history of intuitions
about the relationship of language to music might continue more fruitfully
as part of the semiotic study of cultural forms. The truth of the matter,
however, at least in my view, is that music has only slowly and painfully
taken its place among the other semiotic disciplines.

A critical survey of musical semiotics is not possible here.[3] Indeed, it
may even be premature for such a study: it is still hard to perceive either
well-formulated positions or explicit currents of research that seem particularly meaningful. One distinction that has been suggested for organizing
the different kinds of activity understood as semiotic, and useful enough
for musical semiotics, is that between (1) semiotics as a science of signs, or
of systems of communication, and (2) any attempt at analyzing some domain of interest (for instance, myth, ritual, or musical systems) with the
help of techniques borrowed from linguistics (see Nattiez 1973: 3; Ruwet
1975c: 33). About the first, as it applies to the semiotics of music, I would
agree with Ruwet: " . . . I don't really see what one gains by considering
music as a system of signs or of communication, by speaking of musical
signifiers and signifieds or of musical semantics" (Ruwet 1975c: 33 and
footnote 46).[4] In the second category, however, several trends are noticeable and do warrant discussion. I would identify these as (1) the taxonomic-empiricist view of Nattiez and, to a lesser extent, Molino, Ruwet, and
others, (2) the analogical view, i.e., those studies characterized by the
search for possible analogical connections that might be made between
substantive linguistic categories (e.g., verb, noun, or phoneme and mor-
pheme) and musical patterning, and (3) ethnomusicological studies, which,
often quite independently of contemporary semiotic ideas, have much to
do with the latter.

The first of my distinctions, the taxonomic-empiricist view, is the most
elaborated program of musical semiotics of the three, and I will confine
my discussion here to it alone. My purpose is not to trace the genesis and
development of this view, but rather to characterize its more fundamental
premises and to deal critically with them.[5] The following paragraph, from
a recent article by Nattiez (1974: 155), should give something of the essence of this approach:

> The neutral level is no doubt the one that will cause the most debate.
> Let us say that this is a level of analysis at which one does not decide
> a priori whether the results obtained by an explicit approach are perti-
> nent from the point of view of esthesis and poiesis. The means by

which the description of the material level is achieved are, therefore, not neutral in any absolute sense: disposed, as will be seen, to the analysis of the recurrence of units and their systems of combination, they provide a fixed point for subsequent analyses (poietic and esthesic) of these external and relatively autonomous schemata of decoupage.[6]

A primary distinction thus concerns three distinct but interrelated dimensions of the symbolic object: the poietic level, concerned with the process of production or encoding; the esthesic level, concerned with the perceptual process; and the neutral or material level, which treats the object of study "in its material reality." At first glance, one might be tempted to invoke the Chomskyan distinction of competence and performance. The *niveau neutre*, or "neutral level," could thus be taken to represent an ideal and abstract view of the stimulus object, that is, as a characterization of internalized musical knowledge; the poietic and esthesic levels would then be concerned with the other determinants of a theory of musical behavior—production and perception.

But this is by no means what is involved here. Molino (1975: 48) invokes another comparison, again taken from linguistics, this time phonology, that will take us further: "Phonetic units can be distinguished and defined either at the level of production—articulatory phonetics—or at the level of perception—auditory phonetics—or at the level of the physical substance of the sign—acoustic phonetics."[7] The most important fact about both parts of this analogy is that the three levels do not necessarily coincide: "On the one hand, a sound that produces the same acoustic and auditory effects can be created by different articulatory means; on the other hand, the same unit defined from the acoustic point of view can be interpreted in different ways depending on the listener's perceptual frame" (Molino 1975: 48).[8] Nattiez also draws on this analogy with phonology: "Phonology itself became possible only after a neutral and descriptive science, phonetics, had accumulated several decades' worth of empirical observations of all kinds" (Nattiez 1975: 165).[9] One possible way to understand the purpose of these comparisons is to assume that the *niveau neutre* must be empirically unbiased toward the pertinent distinctions made in the process of perception or production. The claim is that an objective and exhaustive record of the sound stimulus is a necessary preliminary to actual analytic description in the study of language (or music); only then, presumably, will the work of analysis take into account the psychological reality of linguistic (or musical) behavior (whence such notions as contrast, pertinence, and so forth). This view turns out to be, of course, the taxonomic-empiricist position represented, for example, by the period of American linguistics associated with Leonard Bloomfield and his followers. And it is certainly ironic that so many decisions of the taxonomic-empiricist view in musical semiotics are based on the work of the Prague School phonologists. One of their most important and essential claims is that, while an absolutely faithful record of the sound stimulus is possible, for the purposes of phonological analysis, it is utterly useless. Indeed, most phonetic descriptions or inventories have always been concerned, whether explicitly or not, with a double set of constraints; those perceptual limitations of the human organism that might limit the range and number of possible sound contrasts, and the general nature of sound laws, both synchronic and diachronic, which can only be understood and formulated in terms of such restricted phonetic theories. These views are fundamental to all of the current work in generative phonology:

> Our conception thus differs from an alternative view that the phonetic transcription is primarily a device for recording facts observed in actual utterances. That the latter view is not tenable, in any very strict sense, has been known at least since mechanical and electrical recordings of utterances have revealed that even the most skillful transcriber is unable to note certain aspects of the signal, while commonly recording in his transcriptions items for which there seems to be no direct warrant in the physical record. But even if the phonetic transcription were as faithful a record of speech as one could desire, there is still some question whether such a record would be of much interest to linguists, who are primarily concerned with the structure of language rather than with the acoustics and physiology of speech. (Chomsky and Halle 1968: 293)

We must not push these analogies too far. Of the possible meanings that could be understood from such comparisons for the notion of a *niveau neutre*, the strongest possible claim, as we have seen, is the demand for a faithful record of the musical stimulus, a kind of preanalytic level, as it were.[10] Looking further, we are told that the analysis of the *niveau neutre* must be equally useful and applicable to both the poietic and esthesic modes, since it must be possible, subsequent to its description, to relate it to these modes in some meaningful and revealing way. The analytic procedures that underlie descriptions of the *niveau neutre* must be independent (hence objective) of the other modes so as not to favor one over the other. Analytic judgments, therefore, are not ruled out; it simply must not be judged a priori "whether the results obtained by an explicit approach are pertinent from the point of view of esthesis and poiesis." Now it is one thing to argue that a preanalytic, faithful record of the musical stimulus, independent of the other two modes, is attainable (however useless it is); it is much more problematic to argue that the very analytic procedures and, by necessity, that view of musical structure on which such procedures are based, must not take into account intuitions that come from the perceptual or performance modes of musical behavior.

We might then consider this latter view as a weaker claim about the relationship of the musical object, the "objet sonore," to the methodological problems of analysis and description. The claim is that judgments about the internal structure of the musical object can be arrived at independently of any a priori intuitions or premises about the nature of that object or about its behavioral modes. I believe, however, that only the opposite position is tenable. Only some theory about the internal organization of the object, thus making explicit the complexity of that object, will enable one to ask pertinent questions about musical (or linguistic) performance. As Ulric Neisser (1976: xii) has put it, "In particular, the amount and kind of processing that a stimulus is assumed to undergo necessarily depends on related assumptions about the nature of that stimulus; that is, on how the theorist chooses to describe it." Consider, for example, how different is the view of language use that results from the generative point of view about language structure than the one which predominated earlier; or, for that matter, how ideas about musical perception have changed dramatically as a result of the acceptance of at least some version of Schenker's theory of musical structure. We do not, in other words, view the nature of language behavior or of musical behavior as we once did, because we now understand the nature of the object of inquiry, language and music, to be different than we once did.[11]

Perhaps these remarks are enough to help us understand the equivocation that surrounds most discussions of the nature of the *niveau neutre*. Consider again the paragraph of Nattiez with which we began, especially: "The means by which the description of the material level is achieved are, therefore, not neutral in any absolute sense." This comment does not merely impose a matter of degree; the very choice of criteria ("the recurrence of units and their systems of combination") is obviously dictated by the fact that they are able to provide "a fixed point for subsequent analyses (poietic and esthesic)." Indeed Nattiez himself gives the strongest possible statement against the very position he and others seem to be arguing: "... *it is absolutely false to claim that the process of classification*, in Harris as well as the present study, *makes no appeal either to intuitions or hypotheses*" (Nattiez 1975: 256; italics in original).[12] This is echoed, equally strongly, by Molino: "In truth, it is not possible to segment, to reduce to units and to organize a symbolic object only by using as a basis the three dimensions which it necessarily presents ... " (1975: 47).[13] It is hard to know what to make of such claims alongside the following, which surely argues for just the opposite: "A level doubly neutral since it

consists of a description of phenomena in which the conditions of the production and the reception of the message are not considered . . . " (Molino
1975: 58).[14] How exasperating the whole discussion can become is evident
from the following comments by Nattiez about a part of Pierre Boulez's
analysis of *Le Sacre du Printemps*. Nattiez apparently views this analysis as
one that respects the constraints which he wishes to impose on the *niveau
neutre*: "Nevertheless, the study of Boulez, written in 1951, presents
many common features with taxonomic analysis, such as we propose.
First of all, its neutrality, that is, its a priori indifference with respect to
the poietic and esthesic . . . " (Nattiez 1975: 280).[15] This admiration for
Boulez is shortlived, for he takes away from the composer on the very
next page that approbation he had just given him: "Boulez is not disinterested: as a real post-Webernian, he looks for retrograde rhythms, inverted
structures, mirror properties; the influence of Messiaen can be seen here
. . . " (Nattiez 1975: 281).[16] The more general statement is worth quoting: "This is an opportunity to mention that, in the analyses of composers, their own aesthetic conceptions are not without influence on their
methods" (ibid.).[17]

I would argue, then, that the weaker of the two claims about the
nature of the *niveau neutre* is no more tenable than the other. There is,
however, still a weaker claim that could be made explicit, and which is
taken to be fundamental to the taxonomic-empiricist view. The issue involved here is that of discovery procedures. I would characterize it thus:
if there can be no disinterested analytic work, then at least the premises
which underlie analytic judgments must be explicit and objective. It would
be necessary, therefore, to construct a set of analytic procedures which
makes explicit each step of the process of description, so that any researcher, following these same procedures, will come up with the same
analysis. This insistence on discovery procedures is central to the empiri-
cist view. Much of the actual work in analysis that derives from this position is based on the seminal article of Ruwet, "Méthodes d'analyse en
musicologie," where the program of research is clearly stated (1966: 89):
" . . . I have insisted in this article on the necessity of developing an analytic point of view in musicology, in other words, on the urgent need to
elaborate rigorous procedures that can be used to discover codes by starting from messages."[18] Nattiez, strongly influenced by the work of Ruwet,
makes this program the dominant one of his musical investigations: ". . .
he [Ruwet] is developing an approach which has made it possible to
thematize concretely a new area of reflection for musicology: the elaboration of explicit and reproducible analytic methods" (Nattiez 1975:
239).[19]

Thus the real substantive contributions of those who advocate the taxonomic-empiricist view are a rather precise set of analytic procedures and a number of descriptive studies, both of pretonal as well as tonal music in the Western tradition, all derived from these discovery procedures.[20] The status of discovery procedures, so central to this view, is worth considering further. The most important question to ask about them is how they can be criticized. I can think of two ways. One can ask if they are really explicit, if anything else is brought to the process of description except what is contained in the procedures—in other words, do they work automatically? Now while this question might be of some importance to the psychology of problem solving, or to computer problems, it is not the revealing one for us. And it is also interesting to note that most discussions about discovery procedures are really involved with another issue—what they turn up. One obviously cannot construct discovery procedures without somehow knowing, and certainly caring, about the results one is then going to obtain from them. I might, for example, propose a set of procedures which resulted in the most patently absurd claims about musical organization that no one would view seriously for a minute. What usually happens, however, is that discovery procedures do undergo a constant process of criticism and emendation. Now unless one took the view that one set of discovery procedures is as good as any other, criticisms about discovery procedures are really arguments about the results of applying them, what Chomsky would call the realist position about them. Discovery procedures, then, are not ad hoc; they transform some view, often implicit and vague, about the organization of some data into a hopefully effective set of analytic procedures designed to generate just that view of how some data ought to be organized. This means, of course, that the critical issue is not the procedures at all, but the assumptions about how the data which they project are organized. It is, then, apparent how foolish it is to argue that a given analytic judgment must be ruled out because it is not generated by some set of discovery procedures which must supposedly underlie all analytic work.

Some of the points I have tried to make about the taxonomic-empiricist view of musical semiotics, and especially discovery procedures, will emerge with more force by looking at a particular analysis. For this we will have to return to the analytic procedures of Ruwet and one of the analyses discussed by Nattiez in terms of these procedures. One of the examples that Ruwet analyzes (1966: 76-80) is a fourteenth-century *Geisslerlied* (Figure 10-1a). His analysis of it (Figure 10-1b) is to be read in the following way: the temporal dimension is preserved by reading each line across from top to bottom; repetitions or variants of the same segment or phrase are arranged vertically underneath each other. The hierarchical grouping of variants (described by the letter notation) emerges from the

a.

b.

Figure 10-1.   Ruwet's analysis of a fourteenth-century *Geisslerlied*.

application of procedures of segmentation and classification that have much in common with work of the American linguist Zellig Harris.[21] Readers, of course, will have to study the procedures, as well as their application to specific examples, for themselves. Something of their content can be seen from the initial one of the set:

> Our "machine for picking out elementary identities" runs through the syntagmatic chain and picks out identical fragments. Sequences— the longest possible ones—that are repeated in full, either immediately after their first occurrence or after the intervention of other segments, are considered units of level I. This first operation furnishes structures like A+X+A, A+A+X, A+X+A+Y+A, A+A+B+B+X, A+B+A+X+B+Y, etc. (repeated sections, units of level I, are represented by earlier letters of the alphabet, what is left over by later letters).[22] (Ruwet 1966: 74)

All of the procedures, taken together, involve the continuous segmentation of the musical material into repeated or slightly varied segments, and each procedure repeats on a lower level of analysis the kinds of segmentations and classifying that have gone on at higher levels. It could be easily demonstrated that, simply as an algorithm, and apart from the status of the results of these procedures, it is really questionable whether they are automatically and objectively applicable in any global sense. It will be more revealing, however, to presuppose that this is not the case, at least to some degree, and to examine their application in some detail to a specific example—Nattiez's discussion of the first phrase of Stravinsky's *Le Sacre du Printemps*.

Consider first, then, the phrase in question and Boulez's analysis of it (Figure 10-2a), which Nattiez first discusses (1975: 279-285). I think that, for the most part, Boulez's perceptions are correct. The whole example contains four principal phrases (surely not the six phrases of Nattiez's analysis in Figure 10-2c), the first and third of which are nearly identical but for the absence of a_2 in III. All of the phrases except II end with the same note pattern beginning on D, and nearly all of the subphrases (those designated with lowercased Roman letters) begin on C and end on A. In fact, in terms of phrase structure, cadential motives, return, and so on, the whole phrase as Boulez has analyzed it is strikingly traditional in its structure: opening phrase + most varied phrase, return of opening phrase + final phrase = cadential material of I and III.

Figure 10-2b is Nattiez's more rigorous segmentation and grouping, an analysis, in other words, derived from the application of Ruwet's procedures. Even at first glance, it is clear that there are quite arbitrary decisions—for example, the grouping of a_1 and a'_1 together, but not a_4 and a_1, or all of them into the same class of variants. In this case Nattiez prefers to exclude rhythmic distinctions as part of the degree of variation permitted within a class of variants.[23] This is the same kind of decision as one of Boulez's, for which the latter is criticized by Nattiez (1975: 284): "One could say, roughly, that Boulez has defined implicitly his a's by their beginning on C and by their ending on A (except for a_g)."[24] Of course, it would, in principle, be possible to explicitly incorporate a provision that phrases must begin on the same pitch; or, for that matter, to exclude a provision that rejects rhythmic variation as a possible variant feature of a category. The choice, however, can never depend on the procedures, but on the problem of evaluating competing descriptions.

It is also perfectly clear that, because of the additional segment in I (a_2), and the truncated version of IV, Ruwet's procedures, no matter how carefully formulated, will have to entail ad hoc decisions about the relationships of I, III, and IV, which are surely significantly related phrases. Nattiez's first analysis (Figure 10-2c) simply excludes a_1 as part of any phrase and gives it independent status. In Figure 10-2d, Nattiez's alternate analysis, a_2 is simply left out of the description entirely and referred to in the text as an interpolation. Now the first choice is clearly wrong but permitted by the procedures; the second, which is more to the point, is, nevertheless, necessarily excluded by them. Indeed, the concepts of deletion and interpolation are completely at odds with the segmentation procedures of Ruwet: every segment of the musical material must be grouped as a unit or variant of some unit or other. Interpolations and deletions cannot be grouped in this way at all. They presuppose rather that the surface form of a piece is no longer directly and uniquely the object of analysis; a more abstract underlying structure must be presupposed from which the musical surface is then derivable by various operations, such as deletions or interpolations. Notice that Figure 10-2c hedges about a related fundamental issue. In this analysis, a_1 is necessarily a phrase itself, yet the avoidance of the proper letter notation at the node on the same level as A, B, etc., implicitly denies that very choice. The same is true of β and a_4. This device of avoiding higher-level phrase notation simply ignores the issues of wrong decisions and, on a more general level, the question of single constituent units functioning simultaneously on higher phrase levels.

Nattiez's analyses also involve, at least by implication, the concept of deletion, notated by the ϕ's in phrase B of both analyses. In this case, there is obviously a strong feeling on the part of Nattiez that the central phrases (A, B, A^1) are equal in hierarchical status and composed, for the most part, of variant forms of the same segments. He thus must consider the $\frac{3}{4}$ measure of rests as a variant of a_4. Now imagine the problem of

a.

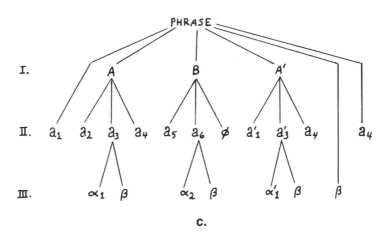

c.

Figure 10-2. Analyses of *Le Sacre du Printemps* excerpt.

b.

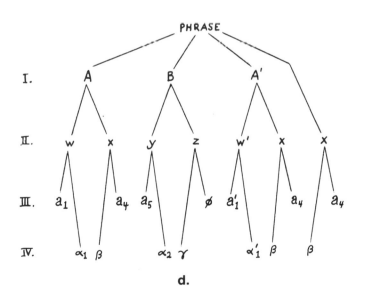

d.

specifying explicitly in such procedures as those of Ruwet the possibility of including some amount of just the time domain alone as variants of phrases. From the strategy of procedures, the arbitrariness is clear from the fact that Nattiez did not choose to equate A and A^1 in the following way:

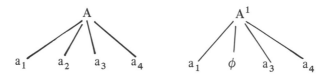

Nor did he choose to consider the sequence of tied notes ♩♩♩♩ as varying musical material relating to a and β.[25] And, finally, consider the different groupings of the a and β variants: in 10-2c, as constituents of the same higher-level group; in 10-2d, as constituents of different but contiguous groups. The fact that both such segmentations could be derived from the same procedures again points out that their use really depends on strong views about desirable structural descriptions.

Let us take stock of what we have. There is no objection to equating discovery procedures with little more than the techniques of trial and error, comparison, and so forth, that are applied within the context of an explicit theory of how some data must be organized—for example, a generative theory of linguistic or musical structure. These techniques would then simply reflect the often automatic and implicit processes that underlie the work of describing and explaining data in terms of explicit structural constraints. The real danger of discovery procedures comes from accepting the structural theory implied by the procedures and then imposing it on the musical object in the interest of empiricism or objectivity—that is, just those claims made for the necessity of discovery procedures in the first place.

The poverty of the taxonomic-empiricist view of musical semiotics is thus embedded in the related problems of accepting a view of musical structure imposed by analytic procedures whose implications remain largely unexamined, and flagrant contradictions of those very same procedures whose justification seems never to be required. As an example of the former, take the argument that, with reference to the Stravinsky analysis, the structural ambiguity of the phrase requires more than a single analysis. Indeed, Nattiez has argued (1975: 283) that this nonuniqueness of solutions is a normal aspect of musical form: "We confirm once again the impossibility of accounting for the phrase uniquely by a single diagram."[26] But the necessity for providing two separate analyses is derived from the impossibility of capturing more than a severely limited kind and number of relationships in any one of them because of the procedures which are supposed to determine analysis. As a result, the shortcomings of these procedures are then attributed to rather fundamental notions of musical structure. As an example of the latter, the use of such analytic notions of deletion and interpolation are a last resort to the impracticability of dealing with the data in some prescribed way. But the use of such devices remains ad hoc so long as the view of musical organization which underlies them is not examined explicitly. For the most part, then, what we are left with is a view of musical organization that cannot seem to go beyond the most elementary and often trivial claims about the importance of musical parallelisms and repetitions. And the universal applicability of the procedures that underlie this view, so inviting to its proponents, is based on the most limited and surface generalizations about musical systems, perhaps different from each other in significant ways, but surely far more rich and complex than any taxonomic-empiricist view of musical semiotics has yet revealed.

Some Properties of the Syntax and Design of Tonal Music

The taxonomic-empiricist view, as I have tried to argue, is to be rejected for a number of reasons. To suggest yet another, it is, in more than one way, a separatist view. There is no principled method for dealing with rhythmic and melodic parameters except as simultaneous features of repeated, varied, or parallel musical segments. And, in the treatment of tonal music, harmonic structure is developed only independently of other parameters and as a process of simple chord labelling. There would be, in other words, no way to consider most complex musical systems in any comprehensive, global way. The issue of musical coherence is thus simply avoided. The desire for general applicability of procedures raises the status of musical repetitions at the expense of other equally fundamental structural components. These components are then demoted in status in quite arbitrary ways.[27] It is just such an overly simple and limited view of musical structure that results from the preoccupation with acceptable discovery procedures—leaving aside the more crucial problem of defining in formal and explicit ways the structural constraints of musical systems in terms of which appropriate generalizations can be formulated.

I would argue rather that the generative approach of contemporary linguistics, and not the taxonomic-empiricist view of language, is likely to be the more useful and revealing one as a model for semiotic musical study. I have discussed elsewhere some of the misuses of linguistics in music theory.[28] My purpose here will be simply to describe something of the formal apparatus that seems necessary to any theory that attempts to deal with the formal coherence of tonal music. This apparatus is to be thought of as describing a part of the musical competence of "native listeners" of Western tonal music and thus a necessary component of a theory of musical behavior.

A fundamental distinction in any theory of tonal music will have to be, I think, one that involves two separate but interrelating hierarchies. The first of these hierarchies, of fundamental importance in revealing part of the coherence of tonal music, is concerned with harmonic structure. The traditional view of harmonic analysis has variously been referred to as Roman numeral analysis, or chord grammar. It is concerned primarily with the labelling of vertical pitch collections according to scale degree and inversion. In Figure 10-3, for example, the Roman numerals below each of the chords in all four of the progressions indicate that the triads (chords built up of thirds) are those belonging to the initial scale degree (tonic), fifth degree (dominant), and second degree of the scale. But it is also understood, but not explicit as part of the labelling apparatus of Roman numeral analysis, that different kinds of relationships exist among members of the complete set of diatonic chords. For example, the dominant relates to the tonic as an essential constituent relationship, but no syntagmatic relationship of this kind obtains between tonic and II; or the syntagmatic relationship between dominant and tonic exists on a lower hierarchical level between II and the dominant. One might say, in other words, that not all possible sequences of triads are grammatical, and the constraints on possible sequences seem to be derived from the possible constituent hierarchical relationships that obtain among the diatonic set of chords. This latter aspect of harmonic structure is thus concerned with chord function and not simply triad identification in terms of scale degree and inversion.[29] And, finally, I think that harmonic function is to a large degree independent of the particular surface form that any sequence of chords might take. In Figure 10-3a and b, the chord labelling as well as chord function can really be abstracted from the different linear patterns of the soprano of each version; similarly, in 10-3c and d, chord inversion and the different melodic pattern of the soprano do not affect the basic chord constituents and their relationships. The invariant feature of these pairs is the constituent relationships of the harmonies; the labelled harmonic constituents can then be understood as the surface constituents of a tree diagram.

In Figure 10-3 the constituent structure of each pair of harmonic sequences is given, and the tree diagrams indicate, just as they do in the anal-

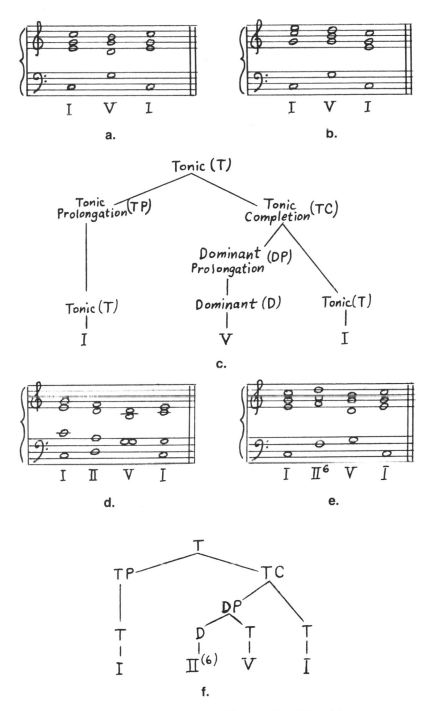

Figure 10–3. Constituent structure of harmonic relationships.

ysis of sentence structure, the syntagmatic and paradigmatic dimensions of (harmonic) structure. In 10-3f, for example, II and V are described as immediate constituents, whereas I and the following II, although contiguous constituents, are described only as ultimate (and in any immediate sense unrelated) constituents of the whole example. On the other hand, the two examples are distinguished by the fact that the Dominant Prolongation (DP) is expanded in a more complex way in 10-3f than in 10-3c. Syntagmatic relationships are thus indicated in terms of the linear association of constituents; paradigmatic relationships are indicated in terms of categories of harmonic expansion—Tonic Prolongation (TP), Tonic Completion (TC), etc.—and the specific ways in which each is expanded in different examples.

The syntactic categories and constituent relationships of harmonic structure are limited; the fundamental process of harmonic prolongation that gives rise to richer and more complex harmonic structures is *embedding*. Consider next Figure 10-4. Embedding is the process by which a syntactic category is replaced by a complete syntactic structure. In Figure 10-4 the TP of the whole example is not expanded by some form of a tonic triad but by a complete syntactic structure TP + TC, the prototypical syntactic structure. This structure, in turn, is expanded by surface triad constituents. In this way, the first dominant chord (V^6), for example, is described as hierarchically less important than the last, which belongs to a more fundamental TC. In Figure 10-5, the beginning of a Handel courante, the process of embedding occurs twice in succession: each newly derived TP continues to be expanded by the embedded structure TP + TC until the level of final constituents is reached. The two skeletal diagrams in Figure 10-5 indicate the degree of embedding abstracted from the more complete constituent analysis shown above the actual musical surface. No-

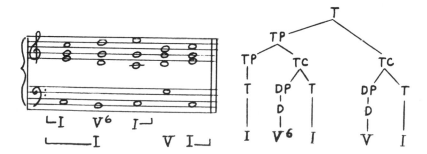

Figure 10-4.   Embedded harmonic structure.

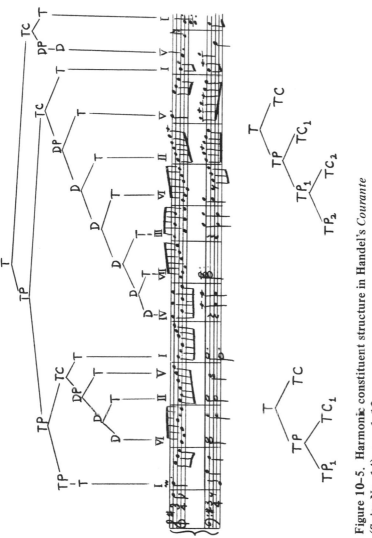

Figure 10–5. Harmonic constituent structure in Handel's *Courante* (Suite No. 14) mm. 1–12.

tice how the constituent structure clarifies the different hierarchical functions of each constituent. Take, for example, the successive dominant (V) chords again. The first one (m. 3), as part of the lowest ranking TC, occurs only in passing, on a weak beat; the next (m. 10) occurs on a strong beat with the leading tone exposed in a higher register and left unresolved; the last dominant (m. 11), as part of the structurally most prominent TC, that of the whole example, occurs with the structural $\hat{2}$ (A) in the soprano, the bass emphasized by octave definition of the fifth degree of the scale.

Two final examples, both from the works of Bach, will illustrate more of the complexity of the syntax of harmony. Consider first Figure 10-6, the first section of a gavotte by Bach. The whole example (mm. 1–8) consists of a TP whose first level of expansion involves the embedding of the TP. Indeed, the constituent analysis of mm. 1–4, abstracted from differences in motivic development, rhythm, and so forth, is very similar in syntactic expansion to the whole of Figure 10-5. Both, for example, have the same degree of embedding, and the projection of the different functional status of chords can be compared. The successive dominant chords of the TP (mm. 1–4) in Figure 10-6, each belonging to higher ranking TCs, are increasingly prominent hierarchically. The dominant in m. 2 occurs on a weak beat in a passing configuration (E-D#-E in the bass, G#-F#-G# in the soprano); the dominant in the next measure is emphasized by the leap to the leading tone in the soprano; the structurally most important dominant (m. 4) of the whole TP arrives on a strong beat, the leap to the leading tone is now increased, and the bass ends a rising stepwise motion to the dominant. This final dominant occurs also as part of a more expanded DP: II^6-V. In this example, notice how the quicker succession of TCs can be related directly to the drive to the dominant of m. 4, an effect quite different from that created by the less frequently occurring dominants in Figure 10-5. The TC of the whole example (mm. 6–8) is expanded differently from any of the preceding examples.[30] The Dominant category (D) is not replaced by some form of V, but by an embedded structure. In this way, the constituent relationships dominated by this embedding can be understood both as being identical relationally to any similar set of constituent relationships and, at the same time, as related to a key or tonal center other than the controlling one of the whole piece; in this case whatever is dominated by the D is realized according to the scale degrees of the dominant key, not the tonic. The traditional term for this is *modulation*—the idea that in some sense, the original key of a piece is given up temporarily in favor of another key. Since, in other words, Roman numeral analysis is, at least explicitly, linear (left to right) in its chord classification, the implication is that a structurally more important key has to be abandoned temporarily and then ultimately regained (one

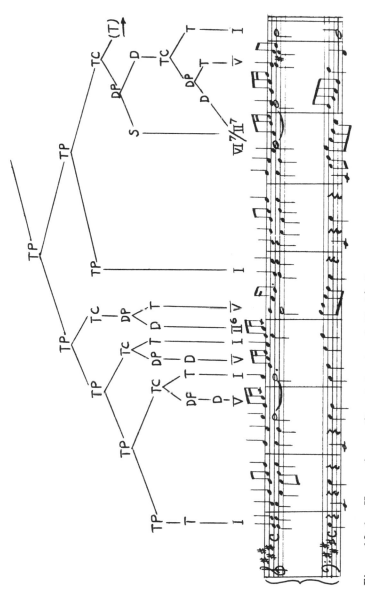

Figure 10–6.   Harmonic constituent structure in Bach's *Gavotte* (French Suite No. 6) mm. 1–8.

cannot, so to speak, be in two keys at the same time). For this reason, it is never possible to avoid the concomitant problem of deciding what temporary key changes constitute a real modulation.[31] But it seems to me that this largely vacuous problem is avoided by a theory of harmonic structure that makes explicit hierarchical constituent relations. In this example, the D and its embedding are organized in terms of the dominant key, but are in their turn part of a DP that is governed by the original key. In other words, the key in terms of which constituent structure is realized as actual pitches is simply a matter of rank; the lowest level TC (mm. 6½–8) is dominated by a Dominant (D) constituent which in turn is governed by a TC still related to the central key of the piece. Notice also that the concept of pivot chord (a chord that belongs simultaneously to the original key and the temporary one, here VI^7/II^7) is made explicit as the simultaneous realization of two constituents, each of which has a different constituent allegiance: the constituent of the second half of measure 6 is both a constituent of the DP of the original key and a constituent of a DP of the temporary key. To a limited degree, then, final constituents are not necessarily realized isomorphically as independent pitch collections; more than one constituent, each uniquely defined syntactically, may be represented by a single pitch collection.[32]

The point of view I have been taking about harmonic structure in the preceding examples is that of finding some means of making explicit how a sequence of harmonic constituents conforms to some general statement about harmonic coherence, rather than simply that of properly labelling pitch collections. The last example (Figure 10-7) should illustrate all of the syntactic devices I have been discussing.[33] What interests me most, taking mm. 1–14 as the unit of analysis here, is what happens with m. 11 to m. 14. The first level of expansion of the whole prelude involves an embedding, the TP of which is the phrase we are considering. The TP on the next level of expansion is similarly expanded by an embedding, which I have divided into TP (mm. 1–8½) and TC (mm. 8½–14). The first part (mm. 1–8½) is clear enough. A complete syntactic unit ($I-II^2-V-I$) is followed sequentially by the same set of constituents in the dominant, and both therefore are described in Figure 10-7 by embedded structures; that is, both the TP and the DP that expand the TP of the next higher rank (that of mm. 1–8½) dominate the same set of constituent relations. But the TC of the next higher rank (mm. 8½–14) again involves a set of constituent relationships in a new (temporary) key, that of the dominant. Now what I have included as part of this TC is nothing more than the beginning of a DP in the old key ($[I^6]$ VI-II) followed by its counterpart (a sequence) in the new key, that of V: ([ ] VI-II). Since II (in E, the principal key) is not followed by V, as one could expect, but with an en-

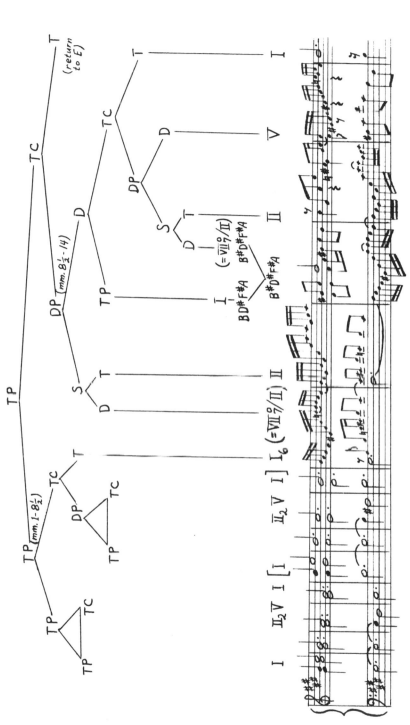

Figure 10–7. Harmonic constituent structure in Bach's *Prelude in E Major* (*WTC II*) mm. 1–14.

tire progression in that key, we can argue that the chord that follows II is
not an immediate constituent of it, but belongs with the following syntactic category, which in this case is the dominant category Dominant (D) expanded by an embedding (TP + TC), rather than simply some form of the
dominant chord. The II (in E, m. 10) is not followed by V, but by an embedded structure expanding the category D. We must add to the possible
categories which can be expanded by an embedding that of D, and consequently there is nothing syntactically irregular about the TC of mm. 8½–
14. The TP of the embedding (which if realized autonomously—B-D#-F#-
A—would have provided a V immediately following the II of m. 10) is here
realized only simultaneously with the VII/II constituent of the embedded
TC. B has been raised to B# so that the surface chord (B#-D#-F#-A) is
realized only as part of the new key. I would say, then, that the expected
dominant chord that would follow the II of m. 10 is realized in two ways:
(1) as part of the simultaneous realization of that constituent and the following VII/II of the embedded structure, and (2) by the strong bass arrival
on the dominant in m. 14, which is related by motion by fifth to the F#
in m. 10. Only the former, however, should be considered the harmonic
satisfaction of the expectation associated with II. The latter realization is
one that forms a part of the design of another hierarchy.

It is this other hierarchy that we come to now. It will be of some use
to look first at Figure 10-5 again, the phrase of a Handel courante, and
particularly at a syntactic property of expansion that we have not yet discussed. The DP (mm. 5-10) at the first level of embedding consists of a
sequence of triads, each one or group of which modifying the next one in
the circle of fifths. The most local constituent relationship, between IV
and VII, is that of a dominant to tonic relationship which that structure
(D) manifests with the next triad in the circle of fifths (III), and this hierarchical duplication of the same basic constituent relationship continues
until m. 10, where the whole DP relates to the following tonic, thus completing the expansion of the TC at that level. This process of successive
modification, in which the modifying element precedes the governing constituent, is known as left-branching. To take an analogy with sentence
structure, one can compare the DP (mm. 5-10) of Figure 10-4 to adjectival phrases like the following:

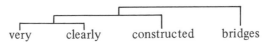

very   clearly   constructed   bridges

which are left-branching structures. The musical effect is quite similar to
the one produced by such left-branching structures of English syntax—that

of heightened anticipation that ends only with the final (and highest level) governing constituent of the whole sequence.

The DP of Figure 10-8 is another such left-branching structure (the 7 indicates those chords which have been altered from simple triads to seventh chords, that is, with the characteristic dissonance of the seventh above the bass). But now the linear patterns of voice-leading and motivic development, which we have kept distinct from the syntactic structure of harmony, are just those features which create the particular hierarchical design projected by a given syntactic structure. In Figure 10-8 an additional pattern exists beyond the left-branching one indicated in 10-8b, one of grouping: each pair of chords is part of a continuous 2 + 2 pattern—the soprano repeats each pitch in a descending sequence as the bass changes direction with each chord and thus reinforces the pattern of grouping in the soprano. One might say that the syntactic pattern is not projected in terms of pitch structure in a neutral way. If one tried to project the syntactic pattern in this way, that is, without any superimposed pattern of regular grouping, one might have something like 10-8c. Of course, one would try to deny the patterns of the outer voices by a continuously descending bass, and contrary motion between it and the upper voices.[34] Exact repetition at a different degree of the scale of the kind in Figure

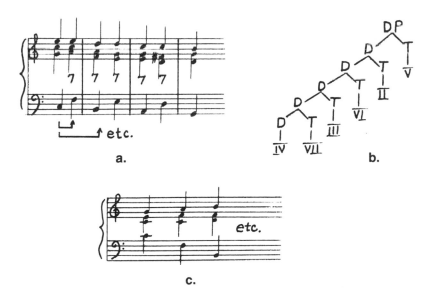

Figure 10-8.   Constituent properties of Circle of Fifths.

10-8, here occurring with each pair of chords, is known as a sequence. It seems to me that this definition, noncontextual as it is, is really not sufficient. It is not simply repetition of old material at a different pitch but the projection of a syntactic pattern (often left-branching) by means of a grouping selected from other possible groupings underlying some set of syntactic choices.

Figure 10-9 will illustrate the selectional process of grouping more clearly. The sequential motivic pattern which recurs with every measure is no less obvious than the fact that the functional sequence of chords (and labelled with the music according to succession of key) is a circle of fifths. These are in fact the two simultaneous structures—design and syntax—which underlie this example. The syntactic left-branching structure is based on the following circle of fifths: $\frac{3}{4}$ D#-G#-P (=passing)/C#-F#-P/ B-E-P/A-D-(G#)//. The pattern selected and projected by this left-branching structure is, like Figure 10-8, a continuous 2 + 2 pattern, each successive pair of chords grouped together. The surface $\frac{3}{4}$ metre is achieved by the passing chord on the third beat of each measure (and which has the same functional root as the following chord). But the design projected here is, of course, infinitely more artful than the illustrative example of Figure 10-8. In the case of the former, the simple descending repeated-note figure of each group of Figure 10-8 is replaced by the melodic-rhythmic figure of the soprano, itself derived from the preceding four measures; the syncopated chromatic descent of the bass replaces the simple device of change of direction in Figure 10-8. And in a more comprehensive study of the piece, it would be shown that the chromatic descent of the bass from A to C# (just as the melodic descent of the soprano from C# to F#) controls in a motivated way this miniature development section leading to the return of the opening phrase of the piece.

Notice that I have not mentioned what would certainly be an important part of any traditional harmonic analysis of the phrase, the sequence of keys C#-B-A-G-(F#), which progresses from the dominant stepwise back to the tonic. It seems to me that, in some ways, this fact is the least determining aspect of the structure of this example. For one thing, this stepwise descent is implicit in any circle of fifths progression. In Figure 10-8, for example, it would be possible to emphasize this kind of pattern by taking every other bass note (starting with either of the first two bass notes would produce the same stepwise descent) and altering the two chords preceding each note of the pattern to form, for example, the dominant-tonic relationship of II^7-V^7. This process of grouping by *association with a specific key* actually reinforces the connection between segments of a group. This point needs to be emphasized. It is not sufficient to claim merely that both facts—the left-branching (circle of fifths) structure and

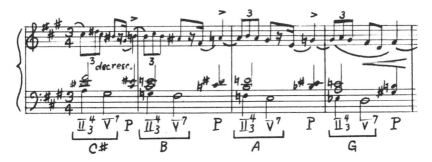

Figure 10-9.   Grouping in Chopin's *Mazurka*, Op. 6/1.

the sequence of descending key areas—are simply part of the harmony of
the piece. Since, in the traditional sense, harmony is understood to mean
the labelling of chords and their relationship to some key, there is no precise understanding, in this point of view, of how each of these facts interacts to create structure. The harmonic coherence of mm. 5–8 is determined by the left-branching succession of dominant to tonic relationships.
There is nothing functionally significant in any syntactic sense in a stepwise succession of keys. The grouping of segments is simply strengthened
by each pair of chords having a precise key relationship; and the particular stepwise key descent in these measures is associated with the chromatic descent from dominant to tonic. It would thus be a pity, in the interests of describing only general properties of tonal grammar, to claim, for
example, as Schenker would, that there is no question here at all of any
local sequence of keys, but rather only voice-leading details within the
frame of reference of a single key. While this is true for the harmonic
structure, local key reference is still an important part of the grouping design of this example—i.e., part of another interrelating hierarchy. In this
way, one can describe the tonal instability of these measures that is associated with this local change of key reference, and at the same time make
explicit the harmonic coherence and stability of the piece as a whole. This
process of key association is essentially one part of the process chosen for
the grouping in Figure 10-9. But this stepwise descent of keys seems to be
only at the service of the more important structural fact of chromatic melodic motion in all of the voices of this section. Only the II^7 has to be altered (to a second inversion chord) to create continuous chromatic descent. It is thus a question of what I would call a conspiracy—the selection
of choices among all of the available constraints and possibilities, only the
sum total and accommodation of which will create a design in every partic-

ular case. I might add that it is not yet possible to indicate explicitly very much of the exact nature that underlies conspiracies.[35]

I have been able to give only the briefest indication of the design hierarchy which interacts in all cases in tonal music with the syntactic hierarchy of harmonic structure. I would emphasize the following points. The design hierarchy is concerned to a much greater degree than the syntactic hierarchy with the particular idiosyncratic aspect of each possible instance of tonal music. There are, in other words, several systems of constraints that appear to be operative. The particular syntactic constituent analysis chosen from the grammar of tonal music limits the kinds of surface designs since each syntactic constituent analysis contains implicitly a limited set of possible groupings (phrase structure, parallelisms, etc.) that could be projected. But the syntactic component itself, simply by virtue of the pitch class content and necessary constituent relationships by which the surfaces of tonal music are constrained, limits in a more global sense how tonal pieces must differ from other musical systems. The interrelation and interaction of these two hierarchies provide what seems to me to be one possible way of making explicit and investigating the complex structure of tonal music. It also seems clear that the taxonomic-empiricist view has put too much importance on the role of repetitions and parallelisms. The crucial functional status that parallelisms achieve as only one possible device of creating structure and grouping at various levels would be missed by insisting that they can provide a completely self-sufficient or even determining role in the structure of (at the very least) tonal music. Neither does the simple letter-labelling of repeated or parallel segments really replace the search for a meaningful analytic vocabulary (motive, phrase, and so on) that will parallel within the hierarchy of design the syntactic categories of expansion that function within the hierarchy of harmonic constituent relationships. The study of music will contribute to semiotic research in a significant way only when we have some viable theories about the complex musical systems of the world; and only this understanding of musical competence will make it possible to deal with the even more intractable cognitive issues of musical behavior.

Notes

1. Daniélou 1968: 8; see also Daniélou 1967. Robin Cooper discusses these sources in her interesting study "Abstract Structure and the Indian Raga System" (1977).

2. There is some valuable discussion on Koch and also on some of the earlier theorists, especially Sulzer, in Baker 1975. Unfortunately, even the

best studies of the aesthetic theories of the period, e.g., Abrams 1953, concentrate on literary theory and neglect almost entirely the musical sources.

3. There are useful surveys that the reader may wish to consult, such as Nattiez 1974 and 1975.

4. " . . . je ne vois pas bien ce qu'on gagne à considérer la musique comme un système de signes ou de communication, à parler de signifiants et de signifiés musicaux ou de sémantique musicale" (author's translations in text here and throughout the essay).

5. Ruwet 1975c is the only real criticism of the taxonomic-empiricist view in music theory, and especially of the work of Nattiez. It is concerned primarily with epistemological issues relating to the Chomskyan paradigm in linguistic theory. I find the article curiously unresolving, both because of its autobiographical approach and the fact that, in the comments about the musical examples, the author seems to have given up very little of his older views. I have discussed the analogical view in Keiler 1978.

6. "Le niveau neutre est sans doute celui qui suscitera le plus de discussions. Disons qu'il s'agit d'un niveau d'analyse où on ne décide pas *a priori* si les résultats obtenus par une démarche explicite sont pertinents du point de vue de l'esthésique et de la poïétique. Les outils de la description du niveau matériel ne sont donc pas neutres dans l'absolu: tournés, comme on le verra, vers l'analyse de la récurrence d'unités et de leurs schémas de combinaisons, ils fournissent un point d'ancrage pour les analyses ultérieures (poïétiques et esthésiques) sur ces schémas de découpages externes et relativement autonomes,"

7. "Les unités phonétiques peuvent être distinguées et définies soit au niveau de la production—phonétique articulatoire—soit au niveau de la perception—phonétique auditive—soit au niveau de la substance physique du signe—phonétique acoustique."

8. "D'un côté un son produisant les mêmes effets acoustiques et auditifs peut être engendré par des moyens articulatoires différents, d'un autre côté, une même unité définie du point de vue acoustique peut être interpretée différemment selon le cadre perceptif de l'auditeur."

9. "La phonologie elle-même n'a été possible qu'après qu'une science neutre et descriptive, la phonétique, eut accumulé les observations empiriques de toute nature pendant des dizaines d'années."

10. I do not discuss the linguistic distinction *etic-emic* taken from the work of Kenneth Pike, which Nattiez and others make use of. It is of relevance only to the ethnomusicological work that I referred to, and would not affect any of my conclusions here.

11. For a fuller discussion of the issues that underlie these remarks, especially as they relate to the empiricist/rationalist controversy in linguistics, see, for example, Chomsky 1972.

12. " . . . *il est absolument faux de prétendre que la démarche classificatoire,* tant chez Harris que dans le présent travail, *ne fait appel ni aux intuitions ni aux hypothèses.*"

13. "A la vérité, il n'est possible de découper, de réduire en unités et d'organiser un object symbolique qu'en se fondant sur les trois dimensions qu'il présente nécessairement . . . "

14. "Niveau doublement neutre puisqu'il consiste en une description des phénomènes dans laquelle on ne fait pas intervenir les conditions de production et de réception du message . . . "

15. "Pourtant, le travail de Boulez, écrit en 1951, présent bien des traits communs avec l'analyse taxinomique, telle que nous la souhaitons. D'abord, sa 'neutralité', c'est-à-dire son indifférence *a priori* vis-à-vis de la poiétique et de l'esthésique . . . "

16. "Boulez n'est pas désintéressé: un bon post-webernien, il recherche des rhythmes rétrogradables, des structures inversées, des miroirs; l'influence de Messiaen se fait ici sentir . . . "

17. "C'est l'occasion de remarquer que, dans les analyses de compositeur, leurs propres conceptions esthétiques ne sont pas sans influence sur leur méthodes."

18. " . . . j'ai insisté dans cet article sur la nécessité de développer le point de vue analytique en musicologie, autrement dit, sur l'urgence qu'il y a à élaborer des procédures rigoureuses destinées à découvrir les codes à partir des messages." This and Ruwet's other articles on music are collected in Ruwet 1972.

19. " . . . il développe une problématique qui a permis de thématiser concrètement un nouveau secteur de réflexion pour la musicologie: l'élaboration de méthodes d'analyse, explicites et réproductibles."

20. See Chomsky 1957: 49ff., where the question of discovery procedures was first raised.

21. The most important work to consult is Harris 1951.

22. "Notre 'machine à repérer les identités élémentaires' parcourt la chaîne syntagmatique et repère les fragments identiques. On considère comme des unités du niveau I les séquences—les plus longues possibles—qui sont répétées intégralement, soit immédiatement après leur première émission, soit après l'intervention d'autres segments. Cette première opération fournit des structures telles que A+X+A, A+A+X, A+X+A+Y+A, A+A+B+B+X, A+B+A+X+B+Y, etc. (les sections répétées, unités de niveau I, sont représentées par les premières lettres, les 'restes' par les dernières lettres de l'alphabet)." The procedures are quoted and discussed in Nattiez 1975: 239ff.

23. It is already clear from Ruwet 1966 that the problem of the independence of musical parameters makes it really impossible to build into a set of procedures of this kind any comprehensive directions about how to treat simultaneous musical parameters differently when deciding on how to group variants together, or how the concept of musical transformations is to be applied properly in every case. Ruwet does make some suggestions about cases in which the differences presented in one parameter (say, rhythm) are to be abstracted from the differences in some other (say, pitch contour), and about which set of variants should be considered trans-

formations of one other. But the suggestions would apply only in a very limited number of cases, and also in only the most simple kind of symmetrical musical phrase structure. In fact, the way in which Ruwet introduces the concept of transformation into his procedures is quite ad hoc. See also Osmond-Smith 1975: 45–55, where the latter problem is raised but, to my mind, trivialized rather than explored fruitfully.

24. "On peut dire que, en gros, Boulez avait défini implicitement ses *a* par leur debut sur un do et leur fin sur un la (sauf pour a_g)."

25. One might be tempted to argue that Nattiez's uses of ϕ are limited to instances where he assigns a variant value to a sequence of rests (or held notes), i.e., where musical time is already provided. It would be easy, however, to give examples (such as the first one I give) where it is necessary to depart from such a constraint to achieve the right kind of generalization.

26. "Nous vérifions une fois encore l'impossibilité de rendre compte de la phrase par un schéma unique."

27. In addition to denying any real independent status to the separate but interrelating parameters of rhythm and pitch contour, and failing to integrate harmonic structure into their view, the taxonomic-empiricist position raises in importance the status of repetitions or parallelisms in quite arbitrary ways. Indeed Ruwet appears to believe that the entire domain of the syntax of harmony has as its object the study of musical parallelisms: "Une théorie de l'harmonie ne peut se justifier que comme une partie integrante d'une syntaxe musicale, dont le seul objet, en définitive, est l'étude des rapports d'équivalence donnés dans la syntagmatique" (1967a: 1703). ("A theory of harmony can only be justified as an integral part of a musical syntax, whose sole object, in the end, is the study of the equivalence relations found on the syntagmatic axis.") How different my view is from the one suggested by Ruwet should become apparent in what follows.

28. See Keiler 1977 and 1978 for a fuller discussion of some of the material discussed here.

29. The work of Schenker, of course, is based on this distinction of chord grammar versus chord function, but it is not possible here to discuss Schenker's theories in relation to my own views. I have discussed this to a limited extent already in Keiler 1977; the reader may wish to consult Salzer 1962 for a cogent presentation of some of Schenker's ideas in this area.

30. I avoid here, because the problem is too complex, any discussion about the presence of tonic (T) constituents in certain constituent environments and their nonrealization on the musical surface. This problem is related to that of the definition and variety of cadences, and their relationship to the harmonic onset of the phrases following a cadence (for example mm. 5–6 in Figure 10-6). In general the issue of cadences seems to me one which is related to the phrase structure or design hierarchy (for which see below) and not to the more general and abstract issue of harmonic relations.

31. Schenker's solution to this problem is not discussed here.

32. The reader will see that it is phenomena such as these that find no place in the view of musical structure implied by the discovery procedures of the taxonomic-empiricist view. The relationship of the two parallel phrases in this example to the overall harmonic structure is too complex to be discussed here. I have really avoided the issue by making them simply parallel TPs on the first level of expansion of the whole structure.

33. I do include, in some of the analyses presented here, the subdominant category (S) as part of the expansional possibilities of the TC category. This is also a problem that cannot be discussed here. In the examples in which I have included it, it should be understood as a principal immediate constituent of the Dominant (D) category.

34. It is not possible to deny entirely the design grouping in this example since, after the third chord, because of voice-leading requirements and other reasons as well, the pitch repetition in the soprano will recur. I have removed the dissonance of the seventh to make the example as simple as possible. Notice that the seventh will introduce a grouping based on the regular downward resolution of that dissonance in every other chord.

35. The concept of conspiracy was developed within generative grammar in phonological research. See, for example, Sommerstein 1977 for discussion of this problem.

CHAPTER 11

Miles Davis Meets Noam Chomsky: Some Observations on Jazz Improvisation and Language Structure

BY ALAN M. PERLMAN AND DANIEL GREENBLATT

It is a commonly-held assumption among people whose acquaintance with jazz is casual or informal that the music is made up out of nothing, invented out of thin air. Musicians and other students of jazz know that this is simply not so, that a jazz solo, though impromptu, is constructed according to specific harmonic and melodic constraints. We will demonstrate that these constraints are in many ways analogous to the syntactic and semantic constraints of natural language and that playing an improvised solo is very much like speaking sentences. Command of the principles that we will describe is equivalent to linguistic competence; executing ideas according to these principles corresponds to linguistic performance.

Syntax: Deep Structure and Harmony

We consider both jazz (excluding atonal and "free" jazz) and natural languages to be describable in terms of three levels of structure—deep, shallow, and surface. It is not our intention to argue the merits of one school of semantic theory over another;[1] rather, we will assume that when a linguist, of whatever persuasion, refers to "deep structure," s/he means a linguistic abstraction, remote from the way a language is spoken or written, related in describable ways to the overt or "surface" structure, and of greater generality or universality than any one surface structure connected to it. The deep structure of *John has a Volkswagen* would, in terms of one linguistic theory, case grammar, contain a verb of existence and a noun phrase, *John*—marked as "dative" or "experiencer" (see Figure 11-1; cf. Fillmore 1968: 47). Such a representation is intended to show the denotative emptiness of *have*, which functions only as a carrier of the tense marker and as the signal of the relationship of possession that obtains between John and his car. Figure 11–1 also symbolizes the underlying similarity of *John has a Volkswagen* to sentences in other languages

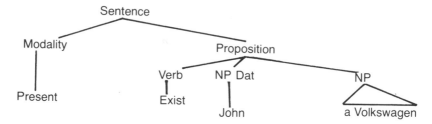

Figure 11-1.   Deep structure of *John has a Volkswagen*.

whose possessive expressions need no overt verb, e.g., Russian *U menja
bol'šoj dom* 'to me [there is a] big house.'

The deep structure of a song is its underlying harmony, as expressed
by the chord symbols found on all sheet music. These constitute a universal structural basis for improvisation. They are among the first topics in
any introduction to the subject of learning to improvise, and anyone who
hopes to be a jazz musician must learn them. "Playing the changes," that
is, improvising on the predetermined harmonic pattern of a song, is the
sine qua non of jazz competence. To play the changes is to involve oneself
in the collaborative effort of a jazz performance. Not to do so is to sound
horribly discordant, even to the most untrained ear; it is like pretending to
speak a foreign language of which one has little or no knowledge.

Just as one linguistic deep structure can be realized by several different paraphrases (*John seems sick ∼ John is seemingly sick ∼ It seems
[that] John is sick*), so can certain chord sequences form the basis of
dozens of songs. The repeated I-VI-II-V of Gershwin's "I Got Rhythm"
is the basis of so many melodies that it has been nicknamed "Rhythm
Changes." Using the changes of the well-known "How High the Moon" (a
"standard," in musicians' terminology), saxophonist Charlie Parker wrote
a new melody, "Ornithology" (Figure 11-2).[2] The progression known as
"twelve-bar blues" is the deep structure for hundreds of songs. Blues
changes, shown in their simplest form in Figure 11-3, are customarily
modified by jazz musicians in order to achieve alternate deep structures of
greater harmonic complexity. We give two examples in Figures 11-4 and
11-5.

The superimposition of different melodies onto the same underlying
harmonic structure is possible in improvisation itself, that is, in the soloing
that takes place after the statement of the melody of the song (or "head,"
as musicians call it). By way of illustration, we consider the changes of
"81," a blues in the key of F (Figure 11-6). The retrogression in bars 9-10

||: Gmaj /// | Gmaj /// | Gm₇ /// | C₇ /// | Fmaj /// | Fmaj /// | Fm₇ /// | B♭₇ /// |

|| E♭₇ /// | D₇ /// | Gm /// | Cm₇♭5/ D₇ / | Bm₇ /// | E₇ /// | Am₇ /// | D₇ /// :||

Figure 11-2. "How High the Moon" / "Ornithology."

|| F /// | B♭₇ /// | F /// | F₇ /// | B♭₇ /// | B♭₇ /// | F /// | F /// |

|| Gm₇ /// | C₇ /// | F /// | Gm/C₇/ :||

Figure 11-3. Blues, basic.

|| F₇ /// | B♭₇ /// | F₇ /// | Cm₇/ F₇ / | B♭₇ /// | B♭m₇ /// | E♭₇ /// | D₇ /// |

|| G₇ /// | C₇ /// | F/ D₇/ | G₇/ C₇ / :||

Figure 11-4. Blues, variation I.

|| F /// | Em₇ /A₇/ | Dm₇ /G₇/ | Cm₇/ F₇/ | B♭m₇/ E♭₇ / | A♭m₇/ D♭m₇ G♭₇ | F / A♭/ | B /D/

|| Gm/C₇/ | C♯m /F♯₇/ | F / A♭/ | D♭ /G♭/ :||

Figure 11-5. Blues, variation II.

||: ¹F /// | ²B♭₇ /// | ³F /// | ⁴F₇ /// | ⁵B♭₇ /// |

|| ⁶B♭₇ /// | ⁷F /// | ⁸F /// | ⁹C₇ /// | ¹⁰B♭₇ /// |

|| ¹¹F /// | ¹²F /// :||

Figure 11-6. "81."

is typical of blues played in the rock-and-roll or rhythm-and-blues genre. Tenor saxophonist Wayne Shorter, improvising on "81" (with Miles Davis on the album *ESP*, Columbia CL2350 or CS9150), plays a simple melodic figure based on the third, second, and root of each chord (Figure 11-7). But it would also be possible to play these same notes against the II-V (here Gm_7-C_7) progression that is more typical of blues played in the bebop genre. The whole sound of the melodic fragment would change; it would become more remote, less obviously related to the underlying harmony, since it would now emphasize higher chord tones—the thirteenth and eleventh of the Gm_7 (E and C, respectively) and the ninth and seventh of the C_7 (D and B♭, respectively). As with grammatical ambiguity, e.g., *Flying planes can be dangerous*, the exact same melodic figure (surface structure) may have a different "meaning," because it derives from a different harmonic deep structure.

Like linguists who postulate an intermediate level of representation between deep and surface structure, we see a second abstract level between the chord changes and the actual improvised solo. In language, this level of "shallow structure" is less universal, more language-specific. The shallow structure of the sentence represented in Figure 11-1 contains *have* (Figure 11-8). Similarly, the shallow structure of a song is neither the harmonic pattern nor the improvised line itself, but rather the array of possibilities that the musician may choose from at any given point. It is derivable from the underlying harmony and, according to conventions described below, is developed into a melodic line. Thus, if the designated chord at some point in a song is G minor, the shallow structure—that is, the cluster of notes upon which improvisation may be built—is either a chord constructed by extending the G minor triad to its upper intervals—G-B♭-D-F-A-C—or a scale, with the key signature of G minor but, according to the conventions of jazz improvising, based on G, A, or D:[3]

G A B♭ C D E♭ F G
A B♭ C D E♭ F G A
D E♭ F G A B♭ C D.

Musicians routinely modify the sheet-music chords in order to create their own possibilities for improvisation. Doing so does not necessarily create a fourth level of structure, however, since many of the modifications, especially those that Mehegan (1975) recommends to the beginner, are virtually obligatory: where the sheet music calls for "C minor," to play C-E♭-G without the minor seventh (B♭) or minor ninth (D) would be unthinkably insipid.[4] However, different players typically select different scales for the same chord, thereby giving the underlying harmony different melodic interpretations. For example, Figure 11-9, a fragment from John Coltrane's

Figure 11-7.   Improvising on "81."

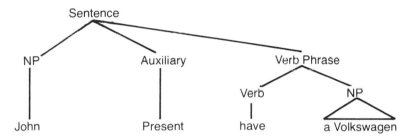

Figure 11-8.   Shallow structure of *John has a Volkswagen*.

Figure 11-9.   "Giant Steps."

solo on "Giant Steps" (*Giant Steps*, Atlantic 1311), draws from a shallow structure that consists of the diatonic scale in the key of B♭, with the natural ninth (C) and thirteenth (G) of that scale. But in the opening phrase of "Donna Lee" (Figure 11–10), Charlie Parker draws from the scale known as "diminished," with the flatted and raised ninths (C♭ and D♭ respectively) of the B♭ scale. These different shallow structures are like intermediate syntactic structures, for example, the active and passive transforms of a single deep structure.

Just as the constituents of the underlying structure of a natural language unite into larger constituents which are themselves basic, so do the chord changes of a song follow recognizable patterns. Specifically, the recursive complexity of linguistic structure is due in large measure to the union of noun phrases and verb phrases and to the embedding and conjoining of these NP-VP sequences at various points in a sentence. In

> We realized that for Bill to hire the man who insulted him was absurd, and we told him so.

there are five NP-VP sequences:
1. the matrix sentence *We realized X*
2. the complement sentence *X was absurd*
3. the subject of *was absurd*: *Bill hire the man*
4. the relative clause modifying *Bill*: *who* (=the man) *insulted him*
5. the second, conjoined sentence: *we told him so*.

The cadence II-V-I is similarly basic to the harmony of most popular and jazz songs. Miles Davis's "Tune-Up" consists exclusively of conjoined II-V-I sequences, with major-to-minor transitions in measures 5 and 9 as the tonic (I) becomes the supertonic (II) of the next II-V-I (Figure 11–11). "Ceora," a Lee Morgan composition, uses stepwise as well as major-to-minor transition in measure 6 (Figure 11–12). As with sentence structure, one cadence may be embedded in another. In measures 10 and 11 of "I'll Remember April," a dominant resolves to a mediant (B minor seventh) instead of the expected tonic (G major); the embedded cadence in measures 11–13 then resolves to a II-V-I in the tonic key, G (Figure 11–13).

Figure 11–10. "Donna Lee."

$$\left\|:\overset{1}{\text{Em}_7}/\!/\!/\right|\overset{2}{\text{A}_7}/\!/\!/\left|\overset{3}{\text{Dmaj}}/\!/\!/\right|\overset{4}{\text{Dmaj}}/\!/\!/\left|\overset{5}{\text{Dm}_7}/\!/\!/\right|\overset{6}{\text{G}_7}/\!/\!/\left|\overset{7}{\text{Cmaj}}/\!/\!/\right|\overset{8}{\text{Cmaj}}/\!/\!/\right|$$

$$\left\|\overset{9}{\text{Cm}_7}/\!/\!/\right|\overset{10}{\text{F}_7}/\!/\!/\left|\overset{11}{\text{B}\flat\text{ maj}}/\!/\!/\right|\overset{12}{\text{B}\flat\text{ maj}}/\!/\!/\left|\overset{13}{\text{Em}_7}/\!/\!/\right|\overset{14}{\text{A}_7}/\!/\!/\left|\overset{15}{\text{Dmaj}}/\!/\!/\right|\overset{16}{\text{Em}_7/\text{A}_7}/:\right\|$$

Figure 11-11. "Tune-Up."

$$\left\|\overset{3}{\text{A}\flat}/\!/\!/\right|\overset{4}{\text{E}\flat\text{m}/\text{D}_7(=\text{A}\flat_{13})}/\left|\overset{5}{\text{D}\flat}/\!/\!/\right|\overset{6}{\text{Dm}_7/\text{G}_7}/\left|\overset{7}{\text{Cm}}/\!/\!/\right|\overset{8}{\text{F}_7}/\!/\!/\right|\ldots$$

$$\qquad\quad\text{II}\qquad\text{V}\qquad\quad\text{I}\qquad\quad\text{II}\quad\text{V}\begin{cases}\text{I}\\\text{V}\end{cases}$$

Figure 11-12. "Ceora."

$$\ldots\left|\overset{9}{\text{Am}_7}/\!/\!/\right|\overset{10}{\text{D}_7}/\!/\!/\left|\overset{11}{\text{Bm}_7}/\!/\!/\right|\overset{12}{\text{E}_7}/\!/\!/\left|\overset{13}{\text{Am}}/\!/\!/\right|\overset{14}{\text{D}_7}/\!/\!/\left|\overset{15}{\text{G}}/\!/\!/\right|\ldots$$

Embedded Cadence

II   V   I

Figure 11-13. "I'll Remember April."

Syntax: Lexicon, Surface Structure, and the Melodic Line

The implicit goal of the jazz improviser is to create an impromptu melody that sounds like jazz and has such coherence and fluency that it appears to have been written beforehand and rehearsed. Just as the speaker of a language makes instinctive use of the lexicon and structure of his/her language when s/he speaks or writes, the musician accomplishes his/her aims through mastery of and spontaneous resort to a basic vocabulary of musical figures, interspersed with quotes and connected by scales and arpeggios.[5] It is the musical figures, or "licks" (played, of course, on the correct scale- and chord-tones) that give a jazz solo its distinctive jazz sound, in the same way that speaking English implies the use of the available word stock of the language, including bona fide loan words and recognizable neologisms. The basic lexicon of jazz licks is not large—there are perhaps two or three dozen that most players rely on—but, since any lick can be played over any chord, beginning with any scale/chord-tone and repeated indefinitely up and down the entire range of the instrument, the number of improvisational possibilities becomes enormous. Figure 11-14 shows five of the most common licks. In order to show how an entire solo can be constructed out of very few different devices, we present in Figure 11-15 a transcription (transposed to concert pitch) of the first few measures of tenor saxophonist John Coltrane's solo on "Giant Steps." Figure 11-16 is our analysis of Coltrane's improvisation in terms of the licks described above.

A "quote" in jazz improvisation is, as the name implies, a melodic motif, usually no more than a two- or four-measure phrase that is lifted from one song and inserted into a jazz solo based on another. Any recognizable melodic fragment is fair game for quoting (the wide syncopated skips of Grofe's "Grand Canyon Suite" are one of the more commonly quoted bits), though quotes usually come from jazz and popular standards. They are customarily played at the beginning of an improvised phrase, perhaps because they are most noticeable there or because the musician has just had an extra moment to think of what s/he will quote. The natural-language analogues of quotes are larger "then-coded" units such as idioms, proverbs, clichés, and collocations. In such cases and in musical quoting as well, creativity consists not in executing the prefabricated unit, but in producing it at exactly the right moment, so that it fits with unmistakable appropriateness at that point in the spoken or musical discourse.

Substitutability and the *allo-/-eme* Principle

Certain linguistic units may replace others as nonfunctional variants. Classifying these variants (allophones, allomorphs) into "*-emes*" (phonemes, morphemes) was one of the major concerns of American structural linguistics of the 1930s, 1940s, and 1950s (cf. Gleason 1961: Chapters 7, 19). The language of jazz also has its *allos* and *emes*, in the form of chord substitutions. In one of the most common substitutions, any seventh-chord[6] may be replaced by a diminished chord built upon a tone that is a full step below the original: F diminished (for G_7) resolves to C, $B\flat$ diminished (for C_7) resolves to F. The logic of this substitution becomes apparent when we consider that the tones of the substitute are an inversion of the original (an analogy to the "phonetic similarity" condition on allophones of the same phoneme): seventh (F), flatted ninth ($A\flat$), third (B), fifth (D). A sev-

a.

b.

c.

d.

e.

Figure 11–14. Five common licks: *a*, an ascending sequence of four notes, the 1-2 and 2-3 separated by an interval of a second, 3-4 separated by a third; *b*, an eighth-note triplet preceded by an introductory note and leading to a naturally accented note; *c*, a triplet arpeggio; *d*, a run based on chromatic neighboring tones; *e*, a mordent-like embellishment on the lower of two notes in a descending line.

Figure 11–15. "Giant Steps."

D♭m₇	G♭₇	C♭	D₇	G	B♭₇	E♭	
Arpeggio		Arpeggio	Figure	Arpeggio	Figure	Scale	Figure
1-3-5-7[a]	3	5-3-1-6	1-2-3-5	8-5-3-1	9-7-6-5[b]	1-2-3-4	5-6-7-9[c]

Am₇	D₇	G	B♭₇	E♭	G♭₇	C♭	Fm₇	B♭₇
Arpeggio	Figure	Arpeggio	Arpeggio	Figure	Arpeggio	Scale	Scale[d]	Scale
5-3-1-7	3-♭9-8-7	3-5-1-3	3-5-7-9	1-2-3-5	7-9-3-5	7-6-5		5-4-3-2

[a] Numbers refer to scale tones for each given chord. The first five notes of Coltrane's solo may be considered a quote from Thelonious Monk's "Round Midnight," inasmuch as they duplicate the initial lick of the melody of that song.
[b] This figure is an *"allo"* of 1-2-3-5 (see 3), played backwards and up a fifth.
[c] Another *"allo"* of 1-2-3-5, played up a fifth.
[d] With chromatic addition.

Figure 11–16. "Giant Steps": analysis.

$$\left|\,^5\text{B}\flat_7\ ///\ \right|\,^6\text{B}\flat_7\ ///\ \left|\,^7\text{E}\flat_7\ ///\ \right|\,^8\text{D}_7\ ///\,\right|$$

Figure 11-17. Variation of twelve-bar blues (cf. Figures 11-3, 11-4).

enth-chord may also be replaced by another seventh-chord built upon a tone that is a flatted fifth higher than the original: $\text{G}\flat_7$ (for C_7) resolves to F, B_7 (for F_7) resolves to $\text{B}\flat$. Here the relationship between the allos is subtle but discernible, since the substitute chord still consists of tones from the original: raised eleventh (F#), seventh (B♭), flatted ninth (D♭), third (E). As with linguistic allos, context is important. Substitutions we have just described are permissible only when the chord in question is a resolving chord, not a chord of rest. Dominant (V) is the most frequent situation in which this happens, but any seventh-chord is a possible context. Thus, in one variation of the twelve-bar blues progression, bar 7 contains, in the key of F, an $\text{E}\flat_7$ rather than the anticipated tonic (F) (Figure 11-17). This choice is the result of a double replacement—A_7 for F (III for I) and $\text{E}\flat_7$ for A_7 (by the flatted-fifth substitution).

Style

As with linguistic creations, style in jazz is a matter of both appropriateness and personal choice. Stylistic constraints, while not as inflexible as such structural requirements as playing the changes, are nevertheless recognized by improvising musicians.

The shape that a solo takes must be appropriate to the subject matter. The songs most frequently adapted to jazz improvisation fall into four rhythmic classifications: ballad (larghetto, ♩ = approx. 80), medium-tempo (andante-adagio, ♩ =100–140), up-tempo (allegro-presto, although in some up-tempo songs, ♩ = well over 200), and Latin (allegro-andante, usually "bossa nova," a Brazilian samba rhythm). Ballads (e.g., "Misty," "Tenderly") are pensive, romantic, lyrical, sometimes mournful; up-tempo songs (e.g., most jazz interpretations of "Cherokee" and "What Is This Thing Called Love?") are rhythmically forceful; medium-tempo songs (e.g., "Satin Doll," "Girl Talk") partake of both qualities. Improvised scales and arpeggios are conventionally composed of eighth-notes. These may be designated by the linguistic term "unmarked": the musician plays his/her licks, scales, and arpeggios in eighth-notes (executed in a characteristically jazz manner; see note 4), with periodic departures, especially at the slower tempos, into rhythmic complexities (triplets; five or more notes played in a four-note span) or accelerations (sixteenth or thirty-second notes). Legato phrasing is more appropriate for ballads; staccato, for Latin-flavored songs. Stylistic patterns occur in melody and harmony as well as in rhythm. A player will readily use the flatted fifth and higher chord intervals—raised eleventh, flatted thirteenth—in improvising on songs that are firmly within the genre of jazz compositions—Dizzy Gillespie's "Night in Tunisia," for example—but s/he might refrain from using them, unless for special effects, in a Richard Rodgers or Beatle song.

Style at the level of individual performance consists in the manner in which a musician combines and recombines existing elements and devices in creating his/her interpretations of a song. As with painting or literature, a performer may be largely derivative and imitative. Or s/he may be highly idiosyncratic: flat-fingered runs, repeated staccato figures, and ingenious uses of silence are the unmistakable components of Thelonious Monk's piano style; Bud Powell created a new approach to jazz piano—as an ensemble rather than a primarily solo instrument—by abandoning the rhythm-keeping function of the left hand in favor of intricate single-note right-hand lines punctuated by quick left-hand chords; John Coltrane produced "sheets of sound" by running up and down scales, climbing and plunging to the outermost ranges of the tenor saxophone.

Semantics and Semiotics: Meaning in Jazz Improvisation

Even though music does not have the same referential function as language, we nevertheless believe that phrases in a jazz solo do have meaning and, furthermore, that the meaning of a phrase is its history, that is, where it comes from. In order to explain what we mean here, we first need to say something about the audience for an improvised solo and about the notion of "competence" as it applies to those who listen to jazz. Our observations of our own and others' reactions to jazz have led us to conclude that there is an important distinction between an "inside audience" and an "outside audience." The inside audience is made up primarily of musicians—of people who know how to improvise themselves or are trying to learn something about improvisation. They have improvisational competence, in the sense that they can "hear" or "understand" an improvised solo. They attend closely to the solos, note by note and phrase by phrase, and they comprehend what is happening, both structurally and historically. When we say that the inside audience has structural competence, we mean that they can recognize basic elements in what is being played *as* it is being played: scales, arpeggios, the A-A-B-A form of thousands of thirty-two-bar popular songs, the repeated twelve-bar structure of the blues. A member of the inside audience who is able to apprehend a jazz solo historically, on the other hand, can recognize stylistic elements from various sources, for example, "That guy sounds like Oscar Peterson in his left hand, but his solo has a lot of Keith Jarrett in it." The structural identification has a great deal of importance to the student learning how to improvise (someone in the position of a foreign-language learner), but it is not the same as understanding the meaning of a solo, since the structural elements exist irrespective of what use the jazz musician makes of them. The inside audience may also include nonmusicians. These individuals are analogous to people who, because they have lived in a foreign country or because their parents speak the language of the old country between themselves, understand a language that they cannot speak. They usually know nothing about structure, or at least nothing consciously, but that does not stop the solo from meaning something to them, since they may recognize licks, quotes, and other stylistic nuances. The inside audience, then, can appreciate—not just in a vague aesthetic way, but specifically—what the jazz musician is doing.

The rest of the listeners—the outside audience—really do not hear or understand improvised solos. For the outside audience, jazz improvisation does not have structural or historical meaning. Once the written melody of the song is over and improvisation begins, the members of this audience stop attending minutely and notice only gross features: "Boy, she plays fast!" or "This guy plays a lot of high notes, doesn't he?" They cannot follow the repetitions of the basic harmonic pattern of the song; in fact, they have no sense at all of what to *expect* from a solo. These people do not have improvisational competence, and, although a jazz performance as a whole may have some significance for them (as it may be meaningful in some way for us to hear an impassioned—but untranslated—speech by the prime minister of Japan, especially if we see and hear it in its original context), they do not understand the intent of the improvised section (we'll never know exactly what the prime minister said).

Returning to the notion of meaning as the musical history of a phrase, we further suggest that weak improvisers tend not to create much meaning in their phrases and solos because they lock into one particular style, and, once that history has been identified, there is not much else to attend to. Such improvisers are competent speakers of the language, but not very meaningful ones: they are always saying the same thing. Strong improvisers —Roland Kirk, Lee Morgan, Marian McPartland—are able to piece together phrases with a variety of different histories and evoke meaning out of their juxtaposition and interpenetration, as well as their presentation. Geniuses

—Charlie Parker, John Coltrane, Clifford Brown, Art Tatum—make startling new phrases which are not immediately comprehensible and whose meaning is the present, since they have no history, or since their history is concealed. People like this quickly become leaders in the musical community: many musicians will gather round and listen, imitate as best they can, and cop licks when they can. In a short while, the innovator's phrases begin turning up in everyone's solos, and new jazz meaning has been created.

Since both jazz and language are products of the human mind, it is not surprising that there seem to be structural similarities between them. Improvising musicians are in much the same position as speakers of a language. They have an underlying message (chords, changes) in the form of a song. How they "say" the song, even the way in which they state the written melody, is up to them. Their improvisations are facilitated by their knowledge of the available harmonic and melodic possibilities and by their technical skill and imagination in combining and recombining these possibilities in novel ways. They are constrained by overriding conventions of permissible melodic lines and harmonic sequence, by the technical skill of the improvisationist, and, of course, by the underlying harmony of the song. The greatest jazz musicians are master technicians who themselves create new harmonic and melodic possibilities. In much the same way do we differentiate the mediocre, the competent, and the excellent users of language.

Notes

1. For a survey of the different theoretical points of view, see Fodor 1977.

2. The song can be heard on *The Charlie Parker Memorial Concert* (Cadet 2CA 60002). The title probably derives from *(Yard)bird*, Parker's nickname.

3. There are other scales that may be used in this context, e.g.,

G A B♭ C D E F♯ G (melodic minor)
A B♭ C D E F G A (dorian mode)

The principles of scale construction are different for major and seventh chords. Since it is not our purpose to explain jazz improvisation per se, we refer the interested reader to Mehegan 1975: 84–100.

4. There are also canons of execution; e.g., eighth-notes are to be played with the rhythm ♪ ♪ (3) or ♫ (3) as opposed to ♫ or ♪. ♪ . Mehegan (1975: 204) describes the characteristic jazz

piano articulation as "wrist legato": "the use of a quick wrist stroke on practically every note, which is cushioned and connected by the finger clinging to the key."

5. Scales and arpeggios are the intermediate or transitional devices that hold the improvised line together and bridge the gap between individual licks. Since the reader may learn about their structure from any introductory book, and since they seem to have no obvious natural-language analogue (unless perhaps conjunctions or function-words), we shall have no more to say about them.

6. In jazz parlance, *seventh-chord* refers to a chord built on a major triad, e.g., C_7 means C-E-G-B♭. *Minor seventh* is used for C-E♭-G-B♭, and *major seventh* denotes a chord with a major third added above the dominant tone, e.g., C-E-G-B.

CHAPTER 12

The Problem of "Ethnic" Perceptions in the Semiotics of Music
BY JOHN BLACKING

The study of music for which there is no written score, and in which the structure emerges only in performance, raises special problems for the semiotics of music. The methodological consequences of these problems are also relevant for the analysis of written music and for semiotics in general.

No study of signs is adequate unless it assumes or includes an account of their meaning. Even an abstract analysis of the phonemic regularities of speech in an unknown language depends on the assumption that certain kinds of regularity of vocal sound have syntactic significance. The mental task of searching for a system in the ordering of vocal signs cannot be achieved without the previous experience of using a particular language.

There is, therefore, in the semiotic enterprise an element of ethnocentricity in the analysts' perception and selection of significant signs. More attention must be paid to the users' views and to contrasts between the different sets of signs that Kenneth Pike has labelled *emic* and *etic*. In this paper, I discuss two issues that have emerged from my studies of African music: (1) the musicologist's perception of a musical structure is only one of a number of perceptions that must be taken into account in arriving at an explanation of the musical product; and (2) the focus of analysis, in written as well as in unwritten music, must be on the creative process, and in particular on performance.

Before discussing the first issue, I suggest that music should be regarded as a special mode of communication and analyzed with a view to finding out what is peculiar to musical behavior and distinct from other behaviors in the society under study.

Music as a Primary Modeling System

There are several reasons why I prefer *not* to speak of "the language of music." First, the phrase tends to give priority to verbal language as a form of human expression; although the term *language* is legitimately used as a synonym for "means of communication," which need not be verbal, the word still has too many overtones to be used confidently in this more general sense. Second, it invokes the notion of direct, translatable representations of ideas, which, in spite of Deryck Cooke's impressive "dictionary" of terms (1959), cannot be supported universally. Third, and most serious, the notion leads us to rely on the tools of linguistics, or on methods developed in the study of language, for progress in the analysis of music.

Music is organized very differently from verbal language, and that is why I welcome the attempts of Nicolas Ruwet, Jean-Jacques Nattiez, and others to identify characteristics that are peculiar to music, and to determine what kind of "gesture" is most likely to follow in response to an initial *musical* idea. Although patterns of musical and verbal discourse in the same society should be closely related to the culture's system of coherence, and essential features of a culture are expressed in its signs (cf. the Venda *tshikona*, Blacking 1973: 50–52, 85–88, 94–95), there are important contrasts between music and verbal language. For instance, even if musical intervals are divorced from the specific meanings that they have in different cultures and it is accepted that a major second is always a major second and a fourth is a fourth, the repertoires of intervals used in musical systems are not like the phonemic sets of different languages.

In language, code and message can be distinguished analytically without the need to invoke facts that are not linguistic. In music, code and message are inseparable: the code is the message, and when the message is analyzed apart from the code, music is abandoned for sociology, politics, economics, religion, and so forth. That is, music is treated as an arbitrary symbol in essentially social, political, economic, or religious interaction, so that it ceases to have meaning as *music*.

Natural language has been the primary modeling system in the intellectual history of semiology and semiotics as scientific modes of discourse, but I am certain it has not been the primary modeling system in the intellectual prehistory of mankind. I even doubt if it is a primary modeling system, and, indeed, wonder if the notion of any *single* primary modeling system is useful. After all, verbal language itself presupposes more fundamental cognitive processes, such as categorization, transformation, and particularly the symbolic transformation of experience (cf. Langer 1948: 35).

I do not wish to invert the order of precedence of language and music, and claim that language is a secondary modeling system and that music is primary, for that would be making the same kind of assumption as those who argue for the primacy of language in human thought. But I would argue that music should be treated as at least *a* primary modeling system, not necessarily on evolutionary grounds (although I myself hold this to be valid) so much as on intellectual grounds. That is, in seeking to understand the elementary structures of human thought, music is in fact more appropriate than verbal language for revealing the purely structural requirements for a symbol *system*, as Susanne Langer has pointed out (1948: 185).

Now I turn to the problem of differential perceptions in the analysis of music, and particularly to problems of definition and selection of units of analysis.

Problems of Definition and Selection of Units of Analysis

There are special problems in the semiotics of music, first, in defining *what is or is not to be treated as music*. Second, there is *the selection of the unit of analysis*: can a movement of a symphony be treated independently any more than a sentence drawn from a paragraph? Third, the *flexibility of meaning in music is generally greater than in language*, and depends almost entirely on the context of performance and the status of performers and listeners. Fourth, the *nonmusical* or *extramusical, components of musical structure must be distinguished from those that are irreducibly musical*.

One solution to all four problems is to employ a method of analysis that is essentially anthropological. Definitions of music and nonmusic, views of what is or is not a musical whole, and meanings, all vary according to the perceptions of composer, performer, listener, *and* analyst (whether "native" or not). Thus, the surest way to understand music and discover what is unique about it is (ideally) to incorporate *all* "ethnic" perceptions of all available musics and to find out on what points they agree. What we are looking for is a musical *process*, which generates the creation and perception of products that are classified as music by some but not by others, and may consist of organized nonsound (such as Cage's silence) as much as sound.

If the same performance or the same score can be understood differently, *all* perceptions must be treated as valid data in finding out more about the musical process. If Serkin, Solomon, Arrau, Ashkenazy, Barenboim, Kemp, and Pollini can perform Beethoven's *Hammerklavier* differently, even to the point of producing different minimal units with their phrasing, is there really such a phenomenon as "the *Hammerklavier*" which can be subjected to semiotic analysis? And which, if any, of these interpretations is Beethoven's? What did he mean when he wrote the music? May not a comparison of the different perceptions of the work tell us more about Beethoven and the musical process than the score itself? After all, the acceptance of a valid grammar depends ultimately on the universal recognition that it is used and carries a message as well as being a code.

The ways in which music is used and defined by its users and the various meanings that are assigned to it provide important clues for semiotic analysis, just as intelligibility and grammatically acceptable sentences are the basis of any analysis of language. The analysis of even an obsolete language depends on assumptions derived from known languages, but in the case of an unknown music similar assumptions cannot be made, because the system may be so different that in terms of known systems it would be defined as non-music, in a way in which an unknown language would not be defined as non-sense.

Definitions of the basic contrasting parameters of music and non-music can indicate which are the critical signs for analysis. For example, in the traditional system of Venda, Southern Africa, one children's "song," (*Tshiḍula tsha Musingaḍi!*) sounds like spoken verse, but another (*Inwi haee Nyamudzunga!*) sounds like a melody (see Blacking 1973: 28 and 70). For the Venda, the former is more musical than the latter, because its monotone is further removed from the patterns of speech tone of the spoken words. It is necessary to know this "ethnic" perception in order to show that in other contexts the rules that generate the "spoken verse" of *Tshiḍula* are more directly responsible than the rules that generate the melody of *Inwi* for the rich melodic elaboration of the response in girls' *tshigombela* songs (Blacking 1973: 70-71) and the singing of European hymn tunes to Venda words without concern for clashes of melodic and speech-tone patterns.

So much for "ethnic" definitions of music and nonmusic. I turn now to the problem of the unit of analysis. Can a semiotic analysis of the *Hammerklavier* Sonata be done independently of other Beethoven piano sonatas, of Beethoven's total output, of the music of his time, and so on?

Analyses of different orders of structure must begin with classifications that are socially accepted, even though these conflict with the analyst's idea of what he is supposed to be studying or seem to have little to do with the music. Thus, most Venda categories of music refer to their social or ritual functions, and at first I thought that people made judgments about music without much attention to musical parameters. But I soon found that social terminology was often used to talk about perceived *musical* phenomena for which there was no special vocabulary. Ankica Petrovic found a similar situation in Bosnia and Herzegovina (1977): people referred to different ways of singing *ganga* in terms of the villages of origin of the singers, and at first Petrovic thought that people made these judgments because of their knowledge of the *social* situation. However, she persevered with the folk categories as a base for her struc-

tural analysis of the music, and after very careful transcriptions of recordings and further questioning and testing of performers and audiences, she
found that there were very small, systematic musical differences and that
people's judgments were based on their discrimination of *musical* features.

This example emphasizes that key parameters in a musical style may
not be revealed as such by strictly semiotic analysis, and that variations
which semiotic analysis reveals may not be significant to the people who
use the music (cf. also *Funguvhu ṱanzwa mulomo*, Blacking 1973: 24).
It also strengthens the case for taking the musical judgment of the "aver-
age" man and woman as seriously as their capacity to recognize and speak
their language grammatically. We generally derive our descriptions and analyses of verbal languages from the judgments and everyday speech of ordinary people, but most analyses of music are based on the performance of
a professional class of musicians or an elite of composers.

Code and Message: Semiotic Analysis and Musical Meaning

My first attempts at analyzing Venda children's songs relied on the identification of minimal units of rhythm and melody that were repeated, inverted, retroverted, and so on. I produced a complex and unwieldy analysis of the music of the songs *independently of Venda classifications and
social function*. Although the songs could be broken down into permutations and combinations of rhythmic motifs and of two-, three-, and four-
tone patterns of intervals, the analysis lacked any of the coherence that I
felt ought to exist in a body of music that was clearly perceived as a single
class and incorporated children's early explorations in the music of their
own society. Then, after more careful attention to the Venda categories,
and particularly to recordings of different performances of the same songs,
I had to revise my whole conception of significant units in the melodies.
In particular, an important clue to the "semiotics" of the songs was provided by an *un*authentic, "wrong" performance of a group of sophisticated
Venda college students, who added variations to a song they had known
since preschool days. The variations brought into the open the song's deep
structure and showed the way to a coherent structural analysis of all the
other songs (Blacking 1967).

Similarly, it was only by bringing together a variety of informants'
views and other ethnographic data related to the *domba* initiation dance of
the Venda that its basic meaning dawned on me, and all the hitherto disparate parts began to fall into place. The coherence of the three main
classes of Venda girls' initiation music had not been apparent until I
started to analyze them (1970) with reference to the deep structure rules

that had been revealed in the analysis of the children's songs *and to the meaning of the music in the lives of all involved in its performance.* For every Venda girl experienced the music as part of a long ritual process of guided physical and social growth from the onset of puberty to marriage, lasting from two to five years (see Figure 12-1), and until I tried to understand the music and dance in those same terms, I could not make sense of it. Moreover, different perceptions had to be differentially weighted according to their social origin: girls, women, and men of different age and status had different perceptions of the music and dance and were differentially involved in its performance. The oldest women had been through every stage of growth and had shared the views of the younger women at one time or another.

This leads to the second issue, the focus on performance. Because in music the code is the message and unwritten music can only be produced by social interaction, in the analysis of oral traditions the *musical product* cannot be isolated as a *niveau neutre* from the performance meanings it has to those who are making it and perceiving it. I have described how the development of a girls' *tshigombela* dance song is as much a function of the people and social events involved in its performance as of the rules of the musical system (1973: 71). No doubt the dozens of permutations and combinations that occur in a series of complete recorded performances *could* be interpreted strictly in terms of the rules of the Venda musical system, without reference to people's perceptions of them or the circumstances of their creation. But the fact is that some of those combinations are more or less acceptable to everyone at the time of performance, and others are much more than that: they are positively transcendental in their effects on audience and performers. And since music is concerned with feelings and transcendence, at least in Venda society, I want to know how the code gets these messages across. I cannot separate music from the apparently contradictory fact that almost identical performances of the same notes do not always generate similar feelings, and yet ultimately as far as *musical* (as distinct from general social) experience is concerned, it is people's response to the notes and the relations between them that evokes the feelings.

Perhaps this contradiction, which we all know from experience as performers, can be overcome if we pay attention to the critical indices of "almost identical," and "relations between them." A fruitful way forward in the semiotics of music will be, perhaps, to look at the structural differences *between* performances, as well as the contrasting relationships between the tones of the musical product, because it is only in performance that we can apprehend the meaning of the model for performance. This approach to the study of music has, of course, been pioneered by ethnomusicologists, who have had to build their models from the evidence of multiple performances, consisting not only of notes sung or played, but also of many different perceptions and explanations of the significant parameters.

If we apply ethnomusicological (or anthropological) methods to written music, then we cannot accept the score of the *Hammerklavier*, or even Beethoven's sketches and opinions of it, as sufficient evidence for understanding it as *music*, as distinct from understanding it as a piano sonata by Beethoven. Different remakings and different perceptions of the sonata become a part of the sonata, just as its original creation and first performance depended on pianistic tradition; and the differences between Arrau's and Pollini's performances or between Arrau's at the age of twenty-five and sixty-five reveal much of importance about music as a human experience, and hence about music making and the choice of structures with which to communicate.

None of this need apply, of course, if music making were a game with arbitrary rules. But, on the contrary, music is the result of intentional interaction, of processes of decision making in society, and both the music and the social interaction are parts of systems of shared communication, or cultures, and so an analysis of what is shared and who shares it is fundamental to understanding the musical product. The "rules" of social life impinge on the "rules" of music making, and many elements of music structures are derived from extramusical or nonmusical sources (Blacking 1973: 12–18) in a way that language codes are not. Nonmusical factors can generate a musical code, so that the message is a sonic transformation of another kind of experience.

If one takes to its logical conclusion the argument that music is always a reflection of something else, then indeed music could become no more than an epiphenomenon of social life, and an anthropology of music would be little more than a crude reductionism. But the emphasis on the analytical value of "ethnic" perceptions makes this impossible, because again and again people insist that music making is a unique form of knowledge and experience. If resort to "popular" opinion should seem unscientific, it is the basis of the science of anthropology. What appears to be its major weakness, namely, its inclusion of variously perceived data that may seem too vague and fuzzy to a musicologist, is in fact its greatest strength and its prior claim to scientific validity. The scientific potential of ethnography is not always appreciated, and it can seem particularly confusing and irrelevant when set beside apparently rigorous analyses, in which the logic of musical structures is exposed for all to see, like the structure of a crystal or a protein. *The scientific rigour of many musical analyses is, in fact, illusory.* The chief difference between a musicological analysis and a

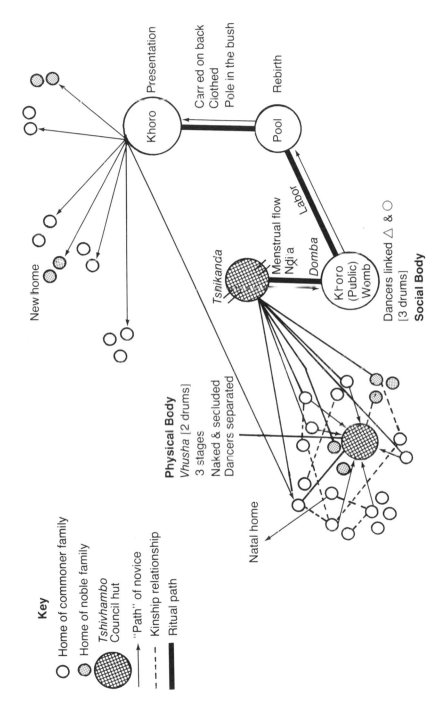

Figure 12-1. *Domba*: movements of novices.

chemical analysis is that, like any other analysis in the human sciences, it may be there for all to see, but it is not necessarily there for all to feel: and if the analytical "experiment" cannot be replicated, it cannot be regarded as scientific. Until a musical analysis can be validated by the corroborative experience of performers and listeners, it remains as it began: an ethnic view of a musical structure which does not necessarily have any more validity than other ethnic views.

The limitations of single "ethnic" views can be overcome by incorporating diverse perceptions in the analytical process. And lest we should think that the view of the trained musicologist or semiotician should always take precedence over those of the untrained, as indeed we would be inclined to prefer the trained engineer's aircraft design, we should recall the conclusions of Crickmore's carefully researched analysis of music appreciation (1968) in which he found that music structures can be comprehended independently of personality, measured intellectual capacity, and musical intelligence as assessed by the Wing test. A full appreciation of Mozart's music does not necessarily require expert knowledge and all the subtleties of understanding that are brought out, for example, in Charles Rosen's analysis (1976).

An analogy from African art may amplify the argument. How do we set about analyzing an object, such as a carved stool, which the makers and users regard as casually as a mass-produced chair in a discount shop but which American connoisseurs see as a work of art? What signs do we look for? First, the "art object" by itself is neither art nor nonart: it only becomes one or the other because of the attitudes and feelings of human beings toward it. Art lives *in* men and women, to be brought out into the open by special processes of interaction. Thus the signs have no meaning until that meaning is shared, so that the *processes of sharing* become as crucial to the semiotics of music as the sonic product which provides the focus for analysis.

Conclusion

Let me try to place what I have been saying about the semiotics of music in relation to what Roland Barthes and Jonathan Culler have written about literature. According to Terence Hawkes, both Barthes and Culler have emphasized that a "science of literature . . . cannot be a science of content . . . but a science of the *conditions* of content, that is, a science of forms" (Barthes, quoted in Hawkes 1977). Culler's concept of *poietics* is concerned with the *process* by which content is formulated. One may compare this notion with the facts of the musical process, especially in oral traditions: just as performers and audience create the work every time they perform it, so the critic becomes a "participant in the works he reads" (Hawkes 1977: 157). We have the notion of critic and readers as performers, and art as available-for-use (cf. Jones 1971). So far, so good.

But two problems arise. First, if we accept, as I do, that our chief concern is with *artistic processes* rather than content, and that ultimately the effect of art *as art* depends on our sensitivity to the different modes of communication that are used—which seems to be the basic point of Judith and Alton Becker's essay—then the question arises: *what* forms is the science of forms to study? Second, what is the epistemological status of a semiotic analysis by a single person? If no readings of a work are "*wrong, they all add to the work*" (Hawkes 1977: 157); a work "is eternal not because it imposes a single meaning on different men, but because it suggests different meanings to a single man" (Barthes, quoted in Hawkes 1977).

The approach I have been advocating concurs with that of Barthes and Culler, but leaves us with no alternative but to treat the semiotic analysis of a "text" (whether music, literature, painting, etc.) as an anthropologist would treat the analysis of a ritual: we must consider *all* "ethnic" perceptions as valid data in discovering the "*process* by which content is formulated" (ibid.), just as a linguist records unknown grammar from the utterances of its native speakers.

Similarly, different "readings" of European music by Africans told me as much about the musical practices of the performers as about the structures of the works they performed. Of course, what it told *me* is in itself only a provisional step forward to understanding. What it told me must then be fed back for comment to the performers. And what it tells others will also have to be included. What a non-Venda hears in Venda music may be just those aspects that are universal: there are many ways in which an outsider can listen usefully to strange music. The process of analysis, even of the same data, is endless, for the analysis itself is part of the artistic process.

It is because of the multiple meanings assigned to music in performance that I am convinced that the key to a semiotics that informs us about what Geertz has called "the social history of the imagination" must rest not so much in a science of forms as in a *science of forms between the forms*. There is nothing essentially new about this, except perhaps the focus on process rather than product. Ruwet argued that it is impossible to represent the structure of a musical piece by means of a unique diagram (1972: 134), and stressed that every work has a multiplicity of interpretations. Barthes has pointed out that a deliberately invoked tension between meanings can reveal a good deal about the nature of language (Hawkes

1977: 111), and Lévi-Strauss has advocated the study of multiple versions of myths to arrive at the bases of mythological thought (1963: 213 ff.). In all three cases, though, attention is focused on the finished product.

I have been suggesting that a focus on musical process requires two different but complementary procedures. On the one hand, detailed analyses of single creative events may be made on the reasonable assumption that there can only be one set of explanations for each occurrence, since each decision in the process of creation involved a choice between alternatives. On the other hand, quasi-statistical analyses of the differences between performances of a given model should reveal which features of musical discourse attract people's attention in their quest for meaning, and hence are most peculiar to music.

In order to reduce the number of variables, the first kind of analysis is best achieved with orally transmitted music and the second with versions of written scores. Both are based on the empirical evidence of performance, and so the primary concern is for human beings as music makers rather than the music that human beings have made.

Note

I am most grateful to Alton and Judith Becker for their criticisms of earlier drafts of this paper. They are not responsible for any of its shortcomings.

CHAPTER 13

Technique and Signification in the Twelve-Tone Method

BY DAVID LIDOV

In the 1920s, late in the fourth decade of his life, Schoenberg developed a new formulation of compositional technique which he called the "method of composing with 12-tones related only to each other." History has made the forcefulness of Schoenberg's invention obvious, but some questions about its meaning remain obscure. Was his new formulation purely a technical matter—a matter of means but not ends—or did it express a change of aesthetic, a change of philosophy? And, if so, what change? For semiotics, the question here is whether the twelve-tone method is a *sign*. Note that we do not ask whether the method is governing or organizing a sign *system* or a linguistic *system*—questions of a very different order. We ask whether the method deployed by Schoenberg may be conceived as a single entity acting as the audible vehicle of a *denotatum* specific to it in its totality.

Schoenberg did address himself to this question. His answers—not entirely consistent—seem to favor the negative: "Form in the arts, especially in music, aims primarily at comprehensibility. . . . Composition with twelve tones has no other aim than comprehensibility" (Schoenberg 1951: 103). And in a letter to Kolisch he writes despairingly of twelve-tone analysis, saying that people must see *what* his music is, not *how* it is made (Schoenberg 1965:164; cf. p. 267).

Needless to say, I would not have chosen to raise this issue if I agreed with Schoenberg, and I am comforted to find at least some ambiguity in his own theoretical writings which supports my belief that a masterful technique is necessarily a communicative sign. He once wrote: "Every man has fingerprints of his own and every craftsman's hand has its personality; out of such subjectivity grow the traits which comprise the style of the finished product" (Schoenberg 1951: 47). However, the personal and expressive traits of Schoenberg's technique are not entirely subjective. Here I will be concerned with their objective formulation and the meanings which attach thereto.

The argument that I will advance belongs to applied rather than theoretical semiotics. Therefore, in indicating the theoretical position from which this application proceeds, I will be as brief as I can and make no effort to justify those methods and assumptions which, for the present study, I take as first premises.

I take the position that musical sense is not confined to the designs that signs make with each other; that music engages an unlimited semantic field. Feelings, qualities of mood and movement, states of consciousness, intentionality and all sorts of other referents lie in that field. By *semantic* I certainly do not mean verbal, but what cannot be translated can, if we work hard enough, be described. Music articulates the continuum of experience into separate thought through the articulations of its various aspects: gesture, color, form, and so on. Musical reference may be extended through any of the relational principles common to signs in general but in this argument I will be particularly concerned with a mode of resemblance which does not usually figure in formal explications of musical aesthetics, but which Nicolas Ruwet described as a homology between musical structures and the structures of other realities and experiences (1972: 14).

In comparison with melodic gesture and harmonic color, so immediately expressive in their sensuous aspect, the more abstract musical facets of form and structure seem often to have a purely technical or merely cabalistic content. In the case of a minor composer, formal questions do slip to the background; form becomes the first aspect of musical expression to be automatized. With a philosophically original composer, formal considerations or considerations of technical procedure enter the foreground. This is the inevitable fact in Bach's music, in Mozart's, Beethoven's, Wagner's, and certainly in Schoenberg's. With composers of the first rank, form and technique become homologous with forms of discourse or structures of belief. They involve music in issues of philosophic stature.

I mentioned that one of the domains of reference particularly accessible to music is that of qualities of consciousness. Images of consciousness are readily evoked by music because, like consciousness itself music is temporal, continuous in its extent, and without spatial boundaries. We will find a key to the philosophic dimension of Schoenberg's musical thought in the qualities of consciousness imagined within the aesthetic frameworks of his styles, beginning with expressionism and proceeding to the twelve-tone method.

Expressionism brought to a climax the development of an idea which was germinal for the Romantic movement, the idea of exotic associations.[1] The early Romantic theory that a state of enthusiasm enables a poet to transcend the logical surface of thought is pushed to new consequences in expressionism. Enthusiasm becomes a frenzied agitation approaching derangement and freedom of association leads not only to exoticism but to an imagery seemingly shorn of all civilizing inhibitions—to what I feel free to term a consciousness of the unconscious. Other writers including Schoenberg himself have suggested a link between psychoanalytic concepts and the aesthetics of expressionism (Schoenberg 1951: 86, 182). This link is no casual hyperbole. A close analysis of the musical technique shows this psychological content as deeply rooted in its stylistic procedure as in the literary texts and subjects to which it is allied.

Musical and literary semiotic structures in expressionist style are homologous with each other in that both proceed by a gross exaggeration of associative or selectional relations and the near eclipse of combinatorial grammar, by a domination of metaphor over metonomy. For music the principle of grammatical combination resided in the principles of consonance and tonality. In terms of Schoenberg's theory of monotonality (a theory which does not seem appropriate for the music of earlier composers but which gives us essential insights into his), all chords belong to each key as representatives of its immediate or distant regions. The distant relations of the tonic are normally comprehended through the mediation of an established logic of harmonic progression. The technique of expressionism is to skip past the mediations—the preparations and resolutions—on the basis of the enthusiasm or agitation captured in its *Einfall*, the motive, which is freely varied to bring distant harmonies and dissonances into immediate apposition.

An early and relatively straightforward example appears in the opening of the Second Quartet, a passage which can even yield its pitches, if not its secrets, to a prolongation analysis.[2] Elements of F-sharp minor are established in hierarchically crucial positions throughout the first forty measures, but the rapid excursions from the tonic key express neither linear nor harmonic requirements. Harmonies switch on and off like stage lights: the tonic minor for four measures, the unison C-natural of measures 6 and 7, the A minor, C-sharp minor, and F major which follow. One can speak of a plan, but it is as tenuous and complex as the plots of dream imagery and as compressed.

The phenomenon of compression is crucial. The appositions of harmonically distant regions or dissonant pitches take their specific semiotic character from their sensuous temporality. Presented in time so that their sequence and duration are imposed on our perception, these appositions provoke a division of attention and pose defiance to memory. Ultimately, it is this music's choreography of our own mental motions between concentration and recollection which become its most intimate sign of a knowledge beyond ordinary knowledge. Of course our understanding of the composer's historical situation, his literary allegiances, and his philosophical commitments play their natural role in our understanding of his musical language, but both the structure and phenomenological character of the technique support our interpretation. The fleeting and irrational harmonies have the form and tempo of free associations in the psychoanalytic sense, those subliminal glimpses of an unknown part of our mind which are available to us when we are in a condition to abandon the inhibitions of rational control. And what are the conditions under which we do abandon rationality? Enthusiasm for the early Romantics, but they had only scratched the surface of free association. Here we have the madness of Pierrot, the insanity of *Erwartung*. Knowledge is gained at a price. The advantage of Schoenberg's harmonic theory is that, unlike Schencker's, it does not portray all possible departures from the key as ultimately strengthening the dominion of the single tonality. His theory of monotonality is compatible with a concept of a weak and fading center. Expressionism accepted weakness as a condition of knowledge. We hear the equation in the Litany of the Second Quartet as the poet sings: "Schwach ist mein Atem rufend dem Träume."[3]

What happens to these signs in twelve-tone compositions? The method first appears in a series of works that have the external trappings of neoclassicism. Is this an apostasy? A retreat from brave adventures to the easy comforts of scholastic routine?

Liebowitz has demonstrated the continuity in Schoenberg's melodic and harmonic manners as his style moved through phases of tonal, freely atonal, and twelve-tone technique, but obviously Schoenberg's style experienced significant changes (Liebowitz 1949: 74–77). What do these changes signify? Schoenberg's expressionism was part of a widely shared and forcefully articulated aesthetic movement, but the philosophical commitment embodied in the new technique was entirely his individual achievement. We have the difficult task of deducing it from the sound and logic of the method itself. This is to say, in effect, that we must deduce the content from characteristics of the vehicle. I think we must begin with some attributes of the technique which were more evident to its critics than to its proponents.

The sound of the twelve-tone method is willful and contrived—and we can hear, if the music sounds artful and spontaneous, that this is so despite the bias of the system, not because of it. Schoenberg threw us off the track with his insistence, rather defensive it seems to me, on the inevitability and naturalness of his invention, as when he offered the unpersuasive simile that compared the manipulations of the tone row to the rotation of a tableknife in the visual field (Schoenberg 1951: 113).

Not only is the argument patently false (the inversion of a theme always changes its character), but other marks of contrivance must not be denied. The rhythm wrestles against the constraints of number magic.

Groupings of pitches into 5 and 7, 6 and 6, four times three and three times four—felt as present or as nearly avoided—establish a subliminal obsession which but for consummate artistry would become a prominent nuisance.

Another false defense of the method was to speak of it as an alternative to tonality. The quality of naturalness in the developed tonal system is an effect or, if you prefer, an illusion which results from values that are largely foreign to Schoenberg's method. His own spontaneity and warmth impose a natural quality on his musical expression, but it is an entirely subjective quality. His naturalness does not result from the twelve-tone method, and furthermore, his analytical essays show no favor to the techniques—won gradually through centuries of experiment—by which classical composition had objectified the concept of musical nature. Although Schoenberg speaks of the twelve-tone method as a substitute for tonality, it is fundamentally unlike tonality in its level of abstract representation. Both are abstract, but whereas a tonality can be represented in the mind in terms of the qualities of a single tone or chord, the tone row is irreducible. In its abstract form as a sequence of twelve pitch classes its mental representation as a single, molar unit is always just beyond reach. Perhaps this has something to do with the capacities which psychologists ascribe to short-term memory. All we can grasp securely are the concrete realizations of the row which impose temporary hierarchical groupings on its elements. Even in its concrete form the consequent tends to obliterate the aural memory of the antecedent. The principle of continuation in twelve-tone music which Adorno claimed to be missing is the need to hear the row another time so we can get it straight, the need to regard a complex object from another angle and for another moment (Adorno 1973: 73-75).[4] Whereas tonality is abstract in the manner of an environment, an orientation, an objective place where things happen, the tone row is abstract in the manner of a *personality*, a subjective force unifying the character of its manifestations but itself never wholly visible or wholly conscious. Considering the twelve-tone technique as a sign vehicle, we find then that two of its most obvious characteristics are its quality of arbitrariness or unnaturalness and its intangibility as an experiential phenomenon.

The intangibility of the row as phenomenon makes it a suitable vehicle for Schoenberg's discourse on unconscious or transcendental knowledge, which continues with heightened profundity in his music. The discourse is further elaborated through the row's thematic content. Schoenberg never abandoned the concept of *Einfall* which sees the theme or perhaps the row as a vehicle of unconscious inspiration. Through the pervasive presence of the row the conscious content of one theme becomes the unconscious content of all others. We find subliminal motivic associations in all sorts of music, but in this music such associations are so dense that all categories of themes, accompaniments, developments, ornaments blend in a constant meld. Every figure has more associations than we can bring to mind.

The difference is that we now find the process of bringing a richer range of associations to mind is not conditional on a weakening of rationality. The genius of the method is to draw its rationality from within the associative process itself. Expressionism opposed motivic association to tonal combinatorial logic, but the new technique takes its logic from the selectional discipline of continuous transformations. To fully grasp this point we must step outside the scholastic conventions of those twelve-tone "analyses" which show merely how the twelve-tone composition can be reduced to transforms of its row. Actually, Schoenberg's compositions in this technique use at least three dimensions of transformations. One is the changing concrete form of the row. Another, derived from the first but not identical to it, is the transformation of compositional functions: themes gradually change into accompaniments and vice versa (a ubiquitous process in composition since, at least, Robert Schumann). And finally there is the transformation of roles in the row as different portions of the row become identified with each other through the resemblances of their concrete forms.[5] In the density of these associations which cut freely across the boundaries of materials and in the potentially irrational contiguity of the variants, the method establishes a further homology with the qualities of unconscious thought. But there is a censor. Despite the density and extremity of variation, all those natural, spontaneous variants of the theme—even very close ones—which do not conform to the row must be excluded. We have a new discipline, purely selective but very tough and very severe. Such a method can have no pretence of imitating nature. What it imitates is the moral will.

> [Moses:] *Dienen, dem Gottesgedanken zu deinen ist die Freiheit.*
> (*Moses and Aaron*, III, 1)

Perhaps we have been so gleeful about the evidence of megalomania —the quarrel with Mann, the too autobiographical portrayal of Moses— that we have failed to confront the moral content of Schoenberg's style. The hyperromanticism of his early compositions yields to a moral imperative in his later work. The willful and contrived sound of the method which we observed before must be understood not as a forgivable fault but as a sign—the index and the icon—of moral will. An idea of will, the given law, the commandment, has taken on the role which classicism had ascribed to nature and the Romantics to enthusiasm. The most intense participation is demanded of the listener, who, following an ideal which is evident in all of Schoenberg's writings on music, must become a student in order to hear anything more than aural wallpaper. What the student hears, provided he or she is in touch with the associative relations of the row is, as in the earlier music, appropriately construed as an image of conscious-ness striving for transcendence, a transcendence which Schoenberg himself identified most often in religious terms. Those who knew him report that he was obsessed with an urge to know.[6] The consistent principle in all of his styles is that the idealization of transcendental knowledge is encoded in the overriding dominance of the selectional principle over the combinato-rial grammar. With the twelve-tone method, the urge to know which had earlier broken the boundaries of consciousness through the medium of madness becomes elevated to a moral principle.

Adorno has criticized this style for its element of mechanical proce-dure and its reliance on neoclassical reflexes. His criticism singled out the Fourth Quartet. We cannot deny the nostalgia for a simpler style conveyed by the phrase rhythm of the opening melody (Adorno 1973: 73-75, 103). How easy it makes the row seem! But our job as listeners is also to hear the accompanying chords which are made of the same stuff, though not so clearly sounded. The music demands constant effort. If, as Adorno sug-gests, the music sometimes seems academic, it may be because we have retreated from it. The complexity, the intensity of vision and of pain in this music, are sometimes more than we can take.

Notes

1. I am indebted to discussions with Tillock Banerjee, York Univer-sity, regarding Romantic aesthetic theories.

2. *Prolongation analysis* refers to reductive procedures which repre-sent a musical composition as a hierarchy of recursively embedded orna-ments and arpeggiations. This mode of analysis, which has roots in Baroque music theory, is primarily associated with H. Schenker (1868-1935). See Keiler's essay in this volume.

3. Op. 7, third movement. This "quartet" is composed for string quartet with solo soprano. (The vocal text is a poem of Stefan George.)

4. Compare "An alert mind will demand to be told the more remote consequences of the simple matters he has already comprehended" (Schoenberg 1951: 55-56).

5. Examples of the three types of transformation from the *Third Quartet*, Op. 30: transforming the concrete form of the row—ubiquitous, but mm. 1-8 (original) vs. mm. 9-12 (inverted retrograde) will do; trans-forming functions—the cello's melody, mm. 13-18, is immediately identi-fied with the opening ostinato accompaniment by virtue of row identity

plus contour identity and registial proximity (one octave lower than viola, m. 2); association of distinct row elements—the same cello melody associates original pitches 1, 2, 4, and 5 with inversion pitches 5, 3, 2, and 1 respectively.

6. This theme recurs throughout Reich 1971, especially in the second half of the biography.

CHAPTER 14

A Musical Icon: Power and Meaning in Javanese Gamelan Music

BY JUDITH AND ALTON BECKER

For several years, we have studied from many different perspectives the traditional music and literature of Java and Bali—traditions as old, rich, varied, and subtle as the European and American traditions we grew up with, though strikingly different from them: different in structure, different in meaning, different in what might be called "writtenness"—that is, the degree to which and the ways in which a written text or score constrains a performance. Recently, a friend asked what in these traditions were and are the sources of power—what made and continues to make a particular kind of music or literature "powerful" (or "true" or "beautiful" or "natural," to suggest some other terms for the compellingness or evocativeness of musical and literary types). We would like to suggest an answer here: that the major source of power of a kind of music or literature is associated with the iconicity or "naturalness" of the coherence system which informs that music or literature. This essay will explain that answer and show how it helps describe the power of Javanese gamelan music.

We might call iconicity the nonarbitrariness of any metaphor. Metaphors gain power—and even cease being taken as metaphors—as they gain iconicity or "naturalness." Consider a term like *orbit* and the power with which that term informs our concepts of nature, from the smallest particles to the spheres themselves, as well as our concepts of political and personal power.

One way to describe what happens to make terms like *orbit* powerful is to say that they operate across epistemologies, from one kind of reality to another kind of reality. Based on the referentiality of human languages, there seem to be four basic kinds of reality we talk about: (1) nature, (2) human relations, (3) language itself, and (4) the supernatural. These categories of referentiality are described clearly by Kenneth Burke. In *The Rhetoric of Religion: Studies in Logology* (1961) he develops an interesting notion of referentiality. In his words,

There are four realms to which words may refer:

First, there are words for the natural. This order of terms would comprise the words for things, for material operations, physiological conditions, animality, and the like. Words like "tree," "sun," "dog," "hunger," "change," and "growth." There words name the sorts of things and conditions and motions there would be in the universe even if all ability to use words (or symbols generally) were eliminated from existence.

Second, there are words for the socio-political realm. Here are all the words for social relations, laws, right, wrong, rule and the like. Here belong such terms as "good," "justice," "American," "monarchy," "out-of-bounds," "property rights," "moral obligations," "matrimony," "patrimony."

Third, there are words about words. Here is the realm of dictionaries, grammar, etymology, philology, literary criticism, rhetoric, poetics, dialectics—all that we like to think of as coming to a head in the discipline we would want to call "Logology."

These three orders of terms should be broad enough to cover the world of everyday experience, the empirical realm of which words are preeminently suited. But to say as much is to realize that we must also have a fourth order: words for the "supernatural." For even a person who does not believe in the supernatural will recognize that, so far as the purely empirical facts of language are concerned, languages do have *words* for the supernatural. (Burke 1961: 14-15)

Burke develops this notion in great detail in his examination of theological logology—words about the supernatural. Whether or not Burke's four realms prove to be the proper number, and no matter how many subclassifications and indeterminacies may be necessary in comparing one culture with another, this scheme suggests several interesting things about languages and musics:

1. That the epistemology appropriate for discussing things is different for each realm: that is, a stone is "real" in a different way than a friend is "real" or divine grace is "real." Sounds made by birds or instruments are "real" in a different way than a dominant seventh chord is "real," and both are "real" in different ways than the music of the spheres or the hum of the void (*Om*) are "real."

2. In a given culture, at a given point in history, one "realm" may be given priority, in the sense that discourse is most convincing if it can be put in terms of one particular realm.

In our culture, Electronic America, we have tended to favor explanations strongly rooted in nature. Things in the other realms are "real" (i.e., convincing) to the extent that they can be seen as iconic with nature. Phonological rules are natural to the extent that they can be shown to be based on physiology. Musical systems are natural, or nonarbitrary, to the extent that they can be shown to be based on acoustics. To see an alternative view, one need only move back in American culture to Emerson, who believed that the whole of nature is a metaphor of the human mind—Emerson is our own radical constructivist. Another way to an alternative view is to move conceptually into another culture, which is often a movement to a new "reality" in which Burke's realms of referentiality are valued differently.

For example, in most dominant language/cultures in Southeast Asia, what we label "language" is called by some variant of the Sanskrit term *bhasa*. What is a *bhasa*? A *bhasa* could be defined as a language which resembles Sanskrit, the language which the gods speak.[1] To "resemble" here means to have word roots close in form to Sanskrit roots, and to thereby be a proper vehicle for translating Sanskrit knowledge—the sastras and mantras. Thus, etymologizing or tracing roots became a major way of gaining knowledge—etymologizing across language families, such as from Javanese to Sanskrit, and tracing Javanese roots back to Sanskrit so that Javanese becomes a *bhasa*. This is a frequent strategy in Javanese/Balinese shadow puppetry, what the Javanese call *jarwa dhosok*—the forced interpretation of old words or a kind of carrying new words to the past and bringing old words to the present—finding in Javanese words the shapes of Sanskrit and, later, Arabic, Dutch, or English words, and vice versa. In these cultures, "truth" and "legitimacy" were features of *bhasa*. (There are true names for things; if you want to understand the thing, you must know its proper name.) History[2] is an account of the state of *bhasa*—i.e., an account of major events in the *third realm*. The pure kingdom becomes more corrupt each time its ruler utters a lie. The history of the decline of the kingdom is the history of the succession of lies uttered by its rulers. (In a logocentric culture, lies are the major source of evil.) Note, now, that the meaning of a Javanese word or a text must entail the way Javanese think words mean—Javanese ideas of referentiality itself. Do stars "follow" calendars or calendars "follow" stars? It's a chicken-or-egg question probably, but you meet the former notion (stars "follow" calendars) far more often, and it is more seriously held in Java and Bali than in Michigan.

3. Iconicity can be defined using Burke's categories as finding the image of something in another realm, for example, finding kinship (realm 2) in nature (realm 1): plants belong to "families"; finding ecological "truths" (realm 1) in human relations (realm 2): intellectual "flowering," an "arid" theory, the "organic" growth of the

university; finding features of language (realm 3) in nature (realm 1):
the "syntax" of DNA, or structuralism, a linguistic model of how
things are.

Among the most *iconic* features of language, for us in the West, are
probably things like tense, location, and being itself. We see these categories as categories of nature rather than categories of language. The past
versus the future, in front of versus behind, and whether or not something
is or *is not* are ordinarily taken to be *facts* about nature (realm 1) rather
than about language (realm 3), until we meet a tenseless language, languages in which deixis is reversed ("here" is near the hearer), and languages
without a copula (the verb *to be*). Note, however, that translating from a
tenseless, hearer-centered, copulaless language (like Javanese or classical
Malay) into English would *require* adding things like *tense*, English *loca-
tionals*, the *copula* (all our most iconic features of language) and *omitting*
things like intricate interpersonal levels, particular sound symbolisms,
hearer deixis, classifiers, degree of intentionality for each act, etc., as non-
essential. Good English is bad Javanese—to the extent that they differ in
the way words mean.

One illustration: a few years ago a graduate student of ours was given
the task of translating a passage on the origin of music in Java into *good*
English. He did. We passed the translation on to a bilingual Javanese
friend, whose reaction was troubled and honest: it sounded strange, deeply
non-Javanese. It took time and patience to find the problem: *good* English
entailed narrative order unless otherwise marked;[3] the Javanese text was a
series of overlays and simultaneous actions, in which a word has multiple
and simultaneous etymologies, an event has multiple and simultaneous
motives.

The fact that we highly value *narrative-causal* structures in our texts
—in our chronological histories, our linear time, our narrative requirement
in courtroom testimony, our novels, our life histories—is probably related
in large part to the fact that we speak a language inflected for tense and
use tense as our predominant mode of textual coherence. It seems safe to
say that a language/culture's predominant mode of textual coherence
would be what is perceived to be one of the more iconic features of that
language/culture.

When we translate a text from an unrelated language we add our systems of coherence in order to make *sense* out of what we are translating.
In so doing we alter to some degree the basic iconicity of the text. It seems
clear we do the same with music; we search out and find the most iconic
elements of our own "music" and judge coherence in terms of our own

coherence. Westerners have been known to assign keys to Javanese gamelan music, and Ravi Shankar assigns ragas to all the world's music.

We are making the claim that the most prominent feature of iconic power in Javanese or Balinese music is coincidence—small coincidence and large coincidence—small coincidings and large coincidings of cycling sounds, all iconic with the cycles of calendars and cosmos and thus, for the Javanese, completely "natural."

The basic unit of all Javanese gamelan music is an entity called a *gongan*, a melodic cycle which can be repeated as many times as one wishes and whose beginning (marked by a stroke on the largest gong) is simultaneously its ending. A gongan can be as short as two beats (*Sampak*) or as long as 1,024 beats (*Minggah, kethuk* 16, *Irama* III). Javanese cyclic systems in whatever cognitive realm—music, calendars, planets—are multiple; more than one cycle is turning within one system. Moreover, these different cycles are not all turning at the same rate. Or, if turning at the same rate, they may be of different sizes or lengths. The primary subcycle of the gongan is a unit called a *kenongan*, named for the *kenong*, a set of large horizontal pot gongs. The kenong plays either two or four times per gong, marking either the halfway point and gong point of the cycle, or marking the four quarters of the cycle (see Figure 14-1).

In many Javanese gamelan compositions, particularly the most archaic pieces, a gongan is simply the sequence of two or four kenongan whose full-cycle return to the beginning is marked by a gong. These are the simplest kind of gongan, in which the second half is a mirror image of the first, and the gong marks the return to the beginning (see Figure 14-2).

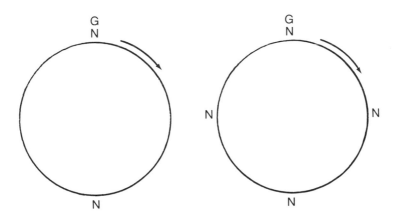

Figure 14-1.   Gong (G) and kenong (N).

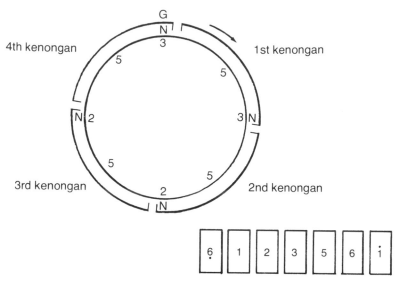

Figure 14–2. The numbers represent pitches as played by a bronze xylophone-type instrument called a *saron*. The keys are numbered as shown at right. 6 = lower octave pitch 6; 1 = upper octave pitch 1.

The coincidence of the kenong with the gong marks the return, the point of stasis and stability. In more complex pieces, many other instruments play melodic sequences which are more or less independent of each other, producing a rich polyphonic texture. Even with their relative independence of each other, these melodic sequences must all conclude at the stroke of each kenong, and on the same pitch as the kenong. Or, the endings of all melodic sequences *coincide* with and play the same note at the kenong.

The word *kenong* comes from the root *kena*, which means 'to strike', 'to touch', and also 'to coincide', 'to come together'. A *kenongan* is the section of the gongan whose end point is marked by a stroke on the kenong, and also that point where melodic sequences come together and coincide on the same pitch.

The multiple cycles of gamelan music, the multiple melodies coinciding at predictable points in the music system, seem related in underlying concept to a similar system of Javanese calendrical cycles. The notion of coincidence and the meanings, the beauty, and the power it generates operate across different kinds of reality. The word *kenong* itself may in Javanese have formerly referred to the coincidence of a particular constellation with the moon which was the beginning of the agricultural cycle. At least that is the case today in North Sumatra where the seasons are regulated by the conjunction of the constellation Scorpio with the moon and the divisions between two such encounters, called *keunong* periods.[4]

In Java, a day is reckoned by describing its position within a number of simultaneous cyclic systems all moving at a different rate or all of different lengths. For us, it suffices to say that today is, for example,

1. Wednesday	= fourth day of seven-day cycle
2. April 5	= fifth day of fourth month of twelve-month cycle
3. 1978	= noncyclic, linear reckoning of the number of complete twelve-month cycles

To designate the same day within the Javanese calendrical system one would have to include the following information:

1. Rebo	= the fourth day of a seven day cycle
2. Kliwon	= the first day of a five-day cycle
3. Pahang	= the sixteenth week of a thirty-week cycle (each year has 210 days within this cycle)
4. Kasepuluh	= the tenth month of a twelve-month cycle (each of the twelve months varies in length with a total of 360 days per year)
5. Panglong	= the descending half of the lunar-month cycle
6. 1910	= linear reckoning of years according to the Caka era, a Hindu system introduced into Java in the seventh century A.D.

The meanings of the different coincidings of calendrical cycles in the life of an individual are complex, sometimes arcane, and constitute a recognized field of study and expertise. Each year, almanacs called *primbon* are published to aid individuals in charting their life course so as to avoid certain activities on days of hazardous coincidence and to take advantage of beneficial coincidings. While not different in concept from Western astrology, Javanese calendrical reckonings differ both in their complexity and in the degree of respect which they command.

It can be argued that musical coincidings constitute a different experience than calendrical coincidings. A musical coincidence is a coming together of simultaneous sounds which may then echo (meaninglessly?) after the moment has passed. Gongs and kenongs are audible and can be *felt* in one's skin, or brain, or heart in a way that calendrical coincidings cannot.

Calendars depend upon numerology and can only be linked metaphorically with musical simultaneities. But metaphoric linkage is one of the most important ways in which artistic forms mean. The iconicity of sounding gongs with calendars (and other systems within the culture) is one of the devices whereby they resonate with import beyond themselves. Coincidence, or simultaneous occurrence, is a central source of both meaning and power in traditional Javanese culture. Coincidings in calendars and in music both represent events to be analyzed and scrutinized because of the importance of the concept which lies behind both. *Kebetulan,*[5] 'coincidence' in Indonesian, and *kebeneran* in Javanese both derive from root words meaning 'truth', *betul/bener.* As pitches coincide at important structural points in gamelan music, so certain days coincide to mark important moments in one's personal life. One might say that gamelan music is an idea made audible and tactile (one hears with one's skin as well as one's ears). Tonal coincidings are no more random than calendrical coincidings, but occur at the severely constrained cycle subdivisions marked by kenong, the word itself suggesting its musical import.

As calendrical cycles ultimately relate to the realm of nature (days and seasons) and the cycling heavens, so gamelan music draws power from its iconicity with the same realm—"the sorts of things and conditions and motions there would be in the universe even if all ability to use words (or symbols generally) were eliminated from existence" (Burke 1961: 14).

Given a cyclic musical system whose meaning and significance are centrally tied to the concept of coincidence, it follows then that the major source of innovation and change in gamelan music has been to add more cycles, thus adding richer possibilities of coincidence. Musically, this means adding more melodic sequences coinciding at kenong and gong and also providing more possible points of coincidence within the gongan. With a very short gongan, it is hardly possible to add more cycles; there isn't room. But if the cycle is expanded, both the number of coinciding cycles and the points of coincidence can be increased.

An example of a more extended cycle than the previous example is the piece called *Puspa Warna*. In this type of gongan, all instruments and voices coincide on the same pitch at each stroke of the kenong (the first subdivision of the gongan), many instruments coincide on the same pitch at the midpoint of each kenongan (the second subdivision of the gongan), and some instruments further coincide at the third subdivision of the gongan, or at each one-eighth gongan. The ciphers on the inside of the circle in Figure 14–3 indicate the saron notes played at each one-eighth subdivision. On the outside of the circle are the notes of an instrument called *bonang*, which in this type of piece coincides with each stroke of the saron as well as with the kenong and gong.

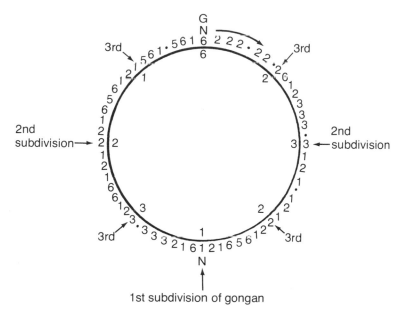

Figure 14-3.   *Puspa Warna.*

With such an expanded structure, more instruments can play, more different sequences are heard, and subdivisions of the kenongan as well as the gongan become opportunities for coincidences. In the history of the development of the gamelan genre, the expansion process has occurred repeatedly until one finds kenongan and gongan of astonishing length and as many as ten layers of melody coinciding at kenong.

In how many ways are these musical coincidences iconic? To repeat our definition of iconicity: iconicity is finding the image of something in another realm. We believe that musical coincidences are iconic with at least one other realm in Java besides the cosmic/calendrical realm, that is, the realm of dramatic plot—Burke's socio-political realm—the realm of human relationships. To extract richer meanings from the coincidence of calendrical cycles, one adds more cycles. In setting a date for an important event such as a wedding, the couple will consult an astrologer to find the day with as full a coincidence of positive days (such as birthdays of the bride and groom in various cycles) as can be expected within a reasonable time.

The plots of the shadow-puppet plays reflect the same overlay of cycles: Sanskrit-speaking gods work their huge plots over slow time; Old-

Javanese-speaking heroes search for their birthrights; low-Javanese-speaking natural demons of all sorts and sizes follow their blinder drives; and modern Indonesian-speaking clowns try to make it all a rustic picnic in the present, like wide-awake men in a dream world.[6] These and other creatures from other times follow simultaneous but separate plots—in different times and different languages—which at some points partially and at one point totally coincide; the structure of the shadow play, like that of the music, is built on cycles and their coincidences, not around a unified causal sequence of actions which reach some climax.[7]

The assertion that longer gongan cycles with more concurrent cycles are "powerful" can be illustrated by the types of gongan and kenongan that accompany persons and events in the shadow-puppet theater. Longer kenongan, with more instruments, more simultaneous melodies, and more coincidences accompany the spiritually refined heroes (pieces like *Puspa Warna*). The less refined the character, the shorter the kenongan, with demons accompanied by the short, fast pieces like *Bendrong*. Likewise, the accompaniment for actions follows the same paradigm. Meditation is accompanied by longer kenongan with more concurrent cycles and more possibilities of meaning. Fights, situations with all options gone but one, are accompanied by the shortest possible kenongan with the fewest possible coincidences (*Sampak*, with the gongan only two beats long).

We began this essay as a search for the naturalness of artistic forms. We have claimed here that this naturalness, which is an essential part of aesthetic experience, grows, at least in part, from the system of coherence which binds together units in that form. The naturalness—i.e., nonarbitrariness/iconicity—of that coherence system varies from culture to culture, and over time within a culture. As cultures come into sustained contact with other cultures, systems of coherence rise and fall, changing among other things language and music. There is time for only a brief look at the way gamelan music has changed over its history and is continuing to change.

The coherencies or iconicities we have been describing for music and calendars inform the symbolic realm of traditional Java. That realm united people, nature, language, and the cosmos, each an icon for the other. From an outside perspective, it is a remarkably integrated world view. In Java today, this kind of coherence of overlaid cycles and their coincidences competes with equally powerful systems, mostly coherence systems from *our* world. Subtle shifts of emphasis and the restructuring and reinterpreting of symbolic forms happen daily. There are indications of deep change in the coherence system of gamelan music. Modern gamelan compositions are often based upon a song, in which the sung melody is the most prominent feature and the gamelan becomes an accompanying ensemble. In these pieces, the kenong and gong almost entirely lose their function as markers of coincidence and instead become punctuation for a verse, essentially no different from commas and periods (*Suara Suling* or *Aku Ngimpi*). The gongan cycle with its rich system of coincidences becomes no more than a strophic verse form.

Deciphering a change in coherence systems, a change in iconicity, comes not only in observing what is being performed. Equally significant is what genres are not being performed, what genres have fallen into disuse, or, to use a metaphor from the realm of nature, what forms are "dying out."

There is a category of very long gamelan pieces, called "great" pieces, which are rarely played in Java today. The reason usually given is that they are "too difficult." But they are not intrinsically more difficult than much shorter pieces, and in some ways they are simpler: the melodic patterns are often more stereotyped than those of shorter pieces. What makes these pieces inaccessible to a modern audience and to modern musicians, we believe, is their absolute resistance to melodic interpretation and their insistence on coincidence as the only thing happening. Within our concept of music as primarily melodic, they are "boring." They are a kind of ultimate realization of coincidence as the primary source of musical meaning and power, the starkest manifestation of a former system of coherence in Javanese music, a kind of iconicity which seems to be losing its power in Javanese symbolic forms.

In Figure 14-4, the outside circle represents the first gongan of the piece *Kiyanggong*. The ciphers represent the points of coincidence, where all instruments play the same note together. For comparison, the gongan cycles of *Bendrong* and *Puspa Warna* are inserted inside the gongan of *Kiyanggong*. In this piece, unlike *Puspa Warna* (and most other pieces in the gamelan repertoire), the other instruments do not play melodic patterns, but simple, predictable formulas leading to the coincidence tone, for example, a formula with the upper neighbor alternating with the coincidence tone (2121   3232).
                              1   2

The effect of a large ensemble playing slow, repetitive, predictable patterns leading to a note which they all play simultaneously, and playing a piece of great length, is either excruciatingly boring or overwhelmingly powerful, depending upon one's musical epistemology. The idea of beauty, or expressiveness, or meaning resides in the relationship between a piece of music and its context.

In conclusion, we wish to reiterate the points made earlier. (1) Systems of musical coherence differ greatly from culture to culture. Cyclicity and coincidence are of low value and low priority in establishing coherence

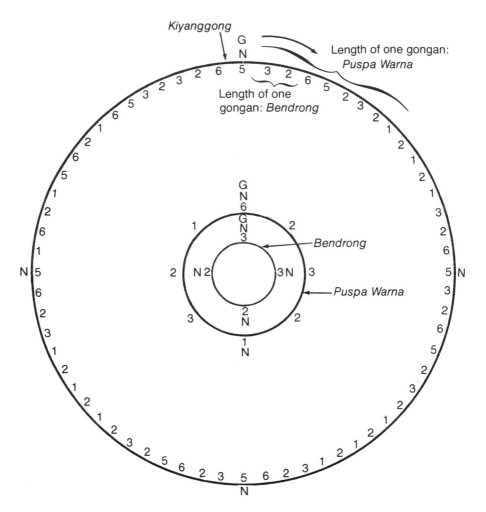

Figure 14-4. Diagram illustrating relative length of gongan between *Bendrong, Puspa Warna,* and *Kiyanggong,* and points of coincidence (ciphers) within the three gongan cycles.

in Western music. On the other hand, the coherence system of harmonic relationships/tonality proves worse than useless in the analysis of gamelan music. (2) Coherence systems in language and music seem natural to their users. A Javanese musician who has studied Western music for over a decade still finds it nearly impossible to compose music (Western or Javanese) which doesn't have a gongan structure. In spite of his years of acculturation, he says of his own nongongan pieces, "They almost don't seem like music." (3) To the extent that the coherence system of Javanese gamelan music is felt to be natural, it is iconic with Javanese conceptions of the workings of time. Musical systems or languages are always more than organized sounds, vocabularies, and syntaxes. They are instances of the way a specific people understand and relate to the phenomenal world.

Notes

We are indebted to several people who have helped us in the course of this study: Madhave Deshpande, Susan Walton, Shelly Errington, Harjo Susilo, and particularly Benedict O'G. Anderson for his initial questions about power in the arts. The original concept of the isomorphism of music drama and calendars came to us after reading Soebardi (1965: 53).

1. We are indebted to Professor Madhave Deshpande for these insights into the concept *bhasa* (see Deshpande 1979). He is currently completing a monograph on sociolinguistics in ancient India in which these notions will be developed more fully.

2. This notion of history first came to our attention in the work of Shelly Errington, particularly her dissertation (1975).

3. Support for this notion is found in the work of William Labov on natural (i.e., nonliterary) narrative, particularly Labov 1972.

4. We are indebted to Professor James Siegel of Cornell University, who suggested we look at the entries under *keunong* in R. A. Dr. Hoesein Djajadiningrat (1934).

5. L. F. Brakel first pointed out to us the importance of this etymology.

6. Old Javanese, or Kawi, is the name of the language of various modes of discourse written in Java from about the ninth to the fourteenth centuries. It is still alive as a literary and ritual language in Bali. Low Javanese, or *ngoko*, is a style of modern, colloquial Javanese which gives no special status to the hearer.

7. During the youth of a now elderly gamelan teacher in Yogyakarta, Bapak Sastrapustaka, when an honored guest would come to the sultan's palace, three ensembles would play at once, each with its own piece. A pelog gamelan would play Ladrang *Raja Manggala*, a slendro gamelan would play Ladrang *Prabu Mataram*, and a Western band would play the Dutch anthem (called "Lagu Raja Wilhelm"), a striking example of the use of simultaneity to honor as well as to invoke power.

CHAPTER 15
Preliminaries to a Semiotics of Ballet
BY MARIANNE SHAPIRO

Like other kinds of dance, ballet is created in relation to other aspects of life, such as communication and belief systems, and political and social relations. It is a kind of cultural behavior that is determined by values and attitudes. The resulting conceptualization involves style, structure, and performance. As I hope to show in the course of this brief study of a representative Romantic story-ballet, classical ballet comments reflexively on modalities of thought and on social institutions, both maintaining and undermining them through its critique of institutions or personages. Moreover, a holistic approach to the material of a ballet, the assumption that it is meaningful in its sociocultural context, has still to deal with the fundamental datum that dance is constituted by the elements of space, rhythm, and dynamics.

For example, it is well known that theatrical classical ballet drew upon the dance steps of rural ethnic groups, systematizing heterogeneous elements of traditional dance cultures. (Pierre Beauchamps is recognized for this kind of codification, accomplished during the seventeenth century in France.) In this way, provincial patterns were transformed into the image of a royal court. Later, American and European "modern" dance developed as a rebellion against ballet traditions (Gregor 1944: Chapters 2-5). Although this development is taken into account in histories of ballet, I know of no work that shows how the placement of the dancers on stage (to take one of several factors) functions in the repertoire of key notions from which the inventors derived their dances. If the physical environment of dance is conceived as a spatial structure, a network of places, and if this network is ultimately not to be distinguished from (or opposed to) the underlying structure of society, then to understand any given portion of such a dance is to remember the "position" of a character in the dance-play, to see his or her "natural" or culturally conditioned place in the order of things.

I can only allude briefly here to such lacunae in the study of dance, which remain to be filled by a happy collaboration of formal and semiotic analyses. Such collaboration will depend on the assumption that mimesis and semiosis are not mutually exclusive but that the latter can ensue from a frank understanding of the former.

In ballet the human body is often used to approximate different kinds of movement that are found outside of ballet itself or in other kinds of bodies. This practice results in variations that actuate the symbolic potential of movement. The movement codes in dance communicate through the ballet affective motivation, cognition, social bonding, courtship and mating, dominance and submission, all aside from the aesthetic pleasure that is shared by dancer and spectators by different means. Ballet both metonymically and metaphorically functions as a model for value and belief, a function that is common to dance as a whole. Anthropology has studied thoroughly the property of dance that marks social and cultural categories and value concepts, and signals status changes such as the passage from childhood to adulthood or class mobility in societies generally distant from the sources of classical ballet (see Hanna 1979, a pioneering work in its thoroughness and comprehensive view of dance). But the anthropology of Western European urban civilization seems to have been largely a matter for sociologists, and sociology has been the anthropology of our own society. From the semiotic viewpoint, it would be valuable to study ballet under conditions analogous to those of other field research in dance—for instance, in terms of rites of passage. The story-ballet *Giselle* contains several, including that from life to death, from natural to supernatural realms, from peasant to (ad hoc) sovereign.

Even in "abstract" ballets like those of George Balanchine for the New York City Ballet, which he composed over a period of more than thirty years, such constraints as production skills, improvisation limits, and rent and lighting costs figure among the production variables. The dance must attract sufficient numbers of people who are willing to attend and to support it financially. Economic conditions constrain ballet at all times. These cannot be detached from the total understanding of a ballet as a communicational act whose goal is a shared set of interpretations that can bridge the gap between intention and understanding, producer and spectator. The economic aspect of production, for example, is rooted together with that of social hierarchization in the beginnings of classical ballet. "One must fit the dancing and the steps to the *airs* and *entrées*," wrote an early explicator of court ballets, "so that a vine-grower or a water-carrier will not dance as a knight or a magician" (Saint-Hubert, "How to Compose Successful Ballets," tr. A. Bergens, in Cohen 1974: 31).

This statement presupposes the arrangement of dance movements according to the minutely defined place in a social hierarchy occupied by the character each dancer is impersonating. A dancer, for example, may occupy any place in the external, mimed hierarchy from that of jongleur to that of the king himself. At the court of Louis XIV dancing became an expression of a formalized style of life to be carried out in entertainments, with the reservation that the king had to appear as the best performer in the court ballets. Gradually, professional dancers took over in performing these ballets and established over the subsequent three centuries the traditions known as classical ballet. But the early concentration of ballet at the court (heralded, in fact, a century earlier by the influential *Book of the Courtier* of Baldassare Castiglione) implies a fundamental opposition that obtains well into our time. Embedded within varying conceptions of ballet is the opposition between dance as an "imitative" art dominated by its quasi-literary aspect, a "picture of life" encompassing at the same time as it tells a story a synthesis of the plastic arts; and on the other hand, dance as a repertoire of schematic formulas of movement, step, and gesture. That dichotomy is with us and continues to rule the various definitions of ballet that I have been able to glean from instructional sources.

One complicating factor that seems to gloss over the difference but actually heightens it is the definition of dancing as the "most intelligible language of gesture." That definition comes from *On Dance*, a dialogue by Lucian (or "Pseudo-Lucian"), composed during the second century A.D. Comprising both an aesthetic and a social analysis of the art of dance, Lucian's description ties the notion that dance is analogous to a linguistic repertoire to what appears to be a concomitant notion, that "the most material and important point of [the dancer's] art consists in the imitation and accurate representation even of the most invisible things" (Lucian 1820: 231–233). Lucian takes the mimetic aspect of language into account without scanting its ability to give codified expression to the "invisible." But it is the imitation of the visible that has the ascendancy in subsequent classical definitions of dancing. To be sure, Lucian was concerned with distinguishing the "noble kind of dancing" from that performed in certain rites of expiation or occasions that licensed lascivious behavior. This had been a chief concern of Plato's discussion of dance in the *Laws* (tr. Bury 1952: 96–97). And it was to this kind of hierarchy that the Renaissance had recourse in justifying its affirmation of the value of dance, with reinforcement from scripture (Huizinga 1967: Chapter 23).

A conception of "pure" or nonimitative dance found theoretical support in the work of a Jesuit who in 1683 published the first history of dance, Claude-François Menestrier. In *Des ballets anciens et modernes selon les règles du théâtre*, Menestrier went so far as to deny the chiefly imitative model and the concomitant rule of preserving in ballets the three

Aristotelian unities of time, place, and action. Ballet would be an independent art with its own rules, not a "mute tragedy or comedy" (in Lange 1976: 7). On the other side of the simplistically posited opposition was one of the best-known dramatic choreographers of the eighteenth century, Jean-Georges Noverre (1727–1810), whose valuable letters on ballet insist that it should represent character, action, and feeling. The question is not an antiquated one, for it underlies the choices of the currently leading ballet companies based in New York City, American Ballet Theatre and Balanchine's New York City Ballet. Moreover, it is one that can include the determination of the balletic movement itself. Noverre went so far as to demand the abandonment of formulaic movement in favor of one that would arise directly from the action depicted.

The controversy calls for a reading in semiotic terms. The fact that motion has inherent value is too often absent from writing on dance. The discussion I have sketched implicitly takes account of the attachment of dance forms to matters of value and, more immediately, of genre. Perhaps of greatest importance to modern analysts is the connection between the apparently rhetorical basis of reasoning on dance and the determination of genre. For the idea of genre is that which rules over the reception of the art, in turn largely determined by expectation. The intensity of disagreement among writers on ballet (who are more often than not practitioners of some aspect of the art) indicates a fundamental and not merely quantitative divergence of expectation and estimation of generic "utility." Yuri Slonimsky writing on the Soviet (probably Bolshoi) ballet of 1960 expounds a programmatic extreme, claiming that the technique and portrayal of character in ballet should only be means to the end of communicating "a message, ennobling and purifying" ("Our Point of View," in Cohen 1974: 164). The need for ballet to serve the needs of the state is grounded in its origins (at least from the days of the Ballet Comique). Further on in his article, Slonimsky reaffirms the ancient connection between this requirement and analogous requirements of the other arts, particularly the literary art: "Together with literature, drama, and opera, ballet is a vehicle of education. . . . Progressive art was always drawn to great literature . . . its ability to penetrate beyond the surface of life cannot be equalled. Soviet ballet sees a life-giving source for further development in joining forces with literature—both classical and contemporary" (ibid.).

It would be impossible to enter into the full implications of such a stance for the question of value in the arts, or even to attempt to characterize the diverse kinds of semiosis involved in evaluation. But the statements of the Soviet *danseur* (all the more, perhaps, for their commonplace character) illuminate the programmatic nexus that conditions ballet production: the determination of what, and how much, is to be imitated.

The question is a penetrating one, for no analysis can ignore the fact that "the classical ballet came into being as a pleasure of the aristocracy and as part of court ceremony" (a particularly literal and contemporary aspect of "noble dancing"), that "the bowing before the public, the addressing of hand movements to them, and the like, are the foundations on which the rules of ballet were built" (Beaumont 1955: 106). While Beaumont is pointing here to the changing composition of ballet audiences, his words aptly characterize the intimacy of the bond between gestural choices and generically founded expectation. Even upon the advent of the Romantic ballet and the various changes it wrought in the totality of production values, the "bowing" and "hand movements" addressed to the audience conferred some sort of vicarious aristocratic status upon it, and generally continue to do so. This trait seems to indicate that mimesis is yielding here to a supervening quotient of semiosis, but also shows that supervention does not equal elimination.

It will take considerable work to disentangle the strands of various levels of imitation in ballet. Suffice it here to recall that the matter of inherent value in balletic movement must be conceived of from other than a sociological (or anthropological) standpoint. Choreographers and dancers disagree sharply on the (often competing) roles of libretto and music. The complications multiply if we remember that rhythm alone comprehends overlapping considerations of tempo, duration, stress, and recurrence. On one side of the question are statements such as that of Ruth St. Denis ("Music Visualization," in Cohen 1974: 130). Whereas this model does not preclude the adaptation of music and movement to the requirements of expression that mimes a narrative, it may be taken to place the imitation of music hierarchically above any other kind. The question of ballet as a theatrical art (on a neo-Aristotelian model) continues to dominate the discussion of *ballets d'action* versus the approximation of "pure form" in the dance. The expressive value of the forms of classical balletic movement continue to attract literary elaboration, and it is a real matter of doubt (apart from preference) whether this issue can ever be eliminated. We note that St. Denis is concerned, as well, with "what is to be imitated."

It was only recently that a preliminary step in the analysis of ballet as a system was provided by the search for a notational metalanguage which could serve (however cumbrously) as a translation instrument. The intricacy and relative obscurity of these methods imply their opposite, namely piecemeal knowledge through empirical observation, by which means ballet movements had always been transmitted to learners (Kleinman 1975).

The most satisfactory conception of the structure and principles of balletic movement was advanced by the work of Rudolf Laban (Laban 1974). He was not limited by the classic division of dance into noble and savage art, nor did he view it as a synthesis of other arts. Rather, using the idea that movement is the common denominator of all action, he developed an entirely empirical approach consisting of scales and models intended to be universally applicable in identifying any human movement in space.

One important factor in the superiority of Labanotation concerns the flow of movement in all dance, which may be said to possess a function of continuity. It is only in duration and flow that the entirety of a dance or a single movement is evoked. Labanotation enables the user to record the three-dimensional aspect of movement, its extension in any direction, its timing and continuity (Preston-Dunlop 1969: Chapter I). Laban's analysis takes account of the amount of technical "effort" sufficient for a given action as measured against other actions; thus he is able to define the "going with" and "going against" aspects of motion factors such as weight, space, time, and flow in proportional arrangement. Another important aid to the semiotic analysis of ballet is provided by the contrastive arrangement of his directional categories, for instance, up/down movement (which he describes as "high/deep") or forward/backward or right/left. Laban's normative analysis provides a means of noting sequences of stress and patterns of movement, amplitude, focus, contour, level, and grouping, which make it possible in turn to report existing relationships of form and function and the extent to which they mirror specific cultural features.

The study of living dance forms sometimes threatens to become an adjunct of literary studies, due partially to the vital connection between basic movement functions and elementary units of rhythm, for example, the use of Latin *pes* (or Greek *pous*) for "foot," referring to metrical units in prosody. And as in the study of any art, the purview of aesthetics is broadened to include ideas of appropriateness (or genre, as above). But the importance of the fact that motion itself has inherent value (Hanna 1979) is too often absent from recorded thinking on ballet. Although the difference of emphasis between "static" and "kinetic" components is included in the standard definition of dance in *Webster's Third International Dictionary*, it does not, of course, suggest the wide (and within exterior limitations, infinitely regressive) range, for example, of inward movement that is possible within the balletic code. Neither the idea of "poses" nor that of "pattern-tracing" would apply here. The implementation of Laban's scheme may come to include a projection for the correlation of affective values with certain types of movement in ballet (Sirridge and Armelagos 1976).

I shall begin the quest for a semiotics of ballet with a brief and, ad-
mittedly, unsystematic analysis of a story-ballet, since the isolation and
codification of balletic movement devoid of "literary" corroborations remains as yet a distant goal. As a product of semiotic invention, a story-
ballet is a complex "text" resulting from many interacting modes of sign
production that participate in a series of hierarchically organized semioses.
The resulting complexity embraces various subsystems including dance,
gesture (mime and nonmime), music, the visual arts (as manifested in stage
setting and costume), and in the case of Romantic story-ballet, plot. The
selection and concatenation of the elements of the balletic vocabulary depend partly upon the choice of conventional movements whereby different elements of the whole system can be manifested to the audience
through iconicity.

As we have noted, ballet does not establish structurally monolithic
oppositions but gradations of opposition. In order to illustrate this as eco-
nomically as possible, I have chosen to focus attention on the Romantic
story-ballet par excellence, *Giselle* (in the standard version, revised by
Petipa).

The choreography of this ballet notably utilizes a sparse lexicon of
balletic movement while the libretto establishes a wide scope of opposition. The palette is limited to a comparatively small number of movements, steps, and poses familiar to students of classical ballet from the
time of its very inception (cf. Lifar 1942). The ability of balletic movements to lend themselves to a great variety of dramatic expression is,
however, exploited by the extensive use of the choreographic leitmotif
(such as the mimed gesture that denotes "dancing" itself). This convention
is supported by musical leitmotifs in the score. Throughout the ballet the
number of leitmotifs alloted to a particular dancer's movements helps define his or her hierarchical status and, moreover, decreases in proportion to
the prominence of the role. Although the *corps de ballet* as a collective
achieves a prominence (in respect to length and frequency of presentation)
unprecedented in story-ballets, its role is revealed as fundamentally con-
text-bound, both by the paucity of dance vocabulary and the frequency
of the leitmotifs applied to it. In view of this status it is relevant to examine the functions that are represented by the *corps de ballet*.

The *corps de ballet* make their first appearance in the beginning of the
second and final act. They are attired in bridal gowns involving minimal
modifications of the costume for *ballets blancs*; that is, the white tarlatan
ballet dress. They wear garlands of flowers on their heads. These modified
coronets constitute a trademark for the ballerina when she is dancing regal
roles, and indicate rank as well as (more generally) radiant beauty. The
corps have a queen among themselves second only to the title role in

prominence. They enter veiled with arms crossed over their breasts, advance from both sides toward the center of the stage (the point of maximal dominance), then face their queen who rises on points and commands them to retire and remove their veils.

The technique of rising *en pointe* (an invention of the new Romantic ballet) promotes the aim of rendering the dancer light and insubstantial and increases the proportion of centrifugal to centripetal movement in the balletic lexicon. Now while centripetal movement clearly portends only its own termination, centrifugal movement corresponds more closely to human ambulation and contains greater dynamic power, providing a greater illusion of continuation. Both the centrifugal *pointe* and that of the *arabesque* are prominently associated not only with Giselle herself but with the *corps de ballet*, so much so that the latter becomes their choreographic sign manual (Beaumont 1945: 88-89).

In terms of balletic vocabulary the position of crossed arms is a centripetal movement clearly implying and entailing its own cessation. In terms of plot it is a leitmotif for the *corps de ballet* (who enter repeatedly in this fashion) having an explicit denotative value outside the balletic code: the culturalized meaning of death, or in Peircean terms, its symbol (conventionally linked with its object). On the level of balletic vocabulary the *pointe* and *arabesque* are centrifugal movements implying dynamism and continuation. They are positions for which the amount of ground support is minimal. On the mimetic level they cannot be interpreted as immanently possessing narrative tags. Semiotically and inherently, they connote immateriality, to which they exist in an iconic relationship (similarity to their object). The overall scheme of the ballet utilizes these positions far more frequently and as independent of the narrative binding of the crossed-arms position. Consequently, the *pointe* and the *arabesque* (and the two jointly) are to be understood as relatively context-free and therefore, as regards the libretto, as having a far higher degree of hierarchical prominence.

In order for the audience to recognize these aspects of balletic vocabulary as utilized by the *corps de ballet* it need not have any prior acquaintance with the libretto of *Giselle*. The libretto follows the Slavo-Germanic legend of the Wilis, spirits of betrothed girls who perished as a result of their having been jilted by faithless lovers. The girls are said to take vengeance on the betrayers by luring them at night to a secluded place and forcing them to dance until they fall dead from exhaustion (Beaumont 1945: 19; cf. Lifar 1942). The audience can be ignorant of this background and still interpret the scene which follows, basing its synthetic inference on a previous set of conventions regarding royalty, another set regarding gestures of anger (a species of ostension), and yet another regarding social behavior between the sexes. It may do so by an intervention consisting of proposing a new rule governing a rarer application of each of the previous sets of rules. This comes about by what Peirce calls abduction, the inference of a case from a rule and a result.

The second act of *Giselle* presents a number of semiotically important contrasts with the first. The *corps de ballet* enters for the first time, attired in what had already established itself as the canonical costume for a ranking ballerina. Each member participates in a shared display of royalty which culminates in the advent of the queen herself. This presentation exists in opposition to the first act, which is almost entirely taken up with peasant and village life and does not prominently display group dances. Given the fact that the fashion for *paysanneries* predates *Giselle* (Lifar 1942), what is innovative here within the context of the nineteenth century in Europe is the pairing of peasant ballet with *ballet blanc* and the concomitant creation of the opposition peasant/noble.

The opposition life/death, clearly mimed in dance and gesture and interpreted by the audience through such events as Giselle's death at the close of the first act, manifests itself as entwined with but subordinate to the peasant/noble opposition. The *corps de ballet*, attired in "nobility," a value accorded to the classic white ballet dress, conveys the fact of death by the crossed-arms position. But since they continue to dance, it becomes clear that they possess a sort of supernatural life. When Giselle enters to become one of them she too participates in that life. Although Albrecht is threatened by an earthly demise as he is constrained to dance by the *corps de ballet*, he is saved by the temporizing of Giselle and her own extension of the dance. Nobility survives both kinds of death. It was rather Giselle *as a peasant* who died, to be resuscitated and ennobled. The prominence of *arabesque* among her movements, initiated only near the end of Act One when she is told of Albrecht's treachery and prepares to die, now comes into full play.

The importance of the *corps de ballet* reinforces the fundamental opposition male/female. It is well known that gender roles in the Romantic repertoire resist change. What Birdwhistell (1969: 11) has called "tertiary sexual characteristics," consisting of sex-linked appearance and behavior, are manifested in a number of ways. For instance, the technique of the pas de deux is based on the assistance a male dancer gives to his female partner in the execution of those dance movements that they customarily perform together. The creation of the *theatrically valid* roles of Romantic ballet reposes upon the dancer's exhibition of socially recognized and conditioned gender differences. Two of four *danseurs* writing in the same issue of *Dance Perspectives* (no. 40, Winter 1969) characterize their partnering roles as analogues of patronage by the stronger of the weaker sex, such as holding doors or relinquishing chairs (Igor Youskevitch and Edward Villella,

both of the New York City Ballet). Allowing for inaccuracies in self-re-
porting and even for considerable variation in the proportion and kind of
sex-linked behavior in ballet, their view helps to corroborate the actual
disposition of movement in male and female roles.

The Romantic period in ballet is known to have ushered in the su-
premacy of the ballerina as heroine. The accompaniment of a foregrounded
female *corps de ballet* underscores this presence of the female. Whereas it
is elements dealing with masculine behavior that furnish propulsive impe-
tus to the libretto in the first act, that function passes to female behavior
in the second act.

The opposition between natural and supernatural life comes to super-
sede that between life and death. It competes with the dramatic link between the acts as the audience would first witness them; and with the
"boy meets girl, boy wins girl, boy loses (leaves) girl" frame of a story-
ballet. Note the subordination of the (reversed) life/death hierarchy to
that of noble and peasant.

The role of the *corps de ballet* also sets in relief a basic opposition in
Romantic story-ballet between the individual and the collective. The first
act counterposes Giselle to her entourage, and second-act Giselle to the
female *corps de ballet*. Numerous plot elements in the first act also juxtapose Albrecht to his social environment, and in turn to Giselle's, while the
second does so between Albrecht and the *corps*. These elements are determined by the frequency of appearance, the extent of domination of center
stage, and the distribution of movements signifying their degree of difficulty or challenge to the materiality of the human body.

As to setting, the opposition peasant/noble is implemented in the
change from the depiction of a peasant village with rustic cottage to that
of an ethereal (silver-white) glade. Every production observes the corresponding change of color. One factor emerges as closely protected in both
acts: lavishness of scene. No bargains, no shortcuts: the stage offers to the
audience the possibility of splendor on both sides of the curtain, as long as
the audience's own habits (such as those of dress) reinforce it.

Indeed, the occasion of ballet, like opera and classical theatre, is culturally marked. Evidence of this can be seen in the persistence of ballets
like *Giselle*, which are not only not contemporary but reflect situations
and paradigms of values having little or no direct connection with the ordinary lives of contemporary audiences. This means that a highly codified
and conventionalized conception of ballet structure and semiosis must find
a common resonance in dancers and spectators alike. Dressing up in particularly festive or glamorous clothing in order to attend these spectacles
becomes a sign of solidarity between performer and audience, a purely
semiotic phenomenon since clothing here is practically devoid of its utili-

tarian function—just as the plots have no utilitarian connection to external life and feed ostensibly on the disjunction between reality and art. There is even a kind of gradience in the customary dress adopted by the audience, depending on the degree of remove from the stage. Those closest to the stage, in the parterre, most closely match the ornamental, even grandiose, mode of dress of the performers. This congruence diminishes as one proceeds backward and upward from the parterre to the rear and roof of the theatre. The fit between performers and spectators with respect to dress is largely independent of factors extrinsic to the occasion (such as economic status).

The opposition of ballerina and *danseur* invests their movements with ostensive meaning for the plot. The interlocking relationship which they establish with respect to movement is determined by the patterns of their trajectories in space as well as by the choice of balletic vocabulary. For example, their frequent mutual *glissade-assemblée*, a coming together from diagonally opposed corners of the stage, describes sympathies and antipathies and constitutes an icon of meeting and parting. The movement is interpreted as melancholy by an audience noting its cyclical repetition. The ensemble of such movements, for example, may be considered an expression unit in itself.

The guiding spirit and colibrettist of *Giselle*, Théophile Gautier, surmounted his obviously literary bias vis-à-vis ballet sufficiently to remark that the sole and unique subject for a ballet is the dance. This sort of principle is carried out on the level of mimesis in the action of *Giselle*, in its abundance of balletic movement as opposed to mime. One subject, however, is constantly mimed (not danced): the dance itself, symbolized by a repeated gesture of revolving arms. Giselle is a young girl with a great desire to dance and a weakness of the heart that makes dancing a danger to her (this mimed by a gesture of hand on heart). The first of these traits belongs to the lore of the Wilis; the second clearly differentiates her from them. The opposition dance/not-dance thus figures among those to be noted as prominent. When Giselle dies, it is of thwarted love and faith, not of physical exhaustion. Her death is preceded by a "mad scene" whose plot motivation is the treachery of Albrecht. Whereas she "loses" him once in each act, and definitively, it is as a dancer that she is kept alive. When dance is itself the signatum, the signans turns away from ballet to mime. Otherwise the semiosis would be rendered purely introversive (as in pure dance), a *modus significandi* quite at variance with the nature of story-ballet. The prominence of the ballet-signans is set in relief by this resort to another set of signantia, a kind of intracode switch.

Elements such as the mad scene, the hierarchical status of the *corps de ballet*, the treatment of the peasant/noble opposition, and the considerable tension placed on the gap between individual and collective are features insufficient in and of themselves to allow the ascription of a revolutionary ideology to *Giselle* as a whole. They do, however, rival the *ballet blanc*, the regal heroine, and self-effacement for love insofar as these features emphasize the roles of the female and the collective as a manifestation of poetically immanent justice.

A more comprehensive study of the semiotics of ballet will go beyond structures localized by time and type to encompass a broader diachronic and typological spectrum. This will ideally involve a detailed investigation of interpretants and interpretive codes, and of the teleology of relations which impart to ballet its aesthetic specificity and continuity. Ballet is a quintessentially syncretic art whose parts articulate a hierarchy of semiotic contexts as well as a calculus of features. Ultimately, it is their coherence that renders the ballet a complex system of iconic relationships.

Bibliography

Abrams, M. H. 1953. *The Mirror and the Lamp*. New York: Oxford University Press.

Adorno, Theodore W. 1973. *Philosophy of Modern Music*. New York: Seabury Press.

Aristotle's Poetics. 1968. Translated by Leon Golden with commentary by O. G. Hardison. Englewood Cliffs, N. J.: Prentice Hall.

Baker, Nancy Kovaleff. 1975. "From Teil to Tonstück: The Significance of the *Versuch einer Anleitung zur Komposition* by Heinrich Christoph Koch." Ph.D. dissertation, Yale University.

Balzac, H. de. 1961. *Eugénie Grandet*. Paris: Editions Garnier Frères.

Barthes, Roland. 1964a. "Eléments de sémiologie." *Communications* 4: 91-144.

―――. 1964b. "Rhétorique de l'image." *Communications* 4: 40-51.

―――. 1970. *S/Z*. Paris.

―――. 1974. *S/Z*. Translated by Richard Miller. New York: Hill and Wang.

Beaumont, Cyril W. 1945. *The Ballet Called Giselle*. London: C. W. Beaumont.

―――. 1955. *Michel Fokine and His Ballets*. London: C. W. Beaumont.

Berne, Eric. 1968. *Layman's Guide to Psychiatry and Psychoanalysis*. New York: Simon & Schuster.

Bersani, Leo. 1969. *A Future for Astyanax: Character and Desire in the Novel*. Boston: Little, Brown.

Birdwhistell, Ray. 1969. "Introduction, the Male Image." *Dance Perspectives* 40.

Blacking, John. 1967. *Venda Children's Songs: A Study in Ethnomusicological Analysis*. Johannesburg: Witwatersrand University Press.

―――. 1970. "Tonal Organization in the Music of Two Venda Initiation Schools." *Ethnomusicology* 14 (1): 1-54.

―――. 1971. "Music and the Historical Process in Vendaland." In *Music and History in Africa*. Edited by K. P. Wachsmann. Evanston: Northwestern University Press, 185-212.

————. 1973. *How Musical Is Man?* Seattle: University of Washington Press.

Booth, Wayne. 1961. *The Rhetoric of Fiction*. Chicago: University of Chicago Press.

Brenner, Charles. 1957. *An Elementary Textbook of Psychoanalysis*. Garden City: Doubleday.

Brontë, Emily. 1972. *Wuthering Heights*. Edited by William Sale, Jr. New York: Norton.

Burke, Kenneth. 1961. *The Rhetoric of Religion: Studies in Logology*. Berkeley: University of California Press.

Cecil, David. 1934. *Early Victorian Novelists*. London: Constable & Co.

Červenka, Miroslav. 1973. "Die Grundkategorien des Prager literaturwissenschaftlicher Strukturalismus." In *Zur Kritik literaturwissenschaftlicher Methodologie*. Edited by Viktor Žmegač and Zdenko Škreb. Frankfurt a. M.: Athenäum Fischer Taschenbuch Verlag, 137–168.

————. 1978. *Der Bedeutungsaufbau des literarischen Werks*. Foreword by W. -D. Stempel. Munich: Fink Verlag.

Červenka, Miroslav, and M. Jankovič. 1976. "Zwei Beiträge zum Gegenstand der Individualstilistik in der Literatur." *Zeitschrift für Literaturwissenschaft und Linguistik* 6 (22): 86–116.

Chaitanya, Krishna. 1962. *A New History of Sanskrit Literature*. Bombay: Asia Publishing House.

Chomsky, Noam. 1957. *Syntactic Structures*. The Hague: Mouton.

————. 1972. *Language and Mind*. Enlarged edition. New York: Harcourt Brace Jovanovich.

Chomsky, Noam, and Morris Halle. 1968. *The Sound Pattern of English*. New York: Harper and Row.

Christiansen, Broder. 1909. *Philosophie der Kunst*. Hanan: Clauss & Feddersen.

Cohen, Selma J. 1974. *Source Readings in Dance History from 1581 to the Present*. New York: Dodd, Mead.

Cooke, Deryck. 1959. *The Language of Music*. London: Oxford University Press.

Cooper, Robin. 1977. "Abstract Structure and the Indian Raga System." *Journal of Ethnomusicology* 21: 1–32.

Cornulier, Benoît de. 1977. "Le Vers français classique." *Le Français Moderne* 45 (2): 97–125.

————. Forthcoming. *Mallarmé, Verlaine, Rimbaud: Méthodes en métrique*. Paris: Editions du Seuil.

Crickmore, Leon. 1968. "An Approach to the Measurement of Music Appreciation." *Journal of Research in Music Education* 16 (3 and 4): 239–253, 291–301.

Daniélou, Alain. 1967. *Sémantique musicale*. Paris: Hermann.

————. 1968. *The Raga-s of Northern Indian Music*. London: Barrie & Rockliff the Cresset.

Delacroix, Henri Joachim. 1927. *Psychologie de l'art: Essai sur l'activité artistique*. Paris: F. Alcan.

Deshpande, Madhave M. 1979. *Sociolinguistic Attitudes in India: An Historical Reconstruction*. Ann Arbor, Mich.: Karoma Publishers, Inc.

Djajadiningrat, R. A. Dr. Hoesin. 1934. *Atjehsch-Nederlandsch Woordenboek*. Batavia: Landsdrukkerij.

Errington, Shelly. 1975. "A Study of Genre: Form and Meaning in the Malay Hikayat Hang Tuah." Ph.D. dissertation, Cornell University.

Ferguson, Donald. 1960. *Music as Metaphor: The Elements of Expression*. Minneapolis: University of Minnesota Press.

Fernández, Henry. 1968-1969. "*Blow-Up*: From Cortázar to Antonioni: Study of an Adaptation." *Film Heritage* 4: 26-30.

Fillmore, Charles. 1968. "The Case for Case." In *Universals in Linguistic Theory*. Edited by Emmon Bach and Robert Harms. New York: Holt, 1-88.

Fodor, Janet Dean. 1977. *Semantics: Theories of Meaning in Generative Grammar*. New York: Thomas Y. Crowell.

Ford, Ford Maddox. 1951. *The Good Soldier*. New York. Alfred A. Knopf.

Fowler, Roger. 1977. "The Referential Code and Narrative Authority." *Language and Style* 10: 129-163.

Geertz, Clifford. 1975. *The Interpretation of Cultures*. London: Hutchinson.

Gleason, H. A. 1961. *An Introduction to Descriptive Linguistics*. New York: Holt.

Golomb, Harai. 1968. "Combined Speech." *Ha-Sifrut* 1: 251 ff. (In Hebrew.)

Gregor, Johann. 1944. *Kulturgeschichte des Balletts*. Vienna: Gallus Verlag.

Greimas, A. J. 1966a. *Sémantique structurale*. Paris: Larousse.

————. 1966b. "Eléments pour une théorie de l'interprétation du récit mythique." *Communications* 8: 28-59. Translated in *Structural Analysis and Oral Tradition*. Edited by Pierre and Elie Maranda. Philadelphia: University of Pennsylvania Press, 1971. Later reprinted in Greimas 1970.

————. 1970. *Du sens*. Paris: Seuil.

————. 1971. "Narrative Grammar: Units and Levels." *Modern Language Notes* 86: 793-806.

————. 1976. *Maupassant. La Sémiotique du texte: Exercises pratiques*. Paris: Seuil.

Greimas, A. J., and François Rastier. 1968. "The Interaction of Semiotic Constraints." In *Game, Play, Literature*. Edited by Jacques Ehrmann. Boston: Beacon Press, 86-105.

Hankiss, Elemér. 1970. "Shakespeare's *Hamlet*: The Tragedy in the Light of Communication Theory." *Acta Litteraria Scientiarum Hungaricae* 12 (3-4): 297-312.

————. 1971. "From Folk Song to Absurd Drama: On a Basic Structural Device of Literary Expression." *Language and Style* 4 (4): 243–263.

————. 1972. "Meaning as a Source of Aesthetic Experience." *Semiotica* 6 (3): 201–211.

————. 1973. "Report of the Investigative Committee on New Research Methods." *Computer Studies in the Humanities and Verbal Behavior* 6 (1): 21–31.

————. 1975. "Death and the Happy Ending: The Value-Structure of Endings in the Novel." In *Toward a Theory of Context in Linguistics and Literature*. Edited by Adam Makkai. The Hague: Mouton, 35–50.

Hanna, Judith Lynne. 1979. *To Dance Is Human*. Austin: University of Texas Press.

Harris, Zellig S. 1951. *Methods in Structural Linguistics*. Chicago: University of Chicago Press.

Hawkes, Terence. 1977. *Structuralism and Semiotics*. London: Methuen.

Hirsch, E. D. 1967. *Validity in Interpretation*. New Haven: Yale University Press.

Holenstein, Elmar. 1975. *Roman Jakobsons phänomenologischer Strukturalismus*. Frankfurt a.M.: Suhrkampf.

Hrushovski, Benjamin. 1968. "Do Sounds Have Meaning?" *Ha-Sifrut* 1: 410 ff.

————. 1976. *Segmentation and Motivation in the Text Continuum of Literary Prose: The First Episode of War and Peace* (=PPS 5). Tel Aviv: Tel Aviv University.

————. Forthcoming. *Integrational Semantics*.

Huizinga, Johan. 1967. *The Waning of the Middle Ages*. Translated by F. Hopman. London: E. Arnold and Co.

Ingarden, Roman. 1931. *Das literarische Kunstwerk*. Halle: M. Niemeyer.

Jakobson, Roman. 1939a. "Zur Struktur des Phonems." In Jakobson 1962: 280–310.

————. 1939b. "Un Manuel de phonologie générale." In Jakobson 1962: 311–316.

————. 1960. "Linguistics and Poetics." In *Style in Language*. Edited by Thomas A. Sebeok. New York and London: MIT, 350–377.

————. 1962. *Selected Writings I*. The Hague and Paris: Mouton.

————. 1963a. "Visual and Auditory Signs." In Jakobson 1971: 334–337.

————. 1963b. *Questions de poétique*. Paris: Editions du Seuil.

————. 1967. "On the Relation between Visual and Auditory Signs." In Jakobson 1971: 338–344.

————. 1971. *Selected Writings II*. The Hague and Paris: Mouton.

————. 1973. *Questions de poétique*. Paris: Editions du Seuil.

Jakobson, Roman, and Morris Halle. 1956. "Phonology and Phonetics." In Jakobson 1962: 464–504.

Jankovič, Milan. 1967. "Dílo jako dění smyslu." *Orientace* 2 (6): 5-8. (Fragment of an unpublished book.)

Jolles, André. 1956. *Einfache Formen*. 2nd. ed. Halle: M. Niemeyer.

Jones, Peter. 1971. "Works of Art and Their Availability-for-Use." *British Journal of Aesthetics* 11 (2): 115-122.

Keiler, Allan R. 1977. "The Syntax of Prolongation, Part I." *In Theory Only* 3: 3-27.

————. 1978. "Bernstein's *The Unanswered Question* and the Problem of Musical Competence." *Musical Quarterly* 64: 195-222.

Kermode, Frank. 1974. "A Modern Way with a Classic." *New Literary History* 5: 415-435.

Kettle, Arnold. 1960. *An Introduction to the English Novel*. New York: Harper & Row.

Kleinman, Seymour. 1975. "Movement Notation Systems: An Introduction." *Quest: The Language of Movement* 23: 33-56.

Laban, Rudolf. 1974. *The Language of Movement: A Guidebook to Choreutics*. Edited by Lisa Ullman. Boston: Plays.

Labov, William. 1972. "Transformation of Experience in Narrative Syntax." *Language in the Inner City: Studies in the Black English Vernacular*. Philadelphia: University of Pennsylvania Press, 354-396.

Lange, Roderyk. 1976. *The Nature of Dance: An Anthropological Perspective*. New York: International Publications Service.

Langer, Susanne. 1948. *Philosophy in a New Key*. New York: Mentor.

————. 1953. *Feeling and Form*. New York: Scribner's.

Lausberg, Heinrich. 1960. *Handbuch der literarischen Rhetorik*. Vol. I. Munich.

Leavis, F. R. 1967. *The Great Tradition*. New York: New York University Press.

Leavis, Queenie D. 1972. "A Fresh Approach to *Wuthering Heights*." In *Wuthering Heights*. Edited by William Sale, Jr. New York: Norton Critical Editions.

Lévi-Strauss, Claude. 1960. "L'Analyse morphologique des contes russes." *International Journal of Slavic Linguistics and Poetics* 3: 122-149.

————. 1963. "The Structural Study of Myth." *Structural Anthropology*. Vol. I. Translated by Claire Jacobson and Brooke Grundfest Schoepf. New York: Basic Books, 206-231.

Liebowitz, René. 1949. *Schoenberg and His School*. Translated by D. Newlin. New York: Philosophical Library.

Lifar, Serge. 1942. *Giselle, apothéose du ballet romantique*. Paris: Albin Michel.

Lotman, Jurij. 1977. *The Structure of the Artistic Text*. Translated by Ronald Vroon. Ann Arbor: Michigan Slavic Materials.

Lucian of Samosata. 1820. *Lucian of Samosata from the Greek with the Comments of Wieland and Others*. Translated by William Tooke. London: Longman.

Lukács, Georg. 1965. *Az esztétikum sajátossága* [The specificity of the aesthetic phenomenon]. Budapest: Akadémiai Kiadó.

Martinet, André. 1966. *Elements of General Linguistics.* Translated by Elisabeth Palmer. Chicago: University of Chicago Press.

Martinon, Philippe. 1912. *Les Strophes.* Paris: Champion.

Mazaleyrat, Jean. 1974. *Eléments de métrique française.* Paris: Armand Colin.

Mehegan, John. 1975. *Jazz Improvisation: Tonal and Rhythmic Principles.* New York: Watson-Guptill Publications.

Meletinskij, E. M., et al. 1969. "Problemy strukturnogo opisania volšebnoj skazki." *Trudy po znakovym sistemam* 4: 86-135.

Merriam, Alan P. 1964. *The Anthropology of Music.* Chicago: Northwestern University Press.

Metz, Christian. 1964. "Le Cinéma: Langue ou langage?" *Communications* 4: 52-90.

————. 1968. *Essais sur la signification au cinéma.* Paris: Klincksieck.

————. 1971. *Langage et cinéma.* Paris: Larousse.

Miller, J. Hillis. 1965. *The Disappearance of God.* New York: Schoken.

Molino, Jean. 1975. "Fait musical et sémiologie de la musique." *Musique en Jeu* 17: 37-62.

Morris, Charles W. 1939-1940. "Esthetics and the Theory of Signs." *Journal of Unified Science* 8: 131-150.

Mukařovský, Jan. 1934a. "Umění jako semiologický fakt" [Art as a semiotic fact]. In Mukařovský 1966: 85-88.

————. 1934b. "Obecné zásady a vývoj novočeského verše" [General principles and evolution of modern Czech verse]. In Mukařovský 1948b: 9-90.

————. 1936. "Estetická funkce, norma a hodnota jako sociální fakty" [Aesthetic function, norm and value as social facts]. In Mukařovský 1966: 17-64.

————. 1938. "Básnické pojmenování a estetická funkce jazyka" [Poetic designation and the aesthetic function of language]. In Mukařovský 1966: 153-157.

————. 1940. "O jazyce básnickém" [On poetic language]. In Mukařovský 1948: 78-108. English translation: *On Poetic Language.* The Hague: Peter de Ridder Press, 1976.

————. 1943. "Záměrnost a nezáměrnost v umění" [Intentionality and unintentionality in art]. In Mukařovský 1966: 89-108.

————. 1944. "K metodologii literární vědy" [On the methodology of literary study]. *Cestami poetiky a esteky.* Prague: Československý spisovatel, 1971, 183-200.

————. 1948a. *Kapitoly z české poetiky, I.* Prague: Svoboda.

————. 1948b. *Kapitoly z české poetiky, II.* Prague: Svoboda.

————. 1966. *Studie z estetiky.* Prague: Odeon.

————. 1977. *The Word and Verbal Art.* Edited by J. Burbank and P. Steiner. New York and London: Yale University Press.

————. 1978. *Structure, Sign and Function.* New York and London:
Yale University Press.

Nattiez, Jean Jacques. 1973. "De l'analyse taxinomique à la caractérisation
stylistique." Mimeograph, University of Montreal.

————. 1974. "Sémiologie musicale. L'Etat de la question." *Acta
Musicologica* 46: 153-171.

————. 1975. *Fondements d'une sémiologie de la musique.* Paris:
Union Générale d'Editions.

Neisser, Ulric. 1976. *Cognition and Reality.* San Francisco: W. H. Freeman.

Osmond-Smith, David. 1975. "Iconic Relations within Formal Transformations." *Actes du 1er congrès international de sémiotique
musicale.* Pesaro: Centro di Iniziativa Culturale, 45-55.

Otruba, M. 1970. "Mýtus a ritus" [Myth and ritual] *Česká Literatura*
18: 213-277.

Petrovic, Ankica. 1977. "Ganga, a Form of Traditional Rural Singing in
Yugoslavia." Ph.D. dissertation, Queen's University of Belfast.

Pfieffer, K. Ludwig. 1978. "The Novel and Society: Reflections on the
Interaction of Literary and Cultural Paradigms." *PTL* 3 (1). 44-69.

Preston-Dunlop, V. 1969. *Practical Kinetography: Laban.* London:
MacDonald and Evans.

Propp, Vladimir. 1958. "Morphology of the Folktale." *International
Journal of American Linguistics* 24 (4). Russian original: 1928.

————. 1971. *Morphology of the Folktale.* Austin: University of
Texas Press.

Reich, Willi. 1971. *Schoenberg: A Critical Biography.* Translated by
L. Black. London: Longman.

Richards, I. A. 1925. *The Principles of Literary Criticism.* London: K.
Paul, Trench, Trubner & Co.

Rosen, Charles. 1976. *The Classical Style.* London: Faber and Faber.

Ruwet, Nicolas. 1966. "Méthodes d'analyse en musicologie." *Revue
Belge de Musicologie* 20: 65-90. Reprinted in Ruwet 1972.

————. 1967a. "Quelques remarques sur le rôle de la répétition dans
la syntaxe musicale." In *To Honor Roman Jakobson, III.* The Hague:
Mouton, 1693-1703.

————. 1967b. *Introduction à la grammaire générative.* Paris: Plon.

————. 1972. *Langage, musique, poésie.* Paris: Editions du Seuil.

————. 1975a. "Parallélismes et déviations en poésie." In *Langue,
discours, société: Pour Emile Benveniste.* Edited by J. Kristeva et al.
Paris: Editions du Seuil, 307-351. English translation to appear in
Modern French Criticism. Edited by T. Todorov. Cambridge:
Cambridge University Press.

————. 1975b. "La Mort des amants." *L'Arc* 60: 70-73.

————. 1975c. "Théorie et méthodes dans les études musicales:
Quelques remarques rétrospectives et préliminaires." *Musique en
Jeu* 17: 11-36.

————. 1979. "Malherbe et le problème des parallélismes en poésie."

In *Mélanges en hommage à Charles Morazé*. Edited by Ph. Wolff.
   Toulouse: Editions Privat.
Salzer, Felix. 1962. *Structural Hearing: Tonal Coherence in Music*. 2 vols.
   New York: Dover.
Saussure, Ferdinand de. 1959. *Course in General Linguistics*. Translated
   by Wade Baskin. New York: McGraw-Hill.
Schlegel, Friedrich. 1882. *Seine prosäische Jugendschriften*. Vol. 2.
   Edited by Jacob Minor. Quoted in *A History of Esthetics*. Edited by
   K. E. Gilbert and H. Kuhn. Bloomington: Indiana University Press,
   1954.
Schoenberg, Arnold. 1912. *Second String Quartet*. Vienna: Universal
   Editions.
————. 1927. *Third String Quartet*. Vienna: Universal Editions.
————. 1939. *Fourth String Quartet*. New York: G. Schirmer.
————. 1951. *Style and Idea*. London: Williams and Norgate.
————. 1965. *Collected Letters*. Edited by E. Stein. Translated by
   E. Wilkins and E. Kaiser. New York: St. Martin's.
Sievers, Eduard. 1924. *Ziele und Wege der Schallanalyse*. Heidelberg:
   C. Winter.
Sirridge, Mary, and Adina Armelagos. 1976. "The Ins and Outs of Dance:
   Expression as an Aspect of Style." *Journal of Aesthetics and Art
   Criticism* 34: 15–24.
Soebardi. 1965. "Calendrical Traditions in Indonesia." *Madjalah Ilmu
   Sastra Indonesia* [Indonesian journal of cultural studies] 3 (1): 49–61.
Sommerstein, Alan H. 1977. *Modern Philology*. Baltimore: University
   Park Press.
Steiner, Peter, and Wendy Steiner. 1976. "The Relational Axes of Poetic
   Language." Postscript to Mukařovský 1940 (English edition).
Steiner, Wendy. 1979. "The Case for Unclear Thinking: The New Critics
   versus Charles Morris." *Critical Inquiry* 6: 257–270.
Steinitz, W. 1934. *Der Parallelismus in der finnisch-karelischen Volksdich-
   tung*. Helsinki: Suomalainen tiedeakatemia.
Tamir-Ghez, Nomi. 1978. "Binary Oppositions and Thematic Decoding
   in E. E. Cummings and Eudora Welty." *PTL* 3 (2): 235–248.
Tamir-Ghez, Nomi, and Benjamin Hrushovski. Forthcoming. "Speech and
   Position: An Outline of a General Theory."
Toland, John. 1977. *Adolf Hitler*. New York: Ballantine.
Vachek, J. 1942. "Psaný jazyk a pravopis." In *Čtení o jazyce a poezii*.
   Edited by B. Havránek et al. Prague: Družstevní práce, 231–306.
Valéry, Paul. 1958. *Collected Works of Paul Valéry*, Vol. 7, *The Art of
   Poetry*. Edited by Jackson Matthews. Translated by Denise Folliot.
   Bollingen Series, vol. 45. Princeton: Princeton University Press.
Van Ghent, Dorothy. 1953. *The English Novel: Form and Function*.
   New York: Harper & Row.
Zich, Otakar. 1918. *O typech básnických*. Reprint, Prague: Orbis, 1937.

Žirmunskij, Viktor. 1964. "Ritmiko-sintaktičeskij parallelizm kak osnova drevnetjurksogo narodnogo èpičeskogo sticha." *Voprosy jazykoznanija* 13 (4): 3–24.